The Net and the Butterfly

The Net and the Butterfly

The Art and Practice
of Breakthrough Thinking

Olivia Fox Cabane
and Judah Pollack

Portfolio/Penguin

An imprint of Penguin Random House LLC
375 Hudson Street
New York, New York 10014

Most Portfolio books are available at a discount when purchased in quantity for sales promotions or corporate use. Special editions, which include personalized covers, excerpts, and corporate imprints, can be created when purchased in large quantities. For more information, please call (212) 572-2232 or e-mail specialmarkets@penguinrandomhouse.com. Your local bookstore can also assist with discounted bulk purchases using the Penguin Random House corporate Business-to-Business program. For assistance in locating a participating retailer, e-mail B2B@penguinrandomhouse.com.

ISBN: 9781591847199 (hardcover)
ISBN: 9780698153448 (ebook)
ISBN: 9780735216778 (international edition)

Printed in the United States of America
1   3   5   7   9   10   8   6   4   2

Set in Adobe Caslon

While the author has made every effort to provide accurate telephone numbers, Internet addresses, and other contact information at the time of publication, neither the publisher nor the author assumes any responsibility for errors or for changes that occur after publication. Further, the publisher does not have any control over and does not assume any responsibility for author or third-party Web sites or their content.

To Dr. Marcus Raichle, discoverer of the default mode network, whose breakthrough made our work possible, whose science underlies this entire book, and for whose guidance we are profoundly grateful.

Contents

Part Two
The Blockers

The Net and the Butterfly

Introduction

IN A SMALL city in Switzerland on a fine spring day in 1905, a young patent clerk left his one-year-old son and wife at home to go see his best friend about a riddle. The two friends loved exchanging ideas, from philosophy to physics, from art to electricity, and this morning our young patent clerk wanted to discuss a problem that had been vexing him for some time.

For the past year, he'd been especially focused on a physics theory he'd begun formulating ten years ago. He laid out every detail of the problem he had been struggling with, and for an entire day the two friends analyzed ideas and rehashed every aspect of the dilemma.

As the sun set, the young man finally concluded that the theory he'd been working on for a decade was going nowhere. It had hit a brick wall. Demoralized and dejected, he declared that he was giving up the entire quest. And so Albert Einstein shuffled home and went to sleep.

You can imagine his friend's surprise the next morning when, answering an urgent knock, he opened the door to see Einstein, who bypassed polite greetings and blurted out, "Thank you. I've completely solved the problem." With that, he returned home and began to write. Einstein spent the next six weeks writing out one of the most important scientific contributions of all time: the special theory of relativity.[1]

What happened inside Einstein's brain that night? After years of effort, why did the answer suddenly appear just when he had given up?

Einstein's experience was a classic example of the way our brain creates breakthrough ideas, completely new and novel ways of solving problems and looking at the world. And believe it or not, if you've ever had a breakthrough, the exact same thing happened inside your brain, too.

This process was deliberately, consciously used by both Salvador Dali and Thomas Edison. Dali would put his elbow on a table and rest his chin on his upturned palm with a spoon between his chin and his palm. He would let himself drift off to sleep. As his muscles relaxed, the spoon would drop and rattle against the table, waking him up. Dali would then sketch the exact concept in his mind at that moment. Edison had a strikingly similar habit of napping in his chair with a handful of marbles. The moment the marbles' clatter woke him up, he would write down whatever was in his mind.[2]

For many, breakthroughs are like butterflies—beautiful and awe-inspiring, yet erratic and elusive. Some people think they happen through hard work and concentration. The harder you focus on the breakthrough you're seeking, the more likely you are to get it. Others think they are spontaneous, inexplicable, and unpredictable. We describe these moments of inspiration as "eureka" or "aha" moments, or we speak of "having a lightbulb go off." They're purely accidental, and there's no way to induce them. Still others believe they are for the lucky and the extraordinary. The truth is that we all can have breakthroughs.

In fact, breakthroughs are *not* accidental, they *can* be induced, and we are going to show you how. Thanks to new neuroscience research, we now know how the breakthrough process works and we have tools to access it.[3] Breakthroughs, like butterflies, may fly an unpredictable path, but it is possible to capture them if we build the right net.

Advances in neuroscience have revealed that these seemingly unpredictable, sudden, and singular flashes are actually a predictable part of an integrated mental process.[4] Einstein described the breakthrough moment as arriving "suddenly, and in a rather intuitive way. That means it is not reached by conscious logical conclusions."[5] But this sudden flash of insight is actually the only visible step of a much longer process, and Einstein knew it. "Thinking it through afterwards, you can always discover the reasons. . . . Intuition is nothing but the outcome of earlier intellectual experience."

Every single person on the planet has the ability to generate creative breakthroughs inside their brains: you can't be born without it. We all have a natural ability to create butterflies. However, you may not know how to get the most out of it, or even how to access it. You need skills and practice to build and wield a net.

Breakthrough thinkers impact the world, whether they're Louis Pasteur, Steve Jobs, or Mahatma Gandhi. Breakthroughs advance science and civilization. Breakthrough thinking gave us modern medicine, from Velcro[6] to the pacemaker.[7] The power of breakthrough thinking is equally valuable at home: you could have a breakthrough about what's been holding you back from getting into a relationship, or what you need to fix in your marriage.

Breakthrough thinking is also critical in business: innovation breakthroughs are worth millions, sometimes billions. Right now, companies are spending time and effort to create a culture of innovation breakthroughs around their employees. But what about the inside of their employees' heads? As it turns out, even if your employees are surrounded by an innovative organization or culture, if their *mental* culture isn't conducive, potential breakthroughs will never be realized.

Are you being asked to be far more creative at work than you signed on for? Does your path forward in your career suddenly depend on your ability to be innovative? Has breakthrough thinking become an expectation rather than an aspiration? Whether you already have regular breakthroughs and want to be able to direct them, or think that you just don't have that kind of brain, we have good news: breakthrough thinking is a skill that you can acquire and practice.

In the following pages, you are going to learn all about how your brain's breakthrough process works, how to access it, what might be holding it back, and how to turbocharge it.

We do, however, want to be clear: we will not be giving you a magic formula. Owning a net isn't sufficient to catch butterflies: you need practice, patience, skill, and a little luck. Because the breakthrough experience varies by individual, there is no guaranteed step-by-step procedure. No one breakthrough looks exactly like any other; they all emerge through their own unique process. That's why the breakthrough experience is not a directed, repeatable, linear one, but rather an evolving, unfolding, creative process with many different elements.

What we are giving you is a framework and a set of tools to

increase the chances of breakthroughs. There's a common saying that "luck is preparation meets opportunity." In this book, you'll learn how to prepare yourself so you can make the most of the opportunities that present themselves. We offer you tools and techniques from a broad range of disciplines—from behavioral and cognitive psychology to neuroscience and meditation, from peak performance athletic conditioning to Hollywood Method acting. In this sense, breakthrough thinking is like mixed martial arts, taking the most effective tools from anywhere, valuing effectiveness over style. This book helps you put the science into practice so that you can accelerate your learning curve.

We know that a person's breakthrough level can be increased with the right methods because we've helped countless clients increase theirs in this way. We've brought these breakthrough tools to the U. S. Army Special Forces and to Stanford's Student Enterprise Accelerator, StartX, in the heart of Silicon Valley.

Through these tools our clients have experienced breakthroughs in areas as disparate as predicting the political outcome of the Arab Spring, creating new medical technology devices, or breaking through executive team deadlocks. They've reported astonishing results that have transformed their practices, and you'll find some of their stories in the pages that follow.

We have both been fascinated with breakthroughs for decades, and in our pursuit of breakthroughs, we've tried some crazy stuff. We've studied sports psychology, Jungian archetypes, depth hypnosis, sensory deprivation, cognitive behavioral therapy (CBT), mindfulness-based cognitive therapy (MBCT), acceptance and commitment therapy (ACT), and an entire alphabet soup of other acronym-worthy experiences. Just as we've passed on the best insights and tools to our clients, we're now giving them to you.

In this book, you'll find unique knowledge drawn from a variety of sciences and the techniques you need to apply this knowledge. Your life will become your lab, and you'll get infinite opportunities to experiment. Becoming a breakthrough thinker does involve work—work that is sometimes hard, uncomfortable, and confronting. But it's also incredibly rewarding.

There is no substitute for doing the exercises in this book. Skimming through them with the earnest intention of completing them "another day" is not enough, nor is doing only the exercises that seem easy or interesting. When an exercise asks you to close your eyes and imagine a scene, really close your eyes and imagine. When we ask you to write out a scenario, grab a pen and paper and write. If we ask you to do something, it's for a good reason, and it will have a real impact on your level of breakthrough thinking.

In part one, we'll talk about what breakthroughs are (and aren't) and look at the inner workings of your brain's breakthrough process. This is where you'll get to feel your breakthrough network in action, and learn to tell the difference between the various modes your brain can switch into.

Then we'll lay out the breakthrough experience for you. You'll learn how to get yourself into the right mental state and collect the facts, stories, knowledge, and experiences needed to fuel your creative process.

You'll learn how to turbocharge your brain's breakthrough power by increasing your level of neuroplasticity, using your brain's ability to constantly rewire itself every time you think a new thought.

Putting It into Practice: A Thirty-Second Neuroplasticity Booster

Every time you think a new thought, all over your brain new structures are created. Yes, really.

Want to know what that feels like? Here you go.

Trace your route to work in your head. Be as specific as you can: imagine the signs, the landmarks, the streetlights and traffic signs. Imagine making the turns you would have to make, the buildings, stores, or restaurants you would pass by.

That feeling of trying to assemble images in your mind, of organizing them in the right order, the slightly awkward feeling of doing something for the first time? That's neuroplasticity at work. Your brain is physically creating new structures.

In part two, we'll talk about your butterflies' natural predators: the forces that prevent breakthroughs from happening inside your mind. Did you know that the three leading causes of butterfly demise are spiders, wasps, and cold? They have equivalents inside your brain: the spiders of fear, the wasps of failure, and the icy cold of uncertainty.

Fear, failure, and uncertainty are the breakthrough blockers that can trap your insights and limit your potential. There are breakthroughs you could be having, right now, that are trapped inside your mind, just waiting to be released. With the right techniques, you can neutralize these negative forces and let your butterflies soar. (If you can't wait to get started, jump straight to page 103.)

Finally, in the last chapter we'll talk about the SuperTools—tools that will supercharge all areas of your breakthrough process. And for the nerds among you, we've included more information about the brain science of breakthroughs in the Science Appendix.

By using the tools in this book, you will open the door to your brain's ability to cut through the noise and see your brilliant breakthrough ideas. These breakthroughs could change your business, your personal life, your physical and emotional well-being, your learning agility, your perspective on the world, your perception of yourself. Exponentially and incrementally, it could change anything or everything about you and who you are. To have breakthroughs, you don't have to be special. You don't have to be brilliant. You don't have to be privileged or even well educated. All you have to know is what you're looking for and how to find it.

Part One

The Butterflies

Chapter 1

The Four Wings

All About Breakthroughs

YET ANOTHER DROP of ink leaked from his fountain pen onto the page, and László Bíró threw down his pen in disgust. A Hungarian newspaper editor who earned his salary by writing, he was frustrated with the tools of his trade. He seemed to spend his time either filling up his fountain pens, or cleaning up the smudges they made.[1]

Of course he was grateful for the invention of the fountain pen: it was a vast improvement over feather quills. But it still meant ink splotches and ruined pages that had to be written all over again.

Why couldn't the ink from his fountain be more like the ink used to print his newspaper? Bíró already knew the answer: newspaper ink was much too thick for his fountain pen. Right ink, wrong pen. Deciding to use the newspaper ink was a good idea. But it wasn't a breakthrough.

The breakthrough came with a new way to deliver the ink. Rather than trying to get the thick ink to flow through a nib, Bíró and his brother figured out how to set a metal ball in a socket and let the thick ink roll out from behind the ball.

Now let's be clear—ballpoint pens had been attempted before. They just hadn't worked until then. Early ballpoints did not deliver the ink evenly; overflow and clogging were just two of the many issues that made them impractical. The breakthrough came when Bíró made the ballpoint pen viable.

In business, a breakthrough is often described as an idea that solves a problem or satisfies a need in an entirely new way. Although there is no single definition of breakthroughs, we define them quite simply as the moment when you *break through* something that was previously limiting you, whether it's a specific problem you couldn't find a solution to, a situation you couldn't understand, or simply an old way of doing or seeing things.

Sociologist and author Martha Beck describes the experience of breakthrough as "a shift in your understanding of the world, because the lens through which you view the world has been suddenly, gloriously changed. And boy, do breakthroughs feel amazing."[2] A breakthrough is a sudden advance in your knowledge or understanding that moves you past a barrier and makes you see things, understand things in a new way. Although all breakthroughs come from the same process in the brain, not all breakthroughs come in the same way.

There are two main kinds of breakthroughs: intentional and unintentional. You'll face some of the same obstacles with both, but these obstacles will play out in different ways. Fear, for instance, impedes both intentional and unintentional breakthroughs—but it rears its ugly head at different stages of the breakthrough experience. For intentional breakthroughs, fear interferes before the breakthrough, bringing up the possibility of failure.

Fear seeps in after unintentional breakthroughs, and it centers on the oncoming challenges of implementing a solution. For instance, you suddenly realize (breakthrough) that you need a divorce. Anxiety might arise as you foresee the unpleasantness that all too often accompanies the process (implementation) of divorcing.

Or perhaps you suddenly realize (breakthrough) you've fallen in love with a close friend. You could fear being rejected after making your new feelings known (implementation), or, confusingly, fear success and the life changes it would entail.

For unintentional breakthroughs, landing on a solution isn't the end goal: you need to act on it. As Beck says, "Having breakthroughs isn't the point. Living them is. Seeing in a new way is only the beginning." Fear is a powerful saboteur of this process.

Although all breakthroughs come from the same process in the brain, not all breakthroughs come in the same way. We have identified four different types: eureka breakthrough, metaphorical breakthrough, intuitive breakthrough, and paradigm breakthrough. Understanding the different kinds of breakthroughs will help you spot them so you don't miss a single one. It will also help you discover the style, or styles, that are most natural to you so you can learn to focus on the way that works best for you.

The key is to understand that no style of breakthrough is better or more productive than another. It is simply best to understand which style or styles come most naturally to you.

Eureka Breakthrough

Eureka translates from the Greek as "I've got it" or "That's it." In popular culture, it has come to describe the moment when someone experiences a sudden, unexpected realization.

Archimedes, the original "Eureka!" shouter, was a Greek mathematician and scientist living in ancient Sicily in the third century B.C. One day, he was asked by King Hiero, ruler of the city-state, to determine whether a crown was made of real gold. Since gold had a known density, all he had to do was measure the density of the crown and see whether it matched up.

The first part of measuring density was easy: determine the crown's weight. But the second part required measuring the crown's exact volume. Now, measuring the volume of an object like a cube is simple. But how do you determine the volume of an object as irregularly shaped as a crown?

Archimedes puzzled on the problem until one day while taking a bath. As he stepped into the bathtub, he watched the water rise, displaced by his leg. He realized that, just as the water had risen to accommodate the new volume of his leg, it would rise in response to the volume of the crown. So he could submerge the crown and measure the amount of water displaced to know the crown's volume, and thus calculate its density. He cried "Eureka!" and jumped out of his bath and ran through the streets of Syracuse stark naked, shouting all the way.

We tend to have eureka insights when we've been mulling over a problem for some time. Take, for example, the time two helicopter mechanics in the Army Reserve saved the army tens of millions of dollars because of their shared love of NASCAR.[3]

During the Iraq War, desert sand and dust were damaging helicopter windshields faster than the army could replace them, and costing hundreds of thousands of dollars every month. Lexan, the shatter-resistant plastic the windshields were made of, tended to scratch easily.

As it happens, Lexan is also used to make NASCAR windshields. But to solve the scratching problem, NASCAR drivers had learned to cover their windshields with thin sheets of transparent Mylar film they called "tearaways." At the end of each race, the used Mylar sheet is torn off, and the Lexan windshield underneath is left without a scratch.

Two national guardsmen on a helicopter maintenance crew in Virginia happened to be big NASCAR fans. As they surveyed the extent of the damage done to their helicopters' Lexan windshields, they were hit with the possibility that NASCAR's solution could solve the army's problem. Creatively reapplying an existing solution is a common type of eureka insight. In fact, NASCAR first borrowed the Mylar technique from motorcycle racers protecting their helmets.

When eureka breakthroughs happen, they happen fast. They are the proverbial lightning bolt over the head. Many people report the sensation of receiving information from a location "above." And this sudden discovery of an immediately applicable solution is incredibly exciting.

Eureka insights are the ones that your author Olivia gets most often (she's ruthlessly pragmatic). These ideas arrive with a clear mental picture of how to execute them and the confidence that they'll work.

They are most likely to come when you have been living with a problem or a block. This problem is interfering with your peace of mind; you think about it often during the day. But the actual breakthrough will most likely occur when you're no longer thinking about the problem.

James Watt did not invent the steam engine.[4] In 1764, at the University of Glasgow, he was repairing what was known as a Newcomen steam engine, which Watt considered very inefficient. He worked on the problem until one spring day in 1765, he was walking through a park when the breakthrough came to him: he needed two cylinders.[5] Eureka! Watt's breakthrough made the engine so much more powerful and efficient that it ushered in the true age of steam.

A century later, the next great breakthrough in power occurred in a remarkably similar way. Nikola Tesla had been working on the concept of an alternating current motor for a few years. One day while walking through a park in Budapest he had a feverish vision of an alternating current motor complete with three slightly out of phase magnetic fields turning the drive shaft.[6] The solution had appeared fully formed. Eureka!

This is part of the grand paradox of breakthrough thinking. In order to have a eureka breakthrough, you have to be deeply immersed in a problem. But then you have to let go of it, let your mind wander off and go do something else. It's while you're otherwise engaged, and *not* focused on the problem, that you will be rewarded with a eureka breakthrough. How to switch between these two modes—focus and lack of focus—is one of the most important things this book will teach you.

"In my experience, eureka moments happen when we face a high level of pressure," explains Victoria Spadaro-Grant, CTO of pasta behemoth Barilla and one of Olivia's favorite clients, "whether the pressure is generated as a by-product of a self-imposed challenge or the result of external circumstances."[7]

When Barilla CEO Claudio Colzani, concerned by the increasing consumption of saturated fats reported by the World Health Organization, ordered a massive reduction in saturated fats across Barilla's entire bakery portfolio, Spadaro-Grant faced a "massive challenge." As head of Research and Development for the Barilla Group, she was in charge of reformulating the portfolio and bringing it to market within five months. "At the time, we did not know how to solve the technical challenge of delivering the same eating experience with less saturated fat, not to mention implementing new manufacturing processes and addressing the multimillion euro cost and profitability impact."

With the clock ticking, Spadaro-Grant assembled "a SWAT team of only six people who were eager to try, test, break rules, and make bold decisions. We realized that with such a short time frame, we *had* to throw the old rule book completely out the window. That realization led to new margins of tolerance across technical solutions, manufacturing setups, formulation costs, and marketing communications. As simple as this sounds, this was the way we changed technical paradigms about how to use fats in our bakery." Eureka!

Metaphorical Breakthrough

In 1782, there was no such thing as a bullet: guns did not shoot small, tapered missiles, but rather lumps of lead known as "shot." Most people produced shot by rolling out a sheet of molten lead, waiting for it to cool, and then chopping it up. This wasn't very effective in producing smooth spheres: the projectiles were misshapen, pitted, or even completely perforated.

As a result, it was nearly impossible for anyone to shoot straight. Because of their irregular shape, the slugs would catch the wind and curve like a paper airplane; their trajectory was always unpredictable. In 1782, hitting your target had more to do with luck than with aim. Since England was in the business of ruling the world at the time, and in the midst of a war with its pesky American colonies, the ability to shoot straight was of great interest.

Producing shot was also expensive, time consuming, and labor intensive. After the chopping method, people tried pouring molten lead into spherical molds. Unfortunately, the cooling process tended to create off-center spheres, and in addition air bubbles left deep, random pits.

Enter William Watts. A prosperous plumber living in a three-story house in the town of Bristol, England, Watts experienced a week of particularly troublesome sleep. Night after night he was puzzled by the same dream: He was walking along a street when it began to rain—only it wasn't raining water, it was raining lead. The drops of lead piled up around his feet. When Watts bent down to pick one up, he saw that it was a perfectly round sphere, the ideal lead shot everyone was chasing after. Watts was dreaming about the perfect product falling from the sky. But what did it mean? Day after day he pondered that question in vain.[8]

After a few days, tired from lack of sleep at night and from puzzling over the dream during the day, Watts went for a walk. As he went down the street he had a flash of insight and suddenly understood the meaning of his dream. He ran home and set to work.

Watts added three floors to his house, making it six stories high. He cut holes in each floor, one atop the other, and put a water tank at the bottom. Then he stood at the top of this shaft with a copper sieve and a bucket of molten lead. He poured the liquid lead through the sieve and watched as lead droplets fell the length of the shaft, landing in the cool water below with a hiss.

He ran downstairs, dipped his hand into the well, and pulled up a handful of beautifully round lead shot. The even pull of gravity in the stillness of the airshaft had produced perfect spheres. Watts had invented a process to make it rain bullets, turning his dream into reality. Patented in 1783, these "shot towers," as they came to be known, sprang up all over England, Europe, and America.

Watts's mind had presented him with a solution indirectly: his brain came up with an analogy and shared it through a dream. Watts dreamed that he was walking in a rain of little lead pellets, had the same dream for a week without knowing what to make of it, then finally had a revelation, and the insight that his mind was trying to communicate became clear.

Metaphorical insights aren't as direct as eureka insights. Answers come to you first as metaphors or analogies, and you must interpret their images before the breakthrough is complete. With Archimedes' eureka insight, the answer came fully formed. There was no need to interpret a metaphor: the submersion of his leg was a direct correlation to the submersion of the crown.

If Watts's insight had been a eureka insight, he would have seen a concrete solution: an image of a tower, of drops of metal falling and being shaped into spheres by friction with the air, landing in water, and cooling down. It would have been a one-to-one correlation. Instead, he had a dream about rain, and then saw that the drops of rain were drops of lead. It was raining lead. The elements were there: the lead, the fall, the water. But there wasn't a direct correlation; a process of interpretation was necessary.

Sometimes, your brain needs to work through various levels of comprehension before you can connect a wordless intuition to a real-life problem. Metaphor works like a wormhole: it can connect things that appear to be incredibly far apart, and it can overlay a pattern on things that appear to be unconnected. Unlike their eureka cousins, metaphorical breakthroughs can be had about subjects we're barely familiar with, like a plumber having an insight about ammunition.

Such insights are often embedded in bizarre dreams. Celebrated inventor Elias Howe dreamed that he was captured by a primitive tribe and held at spear point. Howe, admirably unperturbed in his dream, noticed that the spearheads had holes in them. Thus was discovered the secret to the lock stitch sewing machine—placing a hole on the pointy end of the needle. The improvement in stitching speed revolutionized the clothing industry.[9]

This metaphoric type of insight is also the basis of a process known as biomimicry. In biomimicry, we look for designs already existing in nature that could be useful in a human context. You may have heard that Velcro was discovered by mimicking sticky burrs. But did you know that the tenacious, watertight glue that oysters and barnacles use to adhere to rocks has inspired new ways for surgeons to close wounds on human beings?[10]

The Wright Brothers originally studied the flight of birds to gain insights into how to control powered flight. They noticed the birds twisted their wing tips to keep their balance. But on their lightweight plane, pivoting wing tips would be too fragile. Wilbur Wright, who owned a bicycle shop, had a long inner-tube box in his hands one day. He was absentmindedly twisting the box when the breakthrough suddenly came to him. If the entire wing twisted, you could control flight. His discovery came to be called "wing warping" and was the breakthrough that set the age of aviation in motion.[11]

We have found metaphorical breakthroughs to be a powerful tool when working with leaders. The executive team of a very successful Silicon Valley company asked us to sit in on their meeting when they were facing a block. They had had great success with their core product but could feel their well-funded competitors breathing down their neck. Should they double down on what they were already doing and try to own the market, or should they expand into a more unknown, adjacent area?

The executive team talked and talked. They used logic and linear arguments and lots and lots of words. Some argued they should stay with what they know. Their investors trusted them, their customers trusted them, and they'd spent a lot of time and money building their brand in that direction. Others argued that this was innovate-or-die time, that they had no choice but to spread their wings and fly into the unknown. That's what made companies great. There was a not-so-subtle hint that the other side lacked the courage to be great. That did not go over well. Those arguing to stick with the known product dug in and made their same arguments only more forcefully. Around and around they went, all the time banging up against walls.

Judah went up to the big whiteboard in the front of the room and drew two large boxes. He then split the executive team into their opposing groups, gave them pens, and ordered them to draw pictures of their visions of the future. At first there was grumbling and protests that they didn't know how to draw. Olivia assured them that stick figures were perfectly acceptable. Slowly, the teams began to work.

When the executives finished there was something striking about their two pictures: they weren't very different. Both groups drew a road winding to the horizon, happy faces along the road, and signposts at certain intervals. The farther along the roads you went the more happy faces there were. At first everyone was confused. If their pictures were so similar, why were they arguing?

As each team described their drawings the differences became crystal clear. One group drew bends in the road to represent how they'd have to *react* to the market. The other group drew bends in the road to represent how they wanted to *get ahead* of the market. The room got quiet for moment. A clarity had emerged. In this case the metaphor broke through the disagreement and posturing to reveal the essence of the issue. The group that wanted to stick with the core product and then react to the market saw clearly that they were reacting out of fear. The decision was made to move into the adjacent field. Three years on and the decision has proved a rousing success.

Visual thinking is a common trait among breakthrough thinkers. Many of the people we interviewed carry small sketch pads with them at all times. When they first put their idea to paper it is often as an image or a series of images. Visual thinking accesses different parts of the brain than language and logical argument. And it can be even more powerful when you are not very good at drawing because it forces you to be less literal and more metaphorical.

Intuitive Breakthrough

Imagine a dry lake bed in the high desert of California. This vast wasteland, offering little more than hard red earth, dust, and heat, was the spot the miltary had chosen in 1947 for its top-secret supersonic test flights. The plane being tested, the Bell X-1, was shaped like a bullet, with wafer-thin wings. The U.S. Air Force was experimenting with rocket planes to finally crack the sound barrier.

Unfortunately, every time pilots got close to the speed of sound, their planes' controls would freeze up, their rudders wouldn't move, and they'd be tossed around as if flying through a storm. It wasn't pretty: one plane completely disintegrated. The engineers were wringing their hands. No pilot had yet survived flying even 85 percent of the necessary speed, and the death toll was mounting.[12]

Chuck Yeager, a country boy from West Virginia, was one of the air force's very best pilots. At barely twenty-four years old, Yeager was already a legend. Thanks to his World War II exploits, he was known as an ace fighter pilot who seemed to have been born to fly.

During practice runs, Yeager had experienced all the usual difficulties as he approached the speed of sound: loss of controls, the plane shaking and wobbling, the entire aircraft tossed around in the wind like a rag doll. And yet, despite this evidence, Yeager was convinced that the closer he got to the sound barrier, the easier flying would be.

How could he be so sure? Aerospace engineering barely had a name yet, and he was up against PhDs who safely combined liquid oxygen, cooled to 297 degrees below zero, with ethyl alcohol, and then managed to contain the resulting explosion in a way that created propulsion. They were certain that they had run up against the limits of physics, and that flirting with the sound barrier was a suicide mission.

Yet here was Yeager, the son of a gas driller, with only a high school education, certain that he could make it. He had nothing but an intuition, a hunch so strong he was willing to bet his life on it. He somehow *knew* it would work.

On the fateful morning of October 14, 1947, Chuck Yeager climbed aboard the Bell X-1 and slid into the cockpit. He and his plane were dropped out of the belly of a converted B-29 bomber and rocketed straight up into the sky.

As he approached .9 Mach (90 percent of the necessary speed), the plane tossed and rolled and the controls became unresponsive. But when he reached .96 Mach he informed the ground that he had regained control of the airplane. The country boy had out-predicted the PhDs.

And then all of a sudden, the needle on the machometer fluctuated, then abruptly jumped clear off the scale. On the ground, they heard the famous "sonic boom." Not only had the plane gotten easier to fly, once it got close enough, the plane simply leapt across the sound barrier.

How did Yeager know? And how was he sure enough to risk his life? Intuitive breakthroughs defy logic or explanation. Most of the time, when people experience intuitive breakthroughs they don't know *why* their solution will work, they just know that it *will*.

Achieving a certain level of mastery in one's line of work or craft opens the door to deep insights. Research fellow Tammy Sanders describes intuition as "a nebulous and inexplicable sense of knowing, flowing from expertise and guided by environmental cues."[13] This is the kind of insight that comes to tinkerers, model builders, and product designers. Without even realizing it, you've loaded up thousands of facts, experiences, and case studies over the course of your life, and they're sitting in the back of your mind.

Thomas Edison, the ultimate tinkerer, invented the phonograph with an intuitive breakthrough. As he tinkered with a prototelephone, on a whim, he touched a pinpoint to the vibrating diaphragm he was working with. He had an intuition that, as he spoke, the pinpoint would create indentations in the tinfoil beneath the diaphragm. When the pinpoint played back through the track in the tinfoil, it would vibrate the pin, reproducing the sound. He was right.[14]

Although both eureka and intuitive breakthroughs are characterized by a sense of certainty, there is a finality to a eureka breakthrough; you've arrived at your goal. Intuitive breakthroughs, on the other hand, tend to be more of a beginning; they set you on the path toward the goal. Don't expect a sudden flash of insight. You will, however, experience a quiet calming of the mind and body. It's as though you were standing at a crossroads and suddenly just knew to take the road on the left.

If you're scratching your head, thinking that intuitive breakthroughs don't sound like breakthroughs at all, they're probably not your personal style of breakthrough. If, on the other hand, you read this section and felt truly understood, this might be your native break-through style.

Do you have to be more confident to handle an intuitive insight than a eureka insight? Yes. You have to ascribe legitimacy to a feeling you can't explain, rationalize, or prove.

Leaders must communicate their intuitive breakthroughs clearly and concretely to gain appropriate support in their organizations. But intuition can be difficult to talk about.

Two-star general Dana Pittard was the commanding officer of the army's 1st Armored Division at Fort Bliss in El Paso, Texas. He was in charge of forty thousand people and a massive amount of firepower. So it was odd for Judah, when working with the general and his staff, to hear whispers about the general planting "Charlie Brown Christmas trees" all over the post. Going on his own intuition, Judah asked about the Christmas trees.

After an awkward silence, the general explained that one of his goals was to make Fort Bliss, an army post larger than the state of Rhode Island in the desert of west Texas, a zero-waste facility. Planting trees for soil and water retention as well as shade was part of that mission. It was at this point that the chief of operations said, "Sir, they just look sad along the side of the road. Like rows and rows of Charlie Brown Christmas trees."

Judah asked the general what he saw when he looked at the rows of sad little trees along the road. The general stared off for a few moments. And then it was as if he realized that no one else was seeing what he was seeing. He understood he needed to communicate his intuition.

"I see those trees thirty years in the future. They're spreading their leaves wide across the boulevards providing shade; their thick roots are traveling deep into the ground. Birds and squirrels are making their homes in the branches. As the leaves give off their moisture they cool the sidewalks so more people will walk."

As the general described the post of the future, his staff nodded their heads. But they still were not bought in. Judah could tell from the combination of the general's conviction, yet still vague description, that he had had an intuitive breakthrough. He knew something about the future that went beyond his environmental concern; he just couldn't quite communicate what it was. That's the paradox of intuitive breakthroughs. There was something more to the general's vision than a description of trees. But what was it?

When the group reconvened, Judah asked General Pittard why he was focused on making Fort Bliss a zero-waste post. The general grew very animated. "That's just it. Our military runs on energy, and right now that energy comes from oil. That dependence is a security risk, both from other countries and the environment. Don't you see," he said to his staff, "it's not about the trees. We could have a more peaceful world, a more secure world in thirty years, by changing how we draw energy from the world. The trees are just a first step we can take right now in that direction."

General Pittard was trying to help the military see the inevitability and intelligence of going green. It was an intuitive idea. We may not know if it worked for another thirty years. But his explanation helped his staff understand what his intuition was about (though the Charlie Brown moniker stuck).

Remember, no one style of breakthrough is better than another. Some people experience breakthroughs across multiple styles, and others have a deep relationship with just one. The key is to know which one or two are yours, and to work to cultivate those.

Paradigm Breakthrough

The names associated with paradigm breakthrough are legendary: Newton, Einstein, Heisenberg, Darwin. This is the kind of breakthrough that affects all of humanity and changes the way we see the world.

Paradigm breakthrough is a deep insight about a system of thought that fundamentally changes the rules we assign to that system. When Newton watched an apple fall to the ground and realized that the same force that pulled the apple down was also governing the heavenly bodies, he revolutionized a system.

While eureka breakthroughs and paradigm breakthroughs both tend to arrive in a clear, straightforward fashion, they differ in the type of content they deliver. Paradigm breakthroughs will reveal a grand theory, universal laws, an explanation of multiple phenomena without any immediate concrete application. Eureka breakthroughs, on the other hand, deliver a concrete, immediately applicable answer to a specific problem.

You'll also feel different, physically and mentally, after experiencing these two types of breakthroughs. Eureka breakthroughs deliver a rush of excitement and newfound energy. We heard a story about a scientist who was driving off the NASA campus at the end of the day when a thorny problem suddenly resolved itself—a eureka breakthrough. He stopped his car in the middle of the road, got out, and ran back to his office.

For the rest of the afternoon, his fellow NASA employees simply drove around his car on their way out, swerving extra wide to avoid the driver's side door, which he had left open. Even if you're a generally responsible person, having a eureka breakthrough will bring out the absentminded professor in you.

Paradigm breakthroughs, although far greater in their impact, are a calmer personal experience. They may bring about a sense of awe and wonder rather than excitement. They might be immensely intellectually satisfying, but not necessarily valuable in the financial or practical sense. And they often require additional work to be fully developed, as in the case of Einstein's theory of relativity, which was too complex to have "occurred" to him in its entirety in one moment. Einstein actually spent six whole weeks writing out his theory. The experience was more drawn out than we typically think necessary for breakthroughs, as if the magnitude of the idea was too much to take in all at once.

Paradigm breakthroughs are the most rarely occurring type, and the most powerful. But they have as much to do with luck and timing as they have to do with a single person's abilities. Einstein's paradigm breakthrough came at the end of a long line of smaller breakthroughs going back at least a hundred years, from Alessandro Volta's discovery and description of electrical properties to James Clerk Maxwell's more precise definition of these properties to Albert Michelson and Edward

Morley disproving the existence of aether and more accurately confirming the speed of light, to Ludwig Boltzmann defending the concept of atoms, and finally to Max Planck discovering the law of quanta.

Every single one of these discoveries, these smaller breakthroughs, was a prerequisite for Einstein's paradigm breakthrough. This series of breakthroughs is what Einstein was describing when speaking of his "earlier intellectual experience."[15] Einstein lived at a moment in history ripe for a paradigm shift. He truly "stood on the shoulders of giants."

This is not to take away from Einstein's genius, but it's important to recognize the role of external factors in creating a paradigm breakthrough. And while they may seem like the Holy Grail of breakthroughs, it's something one should neither focus on nor strive after.

The allure of the paradigm breakthrough is obvious. Everyone will know your name. Your face will adorn the walls of dorm rooms. But paradigm shifters don't set out to shift paradigms—a lesson many innovators would do well to learn.

Many people get lost down a rabbit hole chasing a paradigm-shifting idea. NASA scientist Peter Cheeseman talks about seeing colleagues go chasing after the essence of quantum mechanics and never returning. Artificial intelligence expert, serial entrepreneur, and angel investor Barney Pell calls the phenomenon "smart people, stupid problem."[16] Olivia's scientist father recalls: "For the first ten years after my PhD, I was chasing the Nobel Prize and got nowhere. Then I gave up, and finally started doing good science."

Once again, it's important to see the different types of breakthroughs as equally desirable, and you must trust the way your brain delivers a breakthrough to you.

KEY TAKEAWAYS

- A breakthrough is a sudden advance in our knowledge or understanding that moves us past a barrier and allows us to see and understand something in a new way.
- Eureka breakthroughs are clear, sudden, fully formed, immediately applicable, and are most likely to arrive when you're *not* thinking about a problem. They create great excitement in the individual experiencing one.

- Metaphorical breakthroughs usually arrive as metaphors or analogies and require interpretation before they're complete. They are sometimes embedded in dreams, and occur as the brain connects two seemingly disparate items or ideas.
- Intuitive breakthroughs defy logic and explanation and tend to be more of a beginning. They allow us to make progress down a longer path.
- Paradigm breakthroughs arrive in clear, straightforward fashion, similar to eureka breakthroughs. However, these breakthroughs reveal a grand theory or explanation that is without any immediate application. They bring more awe and wonder than excitement. They are the rarest, but also the most powerful, type of breakthrough.
- No specific type of breakthrough is better or more productive than another, it's simply a matter of knowing which type is most natural to you.

Chapter 2

The Chrysalis

Where Breakthroughs Come From

THE YEAR WAS 1965. The place was Clearwater, Florida. In his motel room—the Rolling Stones weren't yet famous enough to afford hotels—Keith Richards woke up on a hot, humid morning to find his guitar and a tape recorder on the bed beside him. Groggy and hung over, Richards rewound the tape and pressed "play." The hourlong tape contained fifty-nine minutes of his own snoring. But the first thirty seconds held the opening bars and first lyric of what became the Rolling Stones's most iconic hit, the song "Satisfaction."[1] He didn't remember even touching the tape recorder.

Believe it or not, Richards's breakthrough moment follows the very same pattern as Einstein's discovery of the special theory of relativity. It's the pattern we heard again and again when we interviewed some of the world's greatest innovators for this book. And it's the same pattern you've experienced if you've ever had a sudden epiphany in the shower.

Whenever you have a "shower moment," chances are something was on your mind, like a problem at work or an issue in a relationship. You'd probably been mulling over the problem, trying to work it out in different ways. Then you stepped into the shower. Your mind wandered off as the water poured over you. You were no longer focused. Suddenly, seemingly out of the blue, the answer came to you.

What do your shower moments have in common with both Keith

Richards's and Albert Einstein's discoveries? When you got into the shower, you unknowingly switched brain modes. Previously, you had been consciously focusing on the problem. But in the shower, your mind was probably drifting, idly daydreaming or seemingly "thinking about nothing." Neuroscientists have recently discovered that the secret to breakthroughs lies in our ability to switch between these two modes, the focused and the meandering.[2]

The focused mode is one you are already familiar with, because it's the one you have been consciously using all your life. You can think of this mode as the "executive mode": it's the one you use to execute, to get things done. Goal oriented and deadline focused, it's a champion at making lists, following timelines, and coming in under budget. The part of your brain responsible for this mode is called the **executive network,** or **EN**.[3]

The EN is a group of brain regions near the front of your skull that help you focus on a task and accomplish a specific goal. You're very well versed in the use of your EN. You did, after all, spend at least a decade in school specifically training those brain regions. As a matter of fact, you're using your EN right now to read this sentence.

The EN allowed our forebears to track the patterns of the stars and the moon, figure out the best time to plant their crops, and organize the immense task of building the pyramids. It's also responsible for "social inhibition," the form of self-control we use to function in society. Without your EN you are a three-year-old. With your EN you are (we hope) a functional, responsible, and productive member of society.

But your EN alone can't create breakthroughs. It needs help from the more meandering network, the one that creates shower moments. This is our creative network, the **default network,** or **DN**. You can think of the DN as a network or council of breakthrough geniuses inside your brain. The geniuses talk and exchange ideas, half-baked theories, and wild speculations.

The DN is the source of all our creativity, all our invention, all our genius—and it hasn't gotten nearly enough recognition. What has the DN accomplished throughout history? A better question would be what great discoveries *hasn't* it played a role in. If the EN gives us the ability to focus and accomplish a task, the DN gives us the ability to look through the complexity of the world to see the patterns underneath.[4]

The DN is a vital component of your brain: research has made clear that this part of your brain is as essential to your survival as your heart or your kidneys.[5] It's so important, in fact, that we could have written this entire book all about the DN. We would have said, "Here it is! Here's how it works, here's how you can access it, here's how you can turbocharge it." But in fact, that's not enough. The DN, alone, can't create breakthroughs.

> It's the ability to use both modes, to switch from one mode to another, that enabled Keith Richards to come up with "Satisfaction" and Albert Einstein to discover the special theory of relativity. In fact, it's what enabled most discoveries in human history.

We will cover how the DN works, how you can access it, and how you can turbocharge it. But we will then take you to the next level and teach you how to get both networks to work together—that is, how to switch from one mode to the other and back again. **This "mode switching" is what it's all about**.

As your brain takes in information via your five senses, some of it is used in immediate circumstances, such as: step over that rock; hit the brakes; someone just walked into the room, so stop singing.

We also use information to build patterns. Some of the patterns are simple, such as: I like pizza from Marcello's, or I don't like it when my mother calls because she gives me guilt for not calling. These patterns are part of life's basics, its essentials. (Especially with a Jewish mother. Trust us.)

Other patterns are more complex, such as: What is the series of notes, chords, and bars that will become a song that will electrify American rock and roll? Try as it might, this was not a pattern that Richards's EN could figure out.

In 1965, on their first American tour, the Rolling Stones were a midlevel group touring the country with their fourth album. They were seriously in need of a breakthrough hit, the kind of number one song that would make them a household name. Richards's EN knew this and had been focusing on it. His executive set a direction and defined a need, but it couldn't come up with a solution.

When Richards fell asleep, his executive was able to take a break from its usual work of thinking and executing. Imagine it taking a walk from its front office in the brain to the deeper, central part of the brain. There's a secret lounge there, where his council of breakthrough geniuses reside. We all have a lounge like that inside our brain.

While Richards's executive was working in the brain's front office, the lights in the genius lounge were dim, because when the EN is focused on accomplishing a specific task, it draws much of the brain's power. But with the front office on break, the power is rerouted to the genius lounge, and when Richards's executive opens the door, things are buzzing.

Imagine a lounge full of plush couches, beanbags, drinks and snacks, whiteboards and sticky notes and different colored pens and pencils. Leonardo da Vinci is sitting in a corner doodling on his sketch pad. Napoleon is playing with toy soldiers. Euclid is dancing with glow sticks that Marie Curie gave him. Michelangelo is wrapping Play-Doh around a pencil. Teresa de Avila is trying to write in her diary, but Erasmus keeps bothering her to ask about the fate of mankind. Steve Jobs is telling Einstein he's not thinking big enough. Sun Tzu is telling a story of his past victory to no one in particular. Joan of Arc is ruminating over her betrayal by the French. Sherlock Holmes is analyzing the environment for clues (To what? It doesn't matter. He just likes analyzing), and Amelia Earhart is taking a nap.

When it walks into the room, Richards's executive asks for their attention. "Listen folks, we need a hit. See what you can come up with." A direction is set, a need is defined. Then—and this is important—the executive heads out to do something else. It knows that it has to let the geniuses do their thing. Maybe it takes a walk, knits a sock, or takes a shower. It can't be something too demanding, or it would draw brainpower away from the lounge.

Meanwhile, back in the lounge, the lights grow bright and the geniuses crank up the espresso machine. They are talking, writing, drawing, building Lego models of their theories, or putting sticky notes up and moving them around. Michelangelo and Leonardo are sketching, Sun Tzu and Napoleon are strategizing, Teresa de Avila and Erasmus are reflecting, Joan of Arc is worrying. (We're not kidding, this is really what the different parts of your DN do.) The ideas are flying. One theory leads to another, which leads to another.

The executive regularly checks back in so that the geniuses can show it what they came up with. The executive might make some comments and suggestions or clarify the direction, and then go back to its crossword puzzle or daydream. Until one moment—during a walk, or in the shower, or in Richards's case, in the middle of the night—when the geniuses get incredibly excited, and the executive sees something spark. Something has come together.

That night in Clearwater, Keith Richards's genius council showed his executive the first eight bars of a song with a single lyric. The geniuses and the executive looked at it together, then looked at each other and said *Yes!* The executive woke Richards up, made sure he recorded it, and then went off-task again so Richards could go back to sleep.

And that, in a nutshell, is the neuroscience of breakthroughs.

Recapping the neuroscience of "Satisfaction":

- The executive sets the direction: Write a hit song!

- Richards falls asleep; his executive leaves the front office.

- Power reroutes to the genius lounge; the brain has switched modes.*

- The geniuses come up with a song that the executive recognizes as a possible hit.

- The executive rouses Richards from sleep and makes sure he records the song.

- Task completed, Richards falls back asleep as his executive leaves the front office.

---

* The salience network is a network of regions that, among other things, focuses our attention on the most salient information at any time. This network has been found to actually direct our attention either to people, facts, or events outside of us, or to things happening inside of us. It mediates between our EN and our DN. It consists of the the anterior insula and dorsal anterior cingulate cortex, the amygdala, the ventral striatum, and the substantia nigra/ventral tegmental area. Things that pique the salience network include anything out of the ordinary, anything that breaks a pattern, anything surprising, pleasurable, or rewarding, anything relevant to the self or which engages the emotions.

The executive, among many other things, sets the direction for your genius council to follow. And once the genius council has come up with something, the executive is the one that puts into practice the ideas the genius council comes up with. It's as if the executive were giving the genius council a bunch of Legos and saying, "See what you can turn these into." The Legos snap together the same way neurons do. Your genius council is constantly trying out new neural connections. Sometimes it makes a multicolored Lego mess, but sometimes it puts together a locomotive, a spaceship, or the special theory of relativity.

If the DN Is So Important, Why Haven't You Heard of It Before?

Since 1929, neuroscientists have known that the brain is in a constant state of activity, and that background noise surrounds our more rational processes, but only recently has that background noise been examined as anything more than a nuisance.[6]

Our modern biases are geared toward the logical, the structured, the efficient—all the things that the DN is not. As the DN's discoverer, Dr. Marcus Raichle, told us, "Up until recently, our focus has been on making the brain do specific things, ignoring the background, default, nonconscious, nondirected activity."[7] The default network is one of the most powerful tools at our disposal, but it is not task focused.

Focus is a positive attribute: a bias for the executive is a bias for what is feasible. But the top performers, the stars, the innovators, the geniuses reach breakthroughs by switching back and forth between the focused EN and the unfocused DN.

Dr. Raichle, who discovered the existence of the default network in 1997, named it thus because it is the mode that the brain *defaults* to anytime it isn't on-task. And this mode never actually shuts off, but rather quiets down when we are focused on something. The moment we switch off a task, we default to this network. Look out the window, bang! Default to the network. Get up to make coffee, bang! We default to the network.

Dr. Raichle told us that this unconscious processing "is truly most of what we really do; because if we didn't we'd be pretty hopeless." The network is always on, always engaged, interrupted only when we have to perform a specific task. And this is why it uses twenty times more energy than the conscious, task-focused part of the brain.[8]

"The brain is active all of the time," Dr. Raichle told us, "whether you are awake or asleep, whether you're engaging in a particular task or you are daydreaming. The brain is operating almost at full capacity or full strength pretty much all of the time."

Unfortunately we are so busy—we have so many tasks to complete to do our jobs, hit our numbers, achieve our goals—that we leave less and less time for our genius council to work its magic. We live in an executive world, which makes it all the more difficult for us to sit still and let power reroute to the genius lounge. But the genius council's participation is essential to breakthrough thinking.

In the mid-1800s, chemists were trying to discover the structure of the molecule benzene, a key component in gasoline. German chemist Friedrich August Kekulé set his executive to the task. But it was one night while dozing off in front of a fire, having switched off his executive mode, that his genius council drew him a picture of a snake eating its own tail.[9]

Kekulé's genius council had given him the metaphor; his executive interpreted the metaphor and solved the riddle: benzene was a ring. With that, Kekulé ushered in the modern age of structural organic chemistry and the rise of the pharmaceutical industry. Ever wonder why so many big pharmaceutical companies are German: Merck, Bayer, Roche, Schering? Kekulé set up his breakthrough lab at the University of Bonn.

Kekulé, like Einstein, Edison, Dalí, Tesla, Watts, and countless other innovators, achieved his breakthrough thanks to the back-and-forth switch between his executive mode and his genius mode. In fact, Dr. Raichle told us that it was after leaving a meeting and walking down the hall that he had the breakthrough leading to the default network's discovery.

So how can you access your genius mode?

Sleep on It (Yes, Really)

Adam Cheyer is the creator of Siri, Apple's artificial intelligence iPhone voice assistant. Building Siri was a Herculean design and programming task. The sheer number of variables—the ability to understand vary-ing speech patterns, the ability to search based on the random ways people would request information, the ability to return answers in a useful way—were each a massive challenge in its own right. Thankfully, Cheyer had a secret weapon: ready access to his genius mode.

Although designing and building Siri was a highly structured task, Cheyer knew better than to try to logically grind out every an-swer. Instead, he told us, "I sleep on the issues I'm wrestling with."[10] Cheyer, like Dalí and Edison, has discovered the incredible break-through power of the hypnagogic and hypnopompic states, the half-asleep periods just before falling asleep and just before waking. These are times when our genius council runs on hyperdrive.

"I go to bed around eleven, noodling on a problem as I fall asleep," he explained. By "noodling" on the problem, Cheyer uses his EN to deliberately and consciously focus his genius council on a question.

He relies on his genius council to make new associations and de-liver breakthroughs while asleep. In the morning he goes to his desk and uses his EN to process the night's harvest of ideas.

Morning after morning while first designing Siri, he would wake up with new insights from his DN. He'd use his EN to integrate them into the prototype he was building. Eventually, he felt that he had something concrete enough to show the rest of the world.

The hypnagogic and hypnopompic states are so fruitful for creativ-ity because our inhibiting frontal lobes—where our EN's front office is located—are quiet, and our DN is running strong.[11]

Falling Asleep: Accessing Your Hypnagogic State

The hypnopompic state is the brief period of time just as you're waking up, while the hypnagogic state is a similarly brief period of time just as you're falling asleep.

Putting It into Practice: How to Enter the Hypnagogic State

- Clear the room of clutter and distractions.

- Have pen and paper, voice recorder, your phone on airplane mode and set to take notes, or . . .

- Dim the lights (or wear an eye mask).

- Ensure you're in a quiet place, or that only white noise is audible.

- Don't get too comfortable—no wearing pajamas or getting in bed.

- Try to find time at midday, or right after you've eaten, when you're just the right amount of tired.

- Set your alarm for ten to fifteen minutes.

- Take a moment to focus your brain on the problem, and then let it go. Relax and drift off.

You'll have better luck with the hypnagogic state if you do some prep work. Sifting through memories of your problem, partial solutions, the contours of your question, and the relevant information you have before you go to sleep is important. It's up to you to set a direction for your brain to wander in. It is as if there were a reception desk in your brain saying, "Welcome to hypnagogic state. What would you like your geniuses to ponder?" You answer the question by thinking about the problem.

Have a pad and pencil or a phone voice recorder nearby, but no other distractions—nothing to get in the way of your recording whatever information comes from the hypnagogic state, whether it's in the form of words or an image.

Dim lighting can help, too. When you're having an insight, your visual cortex goes into alpha waves—that is, your brain actually ceases to process visual information. In order to support the breakthrough ability of the hypnagogic state, you want to enable your visual cortex to go off line unimpeded, and low lighting is just the thing.

We recommend blocking the light rather than turning it off entirely simply because you might need the light to write, and you want to do as few things as possible between waking up and recording your ideas. You might try wearing an eye mask; this will block the light but will be fast and easy to remove, allowing you to begin recording your breakthrough almost immediately.

Sound can be a matter of personal preference. Some people will want to eliminate all sound; others may prefer white noise, a fan, nature sounds, or the television on low volume.

Research strongly indicates that a midday nap enhances most people's cognitive abilities for the rest of the day, and that we get the most benefits from naps that last fifteen to twenty-five minutes. So if you try this exercise and don't awaken with a breakthrough, you'll at least be sharper and more productive for the rest of the day.*

If you want to go high tech, consider Napwell, a napping mask created by MIT and Harvard Medical School students that uses sleep-cycle monitoring to optimize napping. Waking up during the deep sleep portion of your cycle makes you groggy and unproductive, but Napwell monitors your sleep cycle to wake you up at the optimal time, and even uses light to mimic a natural sunrise.

Don't get frustrated if you find you're not actually falling asleep: first, it might take some practice; and second, breakthroughs often come while relaxed and mind-wandering but not asleep.

Waking Up: Accessing the Hypnopompic State

Deep sleep is not only allowed but required to access the hypnopompic state, so fluff those pillows and climb under the blanket. This is the state between rising out of sleep and coming into consciousness.

Presumably, hours will have passed since you fell asleep the night before, so it's imperative that you sent your brain in the right direction.

---

* Some people feel that naps leave them in a zombielike state for the rest of the day. If that's the case with you, just use these tools in the evening at bedtime.

Putting It into Practice: How to Access the Hypnopompic State

---

- Watch a documentary on something you know nothing about. Thinking about new narratives will trip new neural circuits and help your brain form new associations.

- Look through old photos. Your DN might find something valuable in a memory file that you'd forgotten years ago.

- Read a book from your adolescence. Old thoughts and feelings will come rushing in.

- Take a walk outside. You'll simultaneously oxygenate your brain, flip the script on your bedtime routine, and see and feel things more interesting than your bathroom.

- Choose a progressive alarm that starts out quietly and builds in volume. You don't want to be jolted awake, bypassing the liminal state you were trying to take advantage of. Nature sounds work well here.

- Have a recording device nearby, whether to write, type, or record your voice. The breakthroughs emerging from the hypnopompic state can be fleeting and ephemeral, so if you don't record them, they'll retreat from you as you wake up.

It's hard to ignore the number of creative geniuses who credit their successes to the hypnopompic state. "Half the time I get answers in the middle of the night,"[12] said Jeff Hawkins, who started the entire smartphone revolution when he created the Palm and Treo and is now working on Grok, an artificial-intelligence system based on how our brain's neurons actually work. "I think about it while falling asleep, and in the middle of the night I'll wake up and I'll lie in bed silently in the dark and just think. It's very important that it is dark. And then the answer will just come to me."

Sleep is a great tool for accessing your genius mode. Judah has often awoken with great new ideas. He will often finish a conversation with a client by saying, "Alright, I'll have an answer in the morning." His clients often find an answer in their e-mail in-box over breakfast. Olivia, on the other hand, has never woken up with a new insight. When she naps, she rises groggy, hungry, and slightly grumpy. If she fell asleep with marbles in her hand, when they inevitably dropped, bounced, and rolled on the ground, she'd probably startle awake thinking "What idiot is making such a bloody noise?" So don't beat yourself up if the hypnagogic and hypnopompic states don't do much for you.

We made great use of this technique when we worked with a successful start-up's secret skunkworks design studio. One day the small team faced a particularly vexing design challenge. As the energy wound down, Judah opened a few beers to signal a shift. Once everyone had relaxed a little, Olivia tried to casually frame the problem.

"So it seems like you all are trying to figure out how to use superlow bandwidth to create connectivity without cell towers. Does that sound about right?" It did not sound right and the group made sure to be very clear about what the issue was. And that was precisely what we needed them to do: at the very end of the day, they clearly defined the problem they were working on.

That night we sent texts to a few of the team members just before bed to help their ENs focus their DNs before sleep. We framed the problem just as they had earlier. This is more than telling someone to sleep on it. The creation of the clear and concise framing along with focus before sleep is key. We acted as the executives to set the direction for the team's genius lounges. The next morning, one of the engineers showed up with eyes shining. The solution had come to her as she woke up.

KEY TAKEAWAYS

- Our brains have two modes of operation: focused mode and meandering mode.
- Focused mode is the executive mode that helps us get things done

and is powered by the executive network (EN) of the brain. The EN is goal and action oriented.

- Meandering mode is the source of creativity and invention, and is powered by the default network (DN) of the brain. The DN is always running in the background, 24/7.
- Both modes are required for breakthroughs, and therefore we must learn to switch back and forth between them.
- The minutes just before and after sleep can be a fertile environment for breakthroughs. Falling asleep allows us to access DN solutions in the hypnagogic state. Waking from sleep allows us to discover DN solutions through the hypnopompic state.

Chapter 3

On the Hunt

How to Access Genius Mode

IMAGINE A PARTY inside your brain where all your ideas, memories, predictions, feelings, and environmental cues are meeting each other, making small talk, inviting new ideas into the conversation, excusing themselves to go to the bar for another drink, bumping into a new idea on the way to the bathroom, excitedly talking and dancing with each other. That, essentially, is what happens inside your genius lounge.

In this chapter, we'll give you tools to make ideas collide with each other and spark breakthroughs.

Unfortunately, as anyone who zones out all the time can testify, simply taking a break will not lead to inspiration: to stoke creativity, you need to perform tasks that allow your mind to wander.[1]

After an "unusual uses" creativity test ("How many things can you do with a hanger?") students were given a twelve-minute break. One group simply rested; one did an easy, mindless task; one did a demanding memory game; and one group took no break.

When the participants reconvened and retook the creativity test, the "mindless task" group performed an average of 41 percent better. By contrast, participants in the other three groups showed no improvement.

Interestingly, this was only the case for problems that were already being mentally chewed on; doing a mindless task didn't seem to lead to a general increase in creative problem-solving ability. This makes sense: our executive has to have set a clear goal for our geniuses in order for them to be productive.

Where Butterflies Live

Let's say that you're hard at work finishing a report. You feel there's something missing but you don't know what it is. You can't quite make the connection. You could stare blankly at the wall, try to catch up on e-mail, or call a friend who's been guilt-tripping you about returning their voice mail. Or you could allow your executive to wander by performing an undemanding task: water your plants, walk around the building, or make a sandwich. All three have the possibility of helping you get to breakthrough.

When your executive is "distracted" with low-pressure activities, your genius lounge can draw more brainpower.[2]

Science researchers in the field of creativity now recommend the regular inclusion of "mindless" work (i.e., work that is low in both cognitive difficulty and performance pressures) into the standard workday model as a critical component of high-creativity output. Their research suggests that to enhance creativity among chronically overworked professionals, their schedules should alternate between bouts of cognitively challenging, high-pressure work and bouts of mindless work.[3]

Putting It into Practice: Mindless Activities We Recommend

- Doing puzzles or walking labyrinths
- Watching a movie you've already seen countless times
- Throwing a rubber ball against the wall
- Watching sunlight through the trees
- Staring out the window
- Running

- Washing dishes by hand

- Playing video games

- Folding laundry

- Cleaning a cluttered space

- Drawing, doodling, or using an adult coloring book

- Cooking a meal you've cooked many times before

You could also listen to music. If you play an instrument, then by all means go for it, but give your mind a chance to meander by choosing a song you know incredibly well. The music will open your brain into an associative state, while your familiarity with the song will allow you to focus less on the task at hand.[4]

For those of us who are not musicians, just listening to music turns on a host of brain circuits, and listening with headphones helps to block out the outside world. You can sit on your couch, lie down on the floor, or go out for a run. Any music will work as long as it is without lyrics. Sorry, pop-song-loving runners: even if you know the lyrics backwards, they will still grab hold of the verbal part of your brain and activate the EN.

If at any point you feel blocked, stymied, frustrated at your lack of progress, walk away from your desk and start any of the above activities. Each of them will get your executive out of the front office and reroute the power to your genius lounge. The espresso is on and the associating begins.

Try this: Walk to a newsstand or open your computer. Pick a magazine or Web site you'd never usually read. If you usually get *Golf Digest,* get a knitting or architecture magazine. If you're into fashion, buy *Forbes.* Take in information unrelated to the challenge in front of you.[5] You'll be amazed at how quickly an unexpected train of thought can appear and start to snowball.

Olivia sometimes finds herself absentmindedly staring at her vacuuming robot while it cleans the house. Her conscious mind is idly wondering where the robot will go next and trying to predict the patterns. But in the back of her mind, she can often feel her genius

council churning away. Although this completely negates the intended time-saving aspect of the device, it's very beneficial for breakthroughs.

It's not always easy to switch out of our focused, executive mode.

Serena was a social entrepreneur with a company dedicated
to eradicating the lung diseases caused by dusty and muddy
floors in Africa. She was driven by her sense of purpose and yet
kept asking herself whether it was okay to spend all her time
building her company. Shouldn't she be making more time to
meet a nice man and start a family? It seemed everyone put
this question to her, from her mother to her coworkers to her
investors. The question acted as a weight and drain on her cognitive load.

Judah knew the answer to this question lay deeper inside
her than she was comfortable going. He needed to help her
access her genius council. But someone as driven as Serena,
especially when driven by purpose, would not set her executive
to the side easily. He needed to provide her executive with an
easy goal to occupy it so that the power would reroute to her
genius lounge.

At the retreat where we met her, there was a labyrinth made
from stones. A labyrinth is not a maze. Rather, a labyrinth lays
out a single path to follow. Once you enter it, there are no choices
for you to make. All you have to do is follow the contours of the
path as it winds its way inexorably toward the center. The path
gives your executive just enough to focus on, while the lack of
choices leaves plenty of excess power to reroute to the genius
lounge.

Judah set Serena at the start of the labyrinth. He then gave
her executive a little help by focusing it on the question: "Are
you unhappy devoting your life to your work? Do you feel something is missing?" He then ushered her into the labyrinth with a
single command: "Walk slowly." By the time Serena reached the
center her shoulders had relaxed and her brow had unfurrowed.
"I'm happy devoting my life to my work," she said. "It's everyone else who has an issue."

> Afterward, Judah asked Serena what had happened. She said she wasn't quite sure. She was walking the path of the labyrinth looking at the stones and the leaves on the ground. She was wondering at what degree the path curved. Then she said she felt like she just "spaced out. Like I was just walking. And then I knew. I knew." Serena had a eureka breakthrough.
>
> Serena was able to return to building her company with all her energy and dedication and no more doubts nipping at her heels. They were other people's doubts, not hers. She wanted to have an impact on the world through her work.

One of the most interesting ways to let your mind wander is to watch something that is happening in real time. One attraction at the Museum of Modern Art that had people spellbound was a real-time representation of communication patterns between New York and the rest of the world, created by MIT. You can see it at senseable.mit.edu/nyte/visuals.html. Picture it in your mind right now: you're looking at a dark globe, with jets of light emanating from New York to the rest of the world as the city's inhabitants make phone calls. You're seeing exactly what is happening, in the moment, right now. Fascinating, right?

Now, imagine this exact same representation with a year's delay. What you're seeing on the globe is what happened twelve months ago. You will most likely feel your level of interest drop considerably. There is a fascination with the immediate that catches the EN, while letting the DN wander.

"So what's the single best mindless activity I can do?" our clients often ask us. For once, we have a straightforward answer: if we had to choose one single mindless activity for you to do, it would be walking.

Take a Walk

In a recent study, participants walking indoors on a treadmill facing a blank wall or walking outdoors in the fresh air produced twice as many creative responses compared to those who were sitting down.[6]

"I thought walking outside would blow everything out of the

water," said the lead researcher, "but walking on a treadmill in a small, boring room still had strong results." The study also found that creative juices continued to flow even when a person sat back down shortly after a walk. "We know walking meetings promote creativity, but walking before a meeting may be nearly as useful."[7]

From a cognitive angle, walking demands just the right amount of focus from our executive, without asking too much. Walking is a very complex task: we are taking in constant input from our feet, legs, hips, arms, and, of course, our inner ears, the heart of our balance gyroscope. But our brains are experts at this task. Through long familiarity, the executive can do all this with very little energy.[8]

From a physical angle, walking stimulates your brain. Increased blood flow causes a cascade of wonderful changes in the brain, including the release of brain-derived neurotropic factor (BDNF) and other growth factors. BDNF promotes the birth of new neurons and the formation of new synapses, and it also strengthens existing synapses.[9]

Open offices have strong detractors as well as proponents, but with their few inner walls and rolling tables, they're at least walker friendly. In fact, according to research out of Stanford, the most important thing these open spaces offer to creativity is the ability to walk. Doing so increased a person's creative output by 60 percent, the study found.[10]

Darwin famously had a quarter-mile-long walking path called the Sandwalk that was his place to go and think when working on a problem. "So important was walking to his thought processes that Darwin sometimes described a problem he was working on in terms of the number of turns around his path he would need to solve it."[11]

Mason Currey, after studying the habits of nearly two hundred of the world's most prolific inventors and innovators over the ages, found that the single common habit of these great inventors and innovators was walking. As Currey reports, Charles Dickens famously took three-hour walks every afternoon—and what he observed on them fed directly into his writing.

Tchaikovsky made do with a two-hour walk, but wouldn't return a minute early, convinced that cheating himself of the full 120 minutes would make him ill. Beethoven took lengthy strolls after lunch, carrying a pencil and paper with him in case inspiration struck.

Søren Kierkegaard is quoted as saying "I have walked myself into my best thoughts." He is also reported to have often rushed back to his desk and resumed writing, still wearing his hat and carrying his walking stick or umbrella.[12]

Immanuel Kant would take a walk around the town square every day at the same time.

Werner Heisenberg wrote about long, exhausting conversations every night with Niels Bohr as they tried to wrestle with the strange realities of quantum mechanics that "ended almost in despair."[13]

At the end of each of these nights Heisenberg went for a walk alone in the neighboring park all the time asking himself the same question: Could nature really be as absurd as it seemed in his experiments? When Heisenberg came up with his uncertainty principle, now the second most famous and influential scientific theory of the twentieth century, he was walking through the park on his way home.[14] Textbook mind-wandering.

Walking, when used for mind-wandering, works well in quiet, peaceful places; less well when you have to be aware of cars, traffic lights, joggers, and so forth, because your executive mode has to stay active. Whether to meander or to walk with purpose is up to you: Judah is comfortable walking aimlessly, but Olivia needs a route and a destination.

Here's the thing: you don't just take a walk and magically have a breakthrough. Walking is a wonderful way to set the conditions, but there is more to it than simply meandering along.

Putting It into Practice: Creative Walking

- Define your problem. The act of verbalizing what you're looking for can get you started on finding the answer.

- Review your raw material. Read over the latest information you've collected. Check all the random Post-its and slips of paper you've jotted notes on, or any digital equivalent.

- Set a goal. Are you going to walk till you break through the blockage, or just for a set period of time or to a destination?

- Pay attention. It's fine to space out a bit, but don't neglect the scenery entirely.

- Carry a notebook. Always have a way to record your thoughts on hand.

- Keep something in your hand. A coin, a stone, a paper clip, a Star Wars figurine—we won't judge. Our hands send massive amounts of information to our brains, and keeping those channels open keeps our brains in a more associative state. Adam Cheyer always keeps a Rubik's Cube on his desk to play with while thinking.

- Stop and write it down. Don't enjoy the moment of insight so much that you keep playing with it in your head. Few things are as frustrating as forgetting a brilliant thought.

Experiment with Your Environment

The stereotypical image of the mad genius with a messy desk exists for a reason: creative mode is messy. Mess is good for creativity—in fact, it might sometimes be necessary, or as one of our favorite collaborators put it, "Messy is nessy."

Wouldn't you find it more enjoyable to rummage through a chaotic pile of Legos than to be presented with a box of neatly organized pieces? Most of us instinctively want to dump all the Legos into a pile and jumble them together. Minimalism is great for productivity but not for creativity.

One inventor was known to have two very different working rooms; one was Spartan, with almost no stimuli, the other a Wonka-esque madhouse to stimulate creativity. Many tech companies have playrooms for their employees, with grown-up toys like woodworking equipment. What you're aiming for is a contained mess, to stimulate creativity but not hinder productivity.

One very creative young innovator told us he regularly goes through cycles of rearranging everything in his apartment, creating a new environment—disturbing, then reordering, and after a little while doing it all over again. (It drives his roommates insane.)

Putting It into Practice: Change Your Environment

- Put up prisms, which combine the advantages of light, color, and motion.

- Bring nature indoors by filling your creative space with natural elements such as plants, rocks, a small fountain, light, and so on.

- Climb a tree. Yes, we're serious. You probably haven't done it in some time, and that's exactly why you should do it. Seeing the world from a weird angle is surprisingly helpful in unlocking a new perspective.

- If you live in a city, go to the top of a tall building and look out. If your building has windows in public spaces, go up and look out from there. Borrow a colleague's office that looks out a different side of the building than yours. Stare out the window with the new view and notice the differences. How are the streets laid out? What are the trees like? Where are the bodies of water? How would you have designed the city differently?

With all these suggestions, as always, your mileage may vary. Your aim is to find the balance of stimuli that works for you. Olivia likes to reflect on train journeys. The continuously unfolding scenery provides her with something to gaze at while her mind wanders, or fresh stimuli in case her mind gets stuck, but not so much that it is distracting. In addition, being a passenger is a receptive rather than active state, with no immediate action to take and no responsibilities, unlike driving, for example, so it's easier to let your mind wander.

Some people get their best ideas when on planes, others in the shower, others while gardening, running, or sitting still. Some may want to draw, others watch a movie, read something random, or cook. Some people will look out on a vista or the ocean, others may go to a forest. Some will want to walk the beach, others will want to sit with their back against a tree.

The really important thing is to figure out where you tend to get your breakthroughs, and to put yourself in those environments more often.

We often assume that sitting still or performing a repetitive motion like running is the key. But not always. Katashi, a senior vice president at a marketing firm, was trying to figure out what to do with a difficult campaign in Japan. Katashi was a bundle of energy. He talked fast and walked faster. His energy kept his team in a state of agitation.

We knew that telling Katashi to stare out the window or sit under a tree was not going to work. We also knew that he had grown up playing baseball. He had even thought about playing professionally in Japan.

One day we took the whole team to Central Park. Olivia gathered the other members of the team and led them on a wander through the part of the park called the Ramble. She motioned toward trees or benches where people could sit and go quiet. Judah stayed with Katashi and pulled out a reaction ball. It's a hard rubber ball with eight round protrusions and it's used as a training device in baseball. When you throw the reaction ball on the ground it takes crazy bounces, mimicking a baseball taking a bad hop.

Judah stood fifty feet away from Katashi and began to throw the reaction ball at him. Katashi assumed the crouched stance of an infielder. A big smile spread across his face. As the ball hit the ground and veered all over the place, Katashi chased after it, sometimes making spectacular grabs, sometimes getting hit in the shin, sometimes missing it altogether.

Nothing about this activity suggested his genius lounge was getting the energy it needed. But Katashi was so energetic that the activity worked. At one point he stopped and let the ball go right by him. He looked up and said, "That's it."

There are no right ways to do this. You have to find your way.

> ## Putting It into Practice: Play with Your Physical Surroundings
>
> • Right now, find five colors you enjoy around you.
>
> • Touch textures till you find five you find enjoyable.
>
> • Find five different hand movements. Go ahead, we'll wait. Just do different things with your hands.

Your environment, of course, isn't just what you see; it's also what you hear. Here are two exercises to experiment with your auditory environment.

Visualize the music: As you listen to a piece of classical music, imagine a story to go along with it. Is a young hero leaving his small village and encountering pirates and maidens and sea monsters? Is the piece describing the emotional breakdown of an old man after the loss of his wife? (The Disney movie *Fantasia* was written this way.)

Change the soundtrack: This one is Judah's favorite, and it's based on an old film trick by Sergei Eisenstein, a master of Russian film. Play a song while watching a movie scene on mute. Nine times out of ten, Judah says, the music will match the scene so well it's spooky. During an off-site meeting for the drug company Genentech, one executive suggested pairing the final scene from the movie *Casablanca* with "We Are the Champions" by Queen. The experience sparked a conversation about pairing researchers with artists and musicians to help them visualize the chemical structures of key molecules to improve drug delivery.

Putting It into Practice: The Best Background Noises for Creative Work

- An app called Coffitivity recreates the ambient noise of a coffee shop. (The creators originally set out to test the effect of background noise on productivity levels.)

- If you're stuck doing repetitive work, binaural-beat tracks—which play slightly different frequencies into your right and left ear—can help you through the laborious implementation necessary to turn an insight into reality.

- Try electronic music, which features gradually building "narratives" of repeated base melodies.

- The chug-chugging of a train and the churning of a washing machine are incredibly soothing. You can find countless clips online.

- For a choice of ambient sounds try the Web site ASoftMurmur .com. It gives you choices that you can mix and match, like rain and thunder, or waves and wind, or waves and rain.

When you want a fresh insight on a problem, you can also change your social environment. You could run the idea by different nationalities, age groups, or social classes. This is why travel is such a powerful provider of epiphanies: you are surrounded with all new stimuli. Traveling provides a completely different environment in many ways: physical, auditory, social, and so forth.

Interaction exponentially increases your associative power. Just like you, other people's brains bounce between different memories and facts, relating random facts to new endeavors. By sharing your associative ideas with other people, they have a chance of making an association you never would have thought of.

On the other hand, breakthroughs come most often when you're alone: it's hard to dedicate the majority of your brainpower to your internal genius council when other people are around. As with everything else, the best ratio of solo to social time is different for each person. You need to find what works for you.

Albert Einstein considered long walks on the beach to be imperative "so that I can listen to what is going on inside my head."[15] The need for solitude seems to be understood by many of the "greats." Mozart said that it was only when he was entirely alone, whether "traveling in a carriage or walking after a good meal or during the night when I cannot sleep" that his best ideas flowed most abundantly.[16]

Nikola Tesla, inventor of the alternating current that powers our lives, asserted that: "The mind is sharper and keener in seclusion and uninterrupted solitude. . . . Be alone—that is the secret of invention: be alone, that is when ideas are born."[17]

For the greatest possible change of environment, consider experimenting with your psychological environment: become someone or even something else.

A few cutting-edge techniques such as "bodily resonance" can actually simulate this experience. In a fascinating study, researchers used the "rubber hand illusion" to create a greater sense of kinship in people.[18] Light-skinned Caucasian participants were given multisensory stimulation to experience a dark-skinned hand as belonging to them. The more the participants came to experience the dark-skinned hand as their own, the more positive their attitude toward people of another race became. By expanding what people could see and feel as part of their own body, the researchers were able to change their mindset.

The rubber hand illusion can go quite far: you can even "become" an object. People were able to "become" a spoon and feel real empathy for it, even reflexively wincing when it was hit with a hammer!

Putting It into Practice: Change Your Psychological Environment

• Watch a documentary about a topic you'd consider "random." Try to find connections to what you are currently working on. How is this new world of bourbon distillers in rural Kentucky in any way similar to your project on marketing lip balm?

• Spend the day dressed like someone else. If you're usually a casual dresser, wear a suit. If you wear a suit every day, try

> wearing a sleeveless shirt and shorts. How do you feel dif-
> ferent, knowing that you're being perceived differently? (Our
> clothes are an element of our psychological environment.
> Several studies have shown that participants' confidence
> and concentration levels were boosted by wearing a doc-
> tor's white lab coat.)[19]
>
> • For the next twenty minutes, give in to your first impulse.
> Just do whatever you feel like doing. Harder than you thought,
> right? We are constantly stopping ourselves from doing all
> kinds of things.

Constraints Will Set You Free

Creative constraints are what allow you to change your creative environment. Perhaps the most famous (and, unfortunately, probably apocryphal) story of creative constraints was a bet writer Ernest Hemingway made with friends that he could write an entire story in just six words.

How could one possibly introduce characters, explain their relationships, awaken the reader's emotions, and tell a story in just six words? Hemingway did so in one sentence:

For sale: baby shoes, never worn.

When Steve Jobs told the designer of the very first Apple mouse that it had to fit in his hand, work on any surface including his jeans, and cost less than fifteen dollars, he was setting creative constraints.[20]

You can also use time constraints, as in setting a deadline. Some people can be creative on deadline, and many have to be. For many people, work expands to fill the time available, so deadlines help bring focus. "In the software industry," explains engineer Kevin Sauer, part of Microsoft's Black Belt team, "we use what we call iterations or sprints to focus what we are working on at any given time. I personally have experienced how when making these iterations very short (like a week), our teams were hyperfocused and accomplished more than some of the traditional two-week or even one-month sprints. A week is an absurdly short timeline, so the absurdity lowers the stakes. A hundred percent perfection is not on the table, so we are free from fear of failure."[21]

How can you experiment with constraints? You can constrain the time you have to do something, the space you have to do it in, or the resources you have: materials or money.

Our dear friend and creativity expert Tina Seelig, a founding faculty member of Stanford's famous Institute of Design, known as the D-school, was teaching a one-week class to help students understand the general principles of entrepreneurial thinking.

She handed each student an envelope with what they only knew as their "initial funding." She told them they had four or five days to plan, but once they opened the envelope, they had two hours to make as much money as they could.

When they opened the envelopes, they saw they each had five dollars. As Seelig explains it, the teams that made the most money didn't bother using the five dollars. They realized that five dollars framed the problem way too tightly.

One team set up a stand in front of the student union. They offered to measure bicycle tire pressure for free and fill tires for a dollar. About an hour in they realized people were super appreciative and so they pivoted and stopped charging a dollar and instead accepted donations. People donated even more. They walked away with a few hundred dollars. Another team made reservations at many of the popular restaurants in Palo Alto and sold their reservations as the times came up.

But the team that made the most money sold the three-minute presentation time they had in class to a company that wanted to recruit Stanford students. They realized that three minutes was the most valuable thing they had. The lesson here is that we often perceive constraints where there are none.

When filming *Apocalypse Now*, the director Francis Ford Coppola expected his star, Marlon Brando, to show up on set emaciated in order to play the character of Colonel Kurtz. Instead, Brando showed up overweight. So Coppola filmed Brando constantly in shadow. The audience could almost never get a clear look at him. Although this was done to hide the fact that he was too heavy, its effect was to make Kurtz even more menacing. The decision was praised as one of the director's best in the movie.[22]

Seelig uses the example from *Monty Python and the Holy Grail*, where the knights do not ride horses because the production could not afford horses. Instead, the knights pretend-gallop through the forest while their servants follow making the sound of horses' hooves with two coconut shells. It was one of the funnier and most memorable parts of the movie.

The experimentation with various kinds of constraints is also part of what is known as design thinking, an iterative method taught at Stanford's D-school for the practical resolution of problems and the creation of better future situations. Since we could need an entire book to do design thinking justice, you'll find several excellent ones listed in the resources section of this book.

KEY TAKEAWAYS

- To achieve true breakthroughs, we must allow our minds to wander. Research shows that alternating between cognitively challenging work and activities with a low cognitive load enhances creativity.
- Walking is one of the best activities to enhance creativity. Mason Currey found it was the single common factor among nearly two hundred of the world's most prolific inventors and innovators. Be disciplined in your process and always have a way to capture your thoughts along the way.
- Although walking outside may be ideal, don't let the absence of the perfect setting hinder you. Walking around the office or even on a treadmill provides tremendous creative advantages.
- A change of environment sparks creativity. This change can be to your physical environment, or to your auditory, social, or psychological environments.
- Setting constraints can be helpful, whether they are financial constraints, time constraints, or creative constraints. Likewise, removing constraints can also produce unexpected breakthroughs.

Chapter 4

The Butterfly Process

How Breakthroughs Happen Inside Your Head

"CREATIVITY IS JUST connecting things. When you ask creative people how they did something, they feel a little guilty because they didn't really *do* it, they just *saw* something. . . . That's because they were able to connect experiences they've had and synthesize new things."[1]

What Steve Jobs is describing is called "associative thinking," and is essential for breakthrough thinking. Too often, we make the mistake of assuming breakthroughs are freestanding ideas, something never thought of before by anyone in any context. The truth is that almost every breakthrough is a combination of ideas that already existed.

Henry Ford's breakthrough of the assembly line came when he made an association between the Chicago meatpacking industry's use of mechanized hooks and bakeries' use of industrial conveyer belts.[2] He put the two together, applied them to the building of the automobile, and the assembly line was born.

A breakthrough in gun accuracy came when gunmakers looked to the bow and arrow. The feathers on the back of arrows cause the arrow to spin, and the spin makes the arrow fly straight. In the same way, a football flies straight when thrown in a spiral. To make their bullets spin, gunmakers carved spirals inside their gun barrels. Accuracy increased fivefold. Because putting feathers on arrows was called rifling, these guns became known as rifles.[3]

René Laennec was a French doctor who one day observed two young children communicating through a long, hollow piece of wood. One scratched the end of the stick with a pin and the other put her ear to the far end of the stick to hear it. The wood amplified the sound. Laennec went home and invented the stethoscope.[4]

For T. J. Parker, what he did when he was bored helped him start a revolution in the medication industry with his company, PillPack.

In 2006, the Walter Reed Army Medical Center released a study showing that educating patients, and much more importantly, placing their medications in single-serving blister packs, increased proper use of prescription drugs from 61 percent to 96 percent. But the study noted that blister packing was too time consuming to scale.[5]

This matters because a study of patients with cardiovascular conditions showed that nearly half of all hospital admissions were caused by medications being taken improperly.[6] These mistakes cost Americans millions of dollars—by some accounts, billions—every year. If someone could figure out how to scale blister packing medications, millions of people would be healthier and millions of dollars would be saved.

Enter Parker.

With his cofounder Elliot Cohen, he founded PillPack in 2013.[7] PillPack sends people their daily doses of multiple medications in single-serving packs with the date and time of day it is to be taken on the label. How did Parker come up with this?

First and foremost, Parker was steeped in the pharmaceutical world. The reason he heard of the Walter Reed study is that his father, a pharmacist, had started a business prepackaging meds for patients in nursing homes.

Parker had then gone to pharmacy school, but also taken classes in industrial design, furniture design, architecture, textiles, and clothing design. He told us, "I studied design because I was bored. The things you do to waste time because you're bored are the things you care about and will get good at." He also volunteered to help run MIT's entrepreneurship competition and dabbled in tech.

Using his knowledge of pharmacology, operations, technology, and design, Parker created a system that uses robots to sort pills into customized packets. Perhaps some credit for the PillPack idea goes to Parker's pharmacy degree, but a lot of other people with the same degree failed to come up with such an innovative solution to an industry problem.

One of Thomas Edison's least successful inventions was the electric pen, patented in 1876, to help make copies. People just weren't that into it. In 1891, a man named Samuel O'Reilly saw the pen and had a breakthrough. What did O'Reilly figure out?[8]

Here's one way to approach the question. What job could O'Reilly have had that the electric pen would be useful in, but in a different way than Edison intended? When he saw an electric pen place ink on paper, what else could he imagine putting ink on?

Here's another way to approach it. What is the essence of a pen? We think of a pen as something we write with, a way to communicate language on paper. But that is a pen's most common use. Its essence is that it makes ink marks on surfaces. Do those marks have to be made on paper? Do those marks have to be language? Of course not. What other kinds of marks could an electric pen make? And on what other kinds of surfaces?

Sit with that question. See what comes to you. Or start making a list of kinds of marks and surfaces. Even if you guess wrong the guessing itself is great practice.

Here's another hint. Instead of looking at the electric pen, look at Samuel O'Reilly. He worked in downtown New York in the late 1800s. It was a rough-and-tumble place with many unsavory characters, taverns, and oysters sold from carts on the street. The Brooklyn Navy Yard across the river meant there were plenty of sailors walking the streets. Does that help?

Samuel O'Reilly was a tattoo artist. After seeing Edison's electric pen he invented the modern tattooing machine. Instead of ink writing language on paper, he applied ink to skin to create images.

Over a hundred years later, design student Pierre Emm had a similar associative breakthrough. The French Ministry of Culture had challenged students to create remixes of images in the public domain. While riding his bike one day, Emm thought to hack a 3-D printer so it would draw tattoos on skin.[9]

In the 1970s, Southern California suffered a drought that caused people to empty their swimming pools. Skateboarders didn't fixate on the concrete holes in the ground as empty pools. Instead they saw them as proto-skate parks, the kind you see in nearly every city today.

In 1963, another skateboarder, Tom Sims, wanted to combine his two favorite sports, skiing and skateboarding. He also wanted to keep practicing skateboarding during the winter months. In his seventh-grade wood shop class he built a "skiboard." Skateboarding on snow became snowboarding.[10]

Seven Essential Innovation Questions

Here's a tool to help you create associations. It's called the seven essential innovation questions, or SEIQ. This tool does an amazing job of occupying your executive with a goal. Our executives *love* having a goal. When occupied with a goal, our ENs are happy to let our DN geniuses go at full speed.

SEIQ was created at Autodesk, one of the world leaders in 3-D design software, from entertainment to architecture and industrial design. When you walk through the halls of Autodesk, you will encounter some of their 3-D–printed creations, including a dress, jewelry, coral reefs, a fully functional motorcycle, and a full-size jet engine. Autodesk understands creativity.

Their innovation strategist, Bill O'Connor, leads teams through the seven essential innovation questions, which are actually a guide to thinking creatively. The questions point you in fruitful directions. They are helpful even for "creative types" because they help you hit all the different angles.

As always, these questions cannot guarantee an association or breakthrough or a specific outcome. But they are a very helpful framework to set the optimal conditions for breakthroughs to happen. Moving through these questions creates the right space for butterflies to emerge.

O'Connor says that we have all imagined, looked at, moved, used, connected, changed, and made things in our lives—but we haven't done so systematically or consistently. The seven essential questions are about the power of the checklist. "This isn't brainstorming," he told us, "this is brainstreaming."

You take whatever it is you are trying to break through and place it in the room, so to speak, and then ask the seven questions about it—that is, look at it from seven different angles. Not all of them work for everything. All you need is one of them to work for the breakthrough to happen.

The key words of the seven questions are Look, Use, Move, Interconnect, Alter, Make, Imagine. The acronym is LUMIAMI.

1. Look: What aspects of the problem could we look at in a new way, or from a new perspective?

2. Use: What facets of the problem could we use in a new way, or for the first time?

3. Move: What parts of the problem could we move, changing its position in time or space?

4. Interconnect: What could we connect that's not yet connected, or what could we connect in a different way, if it already is connected?

5. Alter: What could we change or alter, in terms of design and performance?

6. Make: What could we make that is truly new?

7. Imagine: What could we imagine that would create a great experience?

Each of the seven essential questions has its own checklist. They're mainly geared toward physical, tangible breakthroughs, so we've starred (*) the ones that also work for intangible products and innovations. You'll notice that almost every question forces you to confront your functional fixedness about an object or concept.

1. Look

Higher: Look at something from a 30,000-foot view.

Reverse: Look at something in reverse, from the back, from the other side.

*Value: Look at something from the point of view of its value.

*Kids: Look at something the way a kid might look at it.

Ignore: Look at something and ignore what you know to be true about it.

Holistic: Look at something from the point of view of the whole thing, from a systems point of view.

When Einstein looked at the universe and said that no matter how fast you are going, light will always move at 186,000 miles per second to you, he ignored what he knew to be true.

2. Use

*Leverage: How could you use this to leverage something else?

*Foundation: How could you use this to build the foundation for something?

*Substitute: How could you use this in place of something else?

*Aspect: How could you use an aspect of this in a new way?

*Change: How could you use this to change something you're doing?

*Apply: How could you apply this in a new way?

When Samuel O'Reilly turned Edison's electric pen into a tattoo machine, he saw how to substitute it for what he was using. And when the Southern Pacific Railroad built a series of microwave towers to facilitate an intercontinental network of telecommunications, they were just focused on improving their trains' efficiency. But this also became the foundation for the telecom company Sprint (**S**outhern **Pa**cific **R**ailroad **I**nternal **N**etwork **T**elecommunications).

3. Move

*Import: What new component could you bring in to make a change?

*Rearrange: What could you rearrange to make a change?

*Replace: What could you swap out and replace to make a change?

*Remove: What could you remove to make a change?

*Speed: What could you make go faster or slower to make a change?

*Frequency: What could you have happen more or less often to make a change?

When Keith Richards first imagined "Satisfaction" that night in Florida, he heard it as a slow, bluesy song. In a Los Angeles studio, the Stones played it faster and it became the iconic song it is.

4. Interconnect

Power: What could you connect to create a more powerful idea?

*Combine: What could you combine with to make something new?

*Network: What could you network into to make something new?

*Transparent: What could you expose to make something new?

*Open: What could you open to the world to see something new emerge?

*Partnership: What could you partner with to make something new?

The bow was created and combined with the spear. Partnership made the spear more powerful and the bow more useful.

5. Alter

*Quality: What could you improve the quality of?

*Design: What could you design differently?

*Performance: How could you increase the performance ability?

*Aesthetics: How could you change the look?

*Experiential: How could you change the experience?

*Standardize: How could you make it fit with other things?

Orville Wright changed the design of their airplane's wings to warp, be movable, and that made controlled, powered flight possible.

6. Make

Processes: What new processes could you create?

Meaning: What new meaning could you create/infuse?

Harness: What could be harnessed to make something new?

Instantiate: What can you instantiate into something new?

Functions: What new functions can you create?

Specialize: What could you make more specialized and focused?

When skateboarders took over empty swimming pools, they created a new function for the pools.

7. Imagine

*Amplify: How can you imagine amplifying this?

*Easier: How can you imagine making this easier to use, buy, sell, assemble?

*Negatives: What are the negatives that you could fix?

*Go: Imagine anything you can.

*Sci-fi: Imagine a sci-fi solution or improvement.

*Try: Try using IT in different ways to see what happens.

Google engineers wondered: What if the car drives itself?

These seven essential breakthrough questions are a guide through the creative process. These are questions the naturally creative ask themselves. But, as O'Connor points out, even they often skip over some of these questions and steps. That's the power of the checklist he referred to. These questions help individuals or teams engage with a challenge in a creative way.

You can import something from another discipline. You can rearrange your concept. You can remove pieces. You can replace pieces. You can make things happen more or less frequently. You can make things happen faster or slower. You can redesign the experience of something, the look of it, the feel of it.

As you move down the questions, they get closer and closer to fully open, no-holds-barred imagination—from simply looking at the thing itself, to connecting it to other things, to altering it, making it into something else, and finally to imagining whatever you can. This progression opens the mind in steps till the last step, imagine, blows the doors off and says "Go!"

Pattern Recognition

In the spirit of experimentation rampant during the early 1970s, Indiana University allowed any student to create and teach a fully accredited course if it was supported by an academic department and approved by the dean.

A lifelong comic-book lover, Michael Uslan knew exactly what he wanted to do. He wanted to teach a course on comic books. He garnered the support of the folklore department, and full of enthusiasm, set out to pitch the dean. It was not an easy sell. Within minutes, the dean cut him off. "Stop. I don't buy any of this. I read every issue of *Superman* I could get my hands on as a kid, but all comic books are cheap entertainment for children—nothing more, nothing less."

"And that," Uslan explained to a fascinated Olivia over lunch, "is when I asked him: 'Are you familiar with the story of Moses?'" When the dean answered that indeed he was, Uslan asked him to summarize it.

"So he tells me: 'The Hebrew people were being persecuted and their firstborn were being slain. A Hebrew couple placed their infant son in a little wicker basket and sent it down the river Nile, where he's discovered by an Egyptian family who raise him as their own son. When he grows up and learns his true heritage, he becomes a hero to his people . . .'"

At this point in the narrative, Uslan interrupted the dean and asked if he would now, as a childhood fan, summarize the story of Superman. "Well, sure," the dean responded. "Planet Krypton was about to blow up. A scientist and his wife placed their infant son in a little rocket ship and sent him to Earth. There he's discovered by the Kents, who raise him as their own son . . ." The dean stopped and stared. The course was approved.

Though it may be hard to remember a time when comic-book heroes were not multimillion-dollar cinema franchises, when Michael Uslan bought the movie rights to *Batman*, superheroes were, in fact, considered as "a kid's thing, dorky, nerdy, like Dungeons and Dragons niche." Comic-book-loving Uslan became the producer of all modern

Batman films to date—starting with Tim Burton's 1989 epic—and ushered in the modern era of superhero movies.

With pattern recognition, you associate two concepts: seeing the underlying patterns and noting their similarity. In recognizing the pattern underlying the stories of Moses and Superman, the dean suddenly understood the point that Uslan was making.

As another example, here's a summary of Disney's vision of the story of Pocahontas:

> *In 1607, a ship carrying John Smith arrives in the lush "new world" of North America. The settlers are mining for gold under the supervision of Governor Ratcliffe. John Smith begins exploring the new territory and encounters Pocahontas. Initially she is distrustful of him, but a message from her Grandmother Willow helps her overcome her reservations.*
>
> *The two begin spending time together, and Pocahontas helps John understand that all life is valuable, and how all nature is a connected circle of life. She also teaches him how to hunt, grow crops, and of her culture. We learn that her father is Chief Powhatan, and that she is set to be married to Kocoum, a great warrior, but a serious man, whom Pocahontas does not desire.*
>
> *Over time, John and Pocahontas find they have a love for each other. Back at the settlement, the men, who believe the natives are savages, plan to attack the natives for their gold. Kocoum tries to kill John out of jealousy, but he is later killed by the settlers.*
>
> *As the settlers prepare to attack, John is blamed by the natives and is sentenced to death. Just before they kill him, the settlers arrive. Chief Powhatan is nearly killed, and John sustains injuries from Governor Ratcliffe, who is then brought to justice. Pocahontas risks her life to save John. John and Pocahontas finally have each other, and the two cultures resolve their differences.*

And here is how an observant movie fan, Matt Bateman, altered that description just slightly to tell the story of James Cameron's *Avatar*.

> *In ~~1607~~ 2194, a ship carrying ~~John Smith~~ Jake Scully arrives in the lush "new world" of ~~North America~~ Pandora. The settlers*

are mining for ~~gold~~ unobtainium under the supervision of ~~Governor Ratcliffe~~ Colonel Quartin. Jake Scully begins exploring the new territory and encounters ~~Pocahontas~~ Neytiri. Initially she is distrustful of him, but a message from ~~her Grandmother Willow~~ the Tree of Souls helps her overcome her reservations.

The two begin spending time together, and ~~Pocahontas~~ Neytiri helps ~~John~~ Jake understand that all life is valuable, and how all nature is a connected circle of life. She also teaches him how to hunt, ~~grow crops~~ tame dragons, and of her culture. We learn that her father is Chief ~~Powhatan~~ Eytucan, and that she is set to be married to ~~Kocoum~~ Tsu'Tey, a great warrior, but a serious man, whom ~~Pocahontas~~ Neyteri does not desire. Over time, John Jake and ~~Pocahontas~~ Neyteri find they have a love for each other.

Back at the settlement, the men, who believe the natives are savages, plan to attack the ~~natives~~ Na'vi for their ~~gold~~ unobtanium. ~~Kocoum~~ Tsu'Tey tries to kill ~~John~~ Jake out of jealousy, but he is later killed by the settlers.

As the settlers prepare to attack, ~~John~~ Jake is blamed by the natives and is sentenced to death. Just before they kill him, the settlers arrive. Chief ~~Powhatan~~ Eytucan is ~~nearly~~ killed, and John Jake sustains injuries from ~~Governor Ratcliffe~~ Colonel Quanitch, who is then ~~brought to justice~~ shot with arrows. ~~Pocahontas~~ Neyteri risks her life to save ~~John~~ Jake. ~~John~~ Jake and ~~Pocahontas~~ Neyteri finally have each other, and the two cultures resolve their differences.

How was the medieval Catholic Church run just like a modern corporation? Think about it. In many ways, the medieval Catholic Church was the world's first corporation, with the pope as its CEO.[11] It had a large sales force and a mission statement—proselytizing—that demanded the expansion into new markets. The product they sold? Salvation.

A transnational entity headquartered in Rome, the Church had franchises in every city, town, and hamlet; from parish churches to Chartres Cathedral. The College of Cardinals acted like a board of directors, archbishops functioned much like a bevy of vice presidents, bishops were the first regional managers, and priests were, of course, salesmen.

And then came the Black Plague. Priests and monks, caring for the sick and dying, died in great numbers, decimating the sales force. The success of any corporation is predicated upon the consumers' belief in the product. The plague caused millions of people to begin to doubt the Church's ability to provide salvation. Monasteries and parish churches sat abandoned like empty stadiums. Cemeteries outside church walls became the scene of orgies. The Church's stock had crashed.

And then came the Reformation, appealing to the Catholic Church's own clientele. What was the Reformation but a loss of market share? The Catholic Church responded to the sudden competition like a good corporation: they launched the Counter-Reformation, which can be seen as a massive marketing campaign. The Church started building huge cathedrals, filling bridges with statues of saints, and commissioning songs.

The Business Case: Million-dollar Patterns

Think of a hotel. Think of what it does, whom it employs, and what makes for high customer satisfaction. Friendly, attentive staff? Attention to detail? Prompt responsiveness no matter what the hour? Easy check-in? Think of what a great hotel CEO would be like. What does he or she do to ensure that guests have a wonderful experience? How does he or she select and train the staff?

Now think of a hospital. What business is it in? What makes for high patient satisfaction? Less time in the admissions waiting room? Friendly staff? Nurses who show up promptly when the call button is pressed?

What do these two businesses have in common? Both have large volumes of people checking in and out every day, for example. Which elements are crucial to the success of both? One could imagine that friendly and attentive staff would be important.

And finally, what if you hired that great hotel CEO for the job of hospital CEO, and asked him to "make it better." What would he do? How would he change staff training? How would he improve staff selection? Which best practices could he bring in from his hotel experience?

Guess what? This entire scenario actually played out in real life. In 2006, the Henry Ford West Bloomfield Hospital hired as its new CEO an executive from Ritz-Carlton hotels who had twenty-five years of experience in the luxury hospitality business, but not a single day in the hospital business.[12]

Gerard van Grinsven focused on the doctor-patient relationship. He had folding metal chairs placed in patient rooms. When doctors came in, they were to open the chairs and sit down beside the bed rather than loom over the patients. It was a simple change that brought the doctors down to the patients' level and created a more human interaction.

Van Grinsven opened a wellness center and a hair salon and made them available to the public. This made the hospital a place for both the sick and the well, and helped integrate the hospital into the community.

He even created a fast check-in system so that when people were admitted to the hospital it was quick and easy, like checking into a hotel, and their room was ready for them. Essentially, van Grinsven brought the concept of customer service to the hospital industry.

Under his tenure, the Henry Ford West Bloomfield Hospital became recognized as one of the best hospitals in the country. Someone's breakthrough council was operating well when they recognized the matching patterns between a hospital and a hotel. That pattern recognition led to a million-dollar breakthrough.

The U.S. Army Special Forces are tasked with complex, often politically delicate missions. Special Forces soldiers are highly intelligent, unusually comfortable with uncertainty, and trained to hold their most primal emotions, like panic, in check. Many of them come through the Army's University of Foreign Military and Cultural Studies, known as Red Team University, under the skeptical if caring gaze of retired Col. Steve Rotkoff, to learn cutting-edge cognitive tools to help them on missions. For the past seven years Judah has been brought in to teach them about the unconscious mental frames that limit their thinking.

During class, the topic of the Arab Spring came up. At this time the uprisings were still taking place. It was an intense conversation. They had almost all lost friends in battle. They were not discussing abstract ideas or names on a map, but real places with smells and hills and dust and people and consequences.

That night Judah was out for beers with three of them. They were still talking about the possible outcomes. It wasn't idle conversation for this smaller group. One of them had come from a scenario-planning group that was tasked with predicting possible outcomes of the Arab Spring in order to plan future strategy. The other two soldiers were going to deploy to the Middle East shortly. When the next round of beers came, they asked Judah what he thought.

Judah knew better then to offer up some armchair opinion. Instead he helped them to see a pattern through association. He pulled up on his phone the Wikipedia entry for the Revolutions of 1848, which included this information:

- The Revolutions of 1848 were a series of political upheavals throughout Europe.

- They were democratic in nature, aiming to remove the old power structures.

- The revolts first erupted in the cities.

- Technological change was revolutionizing the life of the working classes.

- Many in the bourgeoisie feared and distanced themselves from the working poor.

- The uprisings were led by shaky ad hoc coalitions of reformers, the middle classes, and workers, which did not hold together for long.

- Within a year reactionary forces had regained control, and the revolutions collapsed.

The Special Forces soldiers immediately saw the similarities to the Arab Spring. City-centered revolts against the status quo powers; the technological shift of the Internet and social media; economic inequality; and ad hoc coalitions of the young, the liberal, and the workers. Judah pointed to how the revolutions ended, with the old regimes still in power, only stronger.

In typical understated fashion one of the soldiers said, "Thank you, sir. We're tracking." The historical association helped the soldiers create a more effective plan. Rather than arguing about what might happen, they had a breakthrough as to what would most likely happen. And in most places it was exactly what happened, from Iran to Bahrain to Egypt.

KEY TAKEAWAYS

▪ Associative thinking, or making associations between two seemingly unrelated ideas or subjects, is a key attribute of breakthrough thinking.
▪ Use the seven essential innovation questions (SEIQ) to create associations:
  • How could I **look** at this differently?
  • How could I **use** this in a way it was not intended for?
  • What if I **moved** this into a new context?
  • What if I **connected** this to something completely new and different?
  • What if I **altered** a piece of it?
  • What if I **made** something new based on this?
  • How else could I **imagine** using this?
▪ Pattern recognition can help you achieve breakthroughs by seeing the underlying patterns between your current situation and one that has already been solved or come to a conclusion.

Chapter 5

Cultivating Your Garden

Making Your Head an Attractive Place
for Breakthrough Butterflies

Your Truly Amazing Brain

Erik Weihenmayer has climbed the "seven summits," the tallest peaks on all seven continents. He's stood atop Mount Everest in Nepal and Mount Vinson in Antarctica. As a seven-summit climber, Weihenmayer is a member of a very small fraternity of elite climbers. But that's not what is most remarkable about his achievement. Not even close. What is truly remarkable is that Weihenmayer is completely blind.[1]

How did Weihenmayer make his way through ice and snow? He attached a device to his tongue called the BrainPort. The BrainPort takes in visual information and translates it into electrical impulses, which is exactly what our eyes do. The BrainPort replaced Weihenmayer's eyes.[2]

Of course, the BrainPort has no access to the optic nerve, the road your eyes use to send information to your brain, so its electrical impulses hitch a ride along the tongue's nerve road into the brain.

As Paul Bach-y-Rita, the cocreator of the BrainPort, said, "We see with the brain, not with the eyes."[3] If you can get visual information into the brain, no matter what the delivery method, you can see.

Even though Weihenmayer's brain hadn't been built to interpret visual data coming from the tongue, it was able to rewire itself to do just that. Millions of neurons formed new connections with one another as his brain physically reshaped itself to understand the new input.

We used to think that after childhood, our brains stopped changing or developing. This misconception started falling apart when, with the advent of technology that allowed us to see more deeply inside the brain, we noticed that neural connections could actually change. Neuroscientists saw that parts of the brain grow bigger or smaller based on the kinds of activity people were engaged in.[4]

In the fall of 2014, a twenty-four-year-old Chinese woman walked into a hospital complaining of dizziness and nausea. It turned out that her brain had no cerebellum, a part of the brain essential for language, movement, and motor control.[5] It was, in fact, amazing that this young woman was able to walk at all. The fact that she learned not only to walk, but also to speak, use chopsticks, and master complex Chinese calligraphy, are all testaments to the brain's amazing capacity to change itself. Other parts of her brain were transformed in order to do the work of the missing cerebellum.

A 2012 study shows that in deaf people the part of the brain used for processing sound gets rewired to process touch and vision.[6] And on the other hand, a 2005 study showed that in blind people, the visual cortex is rewired to process sound cues.[7] Weihenmayer said it felt like his brain was "rewiring itself."[8] And so it did, because it actually was. This "rewiring" isn't a metaphor: actual, physical structures inside our brain change.

This ability of the brain to change itself to compensate for deficiencies, to change what parts of itself are used for, is just the start of what we now call neuroplasticity. In fact, our brains remain "plastic," changeable, our entire lives. Anytime you encounter a new experience or think a new thought, your brain creates a new physical connection among neurons.[9] Our experiences, the things we pay attention to, and our behaviors are constant feedback loops changing the structure of our brains.

Your Brain Is Constantly Restructuring Itself.
Physically restructuring itself.
Think about that.

Why is this important for breakthroughs? It's very simple: breakthroughs are achieved by the creation of something new, and in our brains, this means the creation of new ideas, new thoughts, new understandings. Having a new thought—any kind of new thought—requires the construction of a new connection inside our brain.[10] How fast, how easily, and how profusely we can create new connections greatly impacts how many breakthroughs we'll have. The ability to create new connections inside our brain—that's neuroplasticity.

The Higher Our Level of Neuroplasticity, the Higher Our Chances of Breakthroughs

When we asked Astro Teller, the head of Google's semisecret research and development facility known as X, how he hires people, he answered, "I hire the most plastic people I can find."[11] This is because Teller knows that having a breakthrough depends upon your ability to physically build a novel set of neural connections.

As babies, our brains are highly plastic because absolutely everything we encounter is new: eating, pooping, language, laughter, crawling, walking. Every single day our brains form new structures to understand what we are encountering: babies perform the equivalent of an Ironman triathlon workout for the brain.

But as we grow up, novelty becomes scarce. Daily routine sets in: same job, same colleagues, same neighborhood, same friends, same TV shows, same politics, and so on. We've gone from doing the equivalent of a daily mental Ironman workout to being neural couch potatoes. Our brains have gotten out of shape when it comes to building neural connections. When learning something new feels hard, we decide that you can't teach an old dog new tricks. In reality, it's not that our brains are no longer capable of change, but that it's out of practice because we haven't been working out.[12]

But thinking that it's too late, that you should have started when you were young, is akin to sitting on your couch watching TV for a year, failing to do a push-up, and saying, "Well, I guess I'm just weak now. I'd better get used to it. I'm going to double down on this couch-sitting thing."

You might be tempted at this point to go join one of the increasingly popular "brain gyms" offering computerized pattern-spotting or memory games. Unfortunately, research so far shows that they make you much better at playing these games, but not necessarily at anything else.[13]

The best way to improve your plasticity is to expose yourself to new things that challenge your brain to build fresh connections. When you keep having the same thought over and over again, and perhaps describe it as being caught in a loop, the physical reality is that you are firing the same path of neurons over and over again. But when you experience or think about something unfamiliar, your brain physically builds a new structure, and it is this ability that enables us to have original thoughts and to create breakthroughs.

Our brains are shaped by the things we pay attention to.[14] *Any* new experience will physically create a new connection. And with your 100 billion neurons, each with the ability to make thousands of connections, there are more potential connections inside your brain than there are stars in the sky.

Before We Start: Getting Your Brain Ready for Breakthrough Thinking

We live in an age of distraction. Before the advent of the Internet, there was a limit to the amount of information we could physically get our hands on. Now, we face an infinite avalanche of information every time we go online. Leo Babauta, author of the *Zen Habits* blog and father of six, told us: "We are increasingly up to our necks in the stream of information, in the crossfire of the battle for our attention, and engaged in a harrying blur of multitasking activity."[15]

What's worse, this battle for our attention is addictive because all our digital communication channels engage our dopamine loops. A common misconception holds that dopamine is related to experiences of pleasure. As increasing numbers of studies show, the famous neurotransmitter is responsible not for pleasure, but rather for motivation, desire, or drive.

With every e-mail, text, Snapchat, or Instagram notification, a dopamine surge drives us to click or open with the anticipation of pleasure. Our electronics have turned us all into gamblers, only instead of pulling the arm of a slot machine or rolling the dice, we check our in-boxes and phones. As Kelly McGonigal explains in her wonderful book *The Willpower Instinct*, evolution is using the *promise* of happiness, not happiness itself, to keep us striving and struggling and checking our phones.[16]

The problem is that breakthrough thinking is driven by this same dopamine-induced expectancy of happiness, excitement, achievement. Dopamine is what drives us to look for solutions, new approaches, or discoveries. It gives us the curiosity that drives so many breakthroughs. But if we get caught in an electronic communications dopamine loop, we are wasting our neurochemical drive.

In essence, dopamine creates the motivation that is needed to create breakthroughs. Don't waste it on e-mail and social media.

Plasticity Exercises

The point of neuroplasticity excercises is not to make you better at the activities themselves. Terry Gross, the famous host of the interview radio show *Fresh Air,* has taken singing lessons for years. She told her teacher right from the start that her goal was not to become a good singer. "I just want to be inside a song, to the extent that I can be. To just have my body inside a song."[17]

In Gross's case, singing does relate to her line of work, as she's the voice of a show. But aside from that, music is one of the great powerhouses for increasing plasticity, and for Gross, who has to interview people from all walks of life, finding connections is a great way to come up with interesting questions.

Anything new you learn will promote your brain's plasticity. But learning something new while doing something physical doesn't just increase plasticity, it also increases the *size* of the neural circuit you are creating, which means—you guessed it—more new connections.

In one study on this subject, when high jumpers imagined themselves clearing the bar successfully, they were 35 percent more successful. But when they imagined themselves clearing the bar and moved one of their fingers at the same time, their success went up by 45 percent.[18] This is why many of the following tools involve some form of movement.

These tools are not exercises in breakthrough thinking, but rather exercises in plasticity. Stronger muscles will help you when the time comes to compete.

• Experiment with movement

Use your nondominant hand for a variety of activities. Brush your teeth, use a fork, use the key to open your house, write your name. This is also a great exercise to experience what it's like to build new connections—you'll really feel neuroplasticity at work.

• Experiment with taste

Go to a restaurant and order something you've never had there before. Really taste it. What's different about it? Your brain has to create new connections in order to build a structure to represent new flavors.

Make a dish, but leave all the salt out of the recipe. Taste it. Notice how the lack of salt changes the flavor. Now add just a little. And taste. Then add a little bit more. Inch your way forward until you've added the perfect amount of salt.

• Experiment with sight

Take a new route to work, the market, or home. Notice as many new things as you can. The next day, take the exact same route, but this time try to predict the landmarks you will see.

Watch twenty minutes of a foreign film without subtitles. See what you can piece together about the plot. Are you watching facial expressions more? How well can you understand the emotional state of the characters even without their words? A few of our favorites are:

- *Life Is Beautiful*
- *Amelie*
- *The House of Flying Daggers*

Sit in a coffee shop while pretending to read this book, and watch the people around you. Don't worry, they'll be too focused on whatever they're doing to notice you. Look at their facial expressions. Look at how they hold their bodies. Are they moving fast or slow? Do they seem jumpy, nervous, neurotic? Now pick one person and imagine what his morning has been like. If he's on a computer, try to imagine what he is typing. Is it for work? Is he searching for a new home? Is he shopping? Writing an old flame? Building a narrative with a who, what, why, when, and how is great plasticity work.

- Experiment with sound

  Listen to music from another culture, whether Bollywood dance music, African blues, or traditional Afghani music. Lose yourself in completely different tempos. If you are home alone, try to dance. When you try to figure out how to move your body to an unfamiliar rhythm, you force your brain to translate new sounds into movement.

Practice Plasticity Like Einstein

Einstein was famous for performing "thought experiments." He would imagine that certain things were true about the universe and figure out what would happen in a universe like that. These thought experiments promote associative thinking. Here are some you can try.

- **Gravity:** Imagine gravity were to stop working after 10 P.M. Now, what does the world look like? Are our beds on the ceiling? How does this change the sports we play? How do we transport goods? Do people have parties in trees covered by nets? Is there a new business making those nets? Are there lawsuits when the nets fail and people end up floating aimlessly all night? Are movies made where true love is found when these people float down in some random place in the morning? Do teenagers sabotage the nets to float off for adventure?

- **Social norms:** Let's say that you are allowed to kick someone if they truly annoy you. Now what does the world look like? How do you prove the person truly annoyed you? Are there special courts to determine whether you were truly annoyed? How hard are you allowed to kick someone? Are special shoes made that allow you to kick without leaving a mark? Is there a social peace movement to stop the kicking?

- **Age:** Imagine you just discovered that you are guaranteed to live to be 130 years old and remain in excellent physical health. You might notice an internal reaction, perhaps a fleeting thought of

"Wait, I thought I would live till . . ." It's natural to unconsciously set expectations. Did you know you had been using that age as a general barometer? Now try to imagine what your life would look like. How does that affect the decisions you make? Will you stay in your current career the whole time? Will you remain in your current marriage or relationship? How would society change if everyone were to live to 130? Would everyone be expected to have more than one marriage? How long would people wait to have children? Would everyone have to wait their turn to have children due to overpopulation from longer life spans? Would people auction off their right to have children to others?

- **Magic:** Maybe you've heard tales of cities that stand entirely on stilts with suspended walkways for sidewalks. Or a city that consists of nothing but plumbing, pipes, showerheads, bathtubs, and valves connected in a maze of metal devoid of any buildings. Other cities trade only in memories, and you can only buy things by sharing memories. Now you design one of these magical cities. What does it look like? How do the people interact in this city? What are the rules?[19] Here's a way to increase your brain plasticity even more: Imagine you are in the scene, like a character in a highly realistic video game. You're walking down the street, opening doors, turning your head left and right to look at new things. Imagine putting your hand up to feel the wind. Walk down one of the main streets and hear the traffic.

Now let's get personal. This exercise is not only great for boosting your plasticity, it's also a great tool in business and in life. Think of the last meeting you attended. Where was it? What was it about? Who was there? Who spoke? How did you feel throughout the meeting?

Now, using your recently heightened powers of imagination, pull back and watch the meeting as if you were an invisible observer who can see the whole group (including you). What do you see now? Look at the faces of everyone around the table, including your own. Remember, you're an invisible observer in the back of the room. Was anyone bored? Disgruntled? How was the leader of the meeting?

Ready for the next jump? This one is key. Think of the most junior person at this meeting. (If this was you, pick the most senior.) Don't just put yourself in her shoes: Get into her skin, see from behind her eyes. How was she feeling? Who was she looking at? What was she concerned about?

If you'd prefer a nonwork situation, imagine a family gathering, such as Thanksgiving or Christmas. How were you feeling? What annoyed you? What made you happy? Now imagine yourself an invisible guest watching the dinner. How is the group experiencing it? Who is looking at whom? Who is eating? Who is serving? Who is bored? Now pick the youngest (or oldest) family member. What was it like for them?

Filling Your Garden: Sow More Than You Need

In the early 1890s, everybody wanted the newest technological marvel. Democratic and affordable, the bicycle could cut people's commute to work in half and enable them to enjoy the countryside on the weekend.

Thousands of bicycle mechanics appeared as if overnight, looking to make bicycles lighter, safer, more comfortable, and easier to produce. They would tinker with ball bearings, rolled steel, differential gears, air-filled tires, and so on.[20]

Many of these enthusiasts would later use what they had learned in bicycle workshops to create greater transportation breakthroughs. The Wright Brothers, for instance, were both bicycle mechanics.

One of these amateur bicycle mechanics watched as mass production took hold in the realm of personal transportation, and cyclists lobbied for better roads to be built. That man was Henry Ford, and by combining the new concepts of mass production with the new tools invented for bicycles, he gave us the modern automobile industry.

The more raw material you give your brain, the more connections it can make. So when you read an article online, follow the hyperlinks and see where they take you. Filling your garden is an experience in meandering. You may end up far afield, and that's okay, because you don't know what might be of interest. You *can't* know. This, of course, can be frustrating to those of us who want to know that what we're doing is generating value, not "wasting time." Unfortunately, if you want to get to breakthroughs, you need to accept that you'll never know what ends up being valuable.

When farmers sow seeds, they don't know which will germinate, which won't, and how many of those that do germinate will actually bear fruit. It's nearly impossible to ensure a 100 percent germination rate. So what do they do? They sow more than they need. In military parlance, this is called redundancy. And unlike in management, where redundancy is assumed to be a bad thing, in the world of technology it's what could save your work (have you ever lost data for lack of a backup?).

"In the technology world of the cloud, we assume the commodity hardware we are building things on will fail, so we have complex failure plans. Data stored in the cloud will often be broken into hundreds of pieces, with three or even six copies of each piece," explains Microsoft's Kevin Sauer.

If you want to have more breakthroughs, you need to accept the need for redundancy. Accept that you won't know which seeds will bear fruit until harvest time. Some may germinate, some may not. Some may germinate, but not bear fruit. You have to be willing to bear that uncertainty. (Chapter 9 will give you the tools to handle it better.)

When we tell you to immerse yourself in your line of work or interest, we don't mean merely working hard at your job in advertising or sitting down at the piano for two hours a day. Get a clear understanding of the underlying principles, the schools of thought, the ways things have been done or attempted, and succeeded or failed.

It's important to talk to people doing the same thing as you are. Bell Labs, the famed research center to which we owe the transistor, the calculator, laser technology, UNIX, and many of today's most essential technologies, was famous for strongly encouraging its newest junior members to knock on the door of Nobel Prize winners and ask questions of "the guy who wrote the book."[21]

As for how to approach people and establish the relationships you need, you'll find information in the resources section of this book, including Olivia's *The Charisma Myth*, of course, and Keith Ferrazzi's *Never Eat Alone*, the "bible of networking." Keith, the CEO of a research institute studying human behavior change, illustrates convincingly that relationships are the backbone of all success in business and in life, and shows you step-by-step how to build the relationships you will need. We highly recommend it.

Popular mythology would have you believe that breakthroughs are a solo endeavor. Most often, there are many contributors to major insights. The garden-filling phase is not just about extracting information from other people. You also have to share your latest challenge: give people the context behind the questions you're asking, the problems you're working on, what's making them so difficult, and what you're hoping to achieve.

Your mindset when sowing seeds must be open and unprejudiced, because you never know who might have an interesting tidbit for you. Remember that early components of breakthroughs don't look like breakthroughs—they look like miscellaneous pieces of information. Be open and curious.

One trick is to keep certain topics at the forefront of your mind at all times so you'll be more likely to notice when relevant pieces of information pass by. Another trick is to draw people into talking about something they're passionate about. Ask them when they first encountered this passion. Did they always love it or did it grow on them? What is it about the activity that speaks to them? You may hear about the history of the thing, the nuances, the best practices. These are excellent ingredients to gather.

You should also read books that are adjacent to your area of interest and talk to people doing something different but related. If you're a manager in a healthcare company, you might talk to a manager at a retail company or at a hospitality company. If you're a business manager, learn about how to run a preschool.

If you're in marketing or sales, it might be helpful to read a book about P. T. Barnum, or about William Randolph Hearst's role in starting the Spanish-American War. But it could also be just as helpful to read about the publication of Thomas Paine's pamphlet *Common Sense* and the American Revolution.

If you're a manager, it could be helpful to read how the Mongols structured their armies and how they created a sense of connection among soldiers from varied cultures. Or about the practices of traditional cultures, from the Iroquois to Australian Aboriginals.

If you're a scientist, it could be helpful to read anything in the history of science. But it can also be helpful to read about the history of philosophy as a way to see the different modes of thought that held people in check. You might discover something about the limits of your own thinking. Science fiction has also been known to be a great inspiration for many scientists.

If you're an entrepreneur, read about the history of Silicon Valley and the entrepreneurs who came before you. You never know what ideas might be sparked by reading about your predecessors.

StartX is Stanford's incubator for new technology companies. It is made up of young, smart, ambitious people looking to disrupt any and every industry. Many of them have more ideas than they know what to do with. One company was working on wearable technology. During a wandering conversation, the co-founders mentioned to Judah they had another idea for smart fabric. It was not the product they were in StartX to develop; it was a new idea. The problem was that although they knew what their technology could do, they had no knowledge about materials and temperature changes.

Judah introduced them to designers of ski clothing at another client of his, the North Face. People who design clothing for skiing have to think a lot about materials and temperature. Its users are in the cold but are very active, which raises their body temperature. The wearable tech founders and the North Face designers were working in adjacent fields. The wearable tech founders were able to take great strides in their designs by learning from the North Face designers.

We'd love to tell you that they are bringing their smart fabric to market, but they found their technology wasn't ready. That's the risk when working with incubators and with breakthroughs in general. Sometimes things don't work out. That's not what breakthrough thinking is about. Breakthrough thinking is about learning and trying again. (Part two digs deep into the skills necessary for breakthrough resilience.)

To create (or discover) his theories of relativity, Einstein didn't just lock himself in a room and think. Instead, he had a group of friends with whom he talked with almost every night.[22] They called themselves the Olympia Academy: Michele Besso, Maurice Solovine, Conrad Habicht, and Einstein's wife, Mileva.

On warm nights, they'd walk the streets of Bern and sit on the riverbank. Other times they'd climb to the top of Mount Gurten, lie on their backs, look up at the stars, and talk until dawn. Then they'd amble back into town and sit at a café, fueling themselves with coffee and ideas.

While the Olympia Academy had very little structure, the members demanded total commitment. When Maurice Solovine skipped a meeting to attend a music recital, Einstein and Habicht went to his house, ate all his food, and smoked a pipe (Einstein) and cigars (Habicht) until the apartment resembled the inside of a chimney. Finally, they piled all his furniture and books on top of his bed. Such was the retribution for giving preference to bourgeois distractions over the Academy.

The group's members were from fields as diverse as poetry and philosophy, and it was these conversations that helped to break open how he thought so that he could then "break open the universe." In order to be innovative, Einstein first had to shift the way he actually thought, and that meant ranging far afield from physics.

Literature, art, and music aren't thought of as "actionable" or "useful" when we're in problem-solving mode, but are extremely useful to our genius council when we're on the road to breakthroughs. Nadya Direkova, an MIT graduate and mathematics whiz who works at Google X and created the Design Sprint program within Google, has been known to take classes ranging from photography to "how to be a mermaid in the world."[23]

If you find yourself in conversation with someone from an adjacent field, here are some good questions to ask:

- If you were describing what you do for a living to a six-year-old, what would you say?
- Do you have any kind of personal philosophy or guiding principles that help you?
- What do you think makes you good at what you do? (They'll demur but be flattered.)
- If I were starting out in your profession, what advice would you give me?
- Did you always know you wanted to be an X, or were you interested in something else? (If they always knew, ask why it called to

them so strongly. If they wanted to be something else, ask what linked their first interest to their second.)

If you're concerned about falling down a rabbit hole, try the Oxford Very Short Introduction Series. These are brief books, each about a hundred pages, that offer concise overviews on myriad topics from rivers to Tibetan Buddhism to molecular biology. Choose two or three of these on varied topics and read them. The advantage is that these booklets are limited, physically, in the amount of information they contain.

When you want a fresh insight, you're guaranteed to be surprised by a different age group, social class, or culture. There's also the option of drawing solutions from nature, the well-known tactic called biomimicry we mentioned earlier.

The first Japanese bullet train, which could reach speeds of up to 180 miles per hour, had a short, snub nose. At such an incredible speed, the train often built up hurricane-force winds when going through tunnels, shaking nearby houses and even shattering windows.

The engineers tasked with redesigning the nose to create less air buildup found the solution in mimicking the beak of the kingfisher.[24]

The kingfisher's beak enables it to dive straight into the water and yet barely make a splash. With its almost Pinocchio-long nose, the new bullet train looks a bit comical. But it no longer causes hurricanes.

It's key to provide your genius council with a wide variety of examples of how others have done what you're seeking to do. The more varied, the better: these "others" who have the solution you need could well end up being insects.

In Harare, Zimbabwe, the Eastgate Centre shopping mall and office building uses only 10 percent of the energy that a similar-sized building would use to heat and cool itself.[25] It does this by mimicking the design of termite castles, which have the remarkable ability to maintain a steady internal temperature regardless of the outside temperature. Like a termite castle, the Eastgate Centre regulates its temperature by drawing cool air in at the bottom of the building while venting warmer air at the top, thanks to large fans at both ends of the building.

One form of breakthrough is simply recognizing the ready-made solutions waiting to be plucked from the natural world. Waste treat-

© Matt Buck

© Piti Sirisriro

ment plants, for instance, used to face the problem of minerals growing on the inside of pipes and slowing down the flow. Traditionally,
engineers had to flush the pipes with toxic chemicals to clean them out.

The buildup is calcium carbonate, which happens to be the exact same material from which seashells are made.[26] During their growing phase, seashells use a template of proteins that pull in ions from the seawater and hold them in place in a self-assembling crystal. When they reach maturity, the shells exude a protein to stop the crystallization. Today, a commercially made and environmentally friendly substance called TPA mimics this protein that inhibits crystallization.

Throughout this process, consider collecting these ideas in a file. This can be in the notes on your phone, a file on your computer, or an old school notebook. You want to create a central place where you can look through the ideas you've gathered in order to focus your breakthrough geniuses and remind them of all the raw material they have to work with. A simple and powerful tool when you're struggling for a breakthrough is reading through your gathered ideas, and then using one of the breakthrough exercises we will recommend in the following chapter.

The breakthrough experience is both a social, outward-focused experience and a solitary, inward-focused one. Gathering information is external: even if you're just sitting at your computer reading articles, the information is coming in from the outside.

We encourage you to go out and talk to other people during the garden-filling phase, because when we engage with other people, we connect our associative networks to other associative networks, and that creates a whole new field of possibilities. So we research, we read, we listen, we talk, we argue, we explain, we get pointed to new sources of information, we watch videos, go to lectures, have lunch with different people, all in the service of collecting ideas, facts, and information.

KEY TAKEAWAYS

- Brains remain plastic throughout life. We all have the ability to think new thoughts. Although most of us are out of shape neurologically, we can increase our plasticity.
- Don't waste your breakthrough dopamine, your internal drive, on e-mail and phone distraction overload.
- Exercise is a magic bullet for raising plasticity and mood. Just five minutes at a time can help.
- Plasticity rises when doing, learning, and experiencing new things. Experiment with new movements, new tastes, new sights, new sounds,

new stories. Moving while experiencing something new turbocharges the plasticity.

- Try Einstein-style thought experiments. Imagine crazy situations or worlds with different laws and see where it takes you.
- Gather large amounts of information on a chosen subject or problem so you can immerse yourself in that field of knowledge. Some of what you gather will be useful and actionable. Most of what you gather will not directly lead anywhere, and this is okay.
- Look to others. Engaging others will allow you to learn from their perspective and insights. Seek input from people in other fields and professions, even if it may seem they cannot help you.
- Look to nature. Mother nature is a 4.5-billion-year research and development project. The practice of biomimicry can teach us a lot.
- Remember to keep notes in a central place for later reference. Consider a notebook, or an online app like Evernote, which allows you to sync notes to multiple devices (phone, laptop, desktop) simultaneously.

Chapter 6

What's in Your Net?

How to Evaluate the Output of Genius Mode

SO YOU'VE GONE through the breakthrough experience, and you've come up with one—or many!—ideas that have breakthrough potential. Do you go right out into the world and bet the house on it? No. This is where you bring your executive back to the front office. You may have heard the saying "Write drunk, edit sober." Now is the time to edit sober.

Edward de Bono is one of the world's foremost experts on how we think. He is a psychologist, a physician, and an author who teaches at the universities of Oxford, Cambridge, and Harvard. One of his most famous tools is called Six Thinking Hats. In this classic tool, a team that wants to brainstorm is given six different-colored hats, each standing for a different frame of mind, a different way of looking at a situation and generating possible solutions.

The **blue** hat focuses on the process, managing time, keeping the big picture in mind.

The **white** hat focuses on facts on the ground, figures, metrics, the reality of the situation.

The **red** hat focuses on the emotional resonance of the situation and the solution, and how others might be impacted, including your empathy and fears.

The **green** hat focuses on creative thinking, new possibilities, new perspectives on the situation and the solution, and on refining new ideas.

The **black** hat has a skeptical outlook and considers risks, potential problems and obstacles of the solution, or weaknesses in the plan.

The **yellow** hat, on the other hand, is an optimistic outlook, positive thinking, a focus on the benefits and best-case scenarios of possible solutions.

Using the Six Hats to Evaluate Potential Breakthroughs

We've adapted these tools to help you sift through different ideas, to catch which are the potential breakthroughs and which are not.

Though some breakthroughs are immediately recognizable as such, often major breakthroughs come through a series of smaller breakthroughs. We wind our way along the path, eventually coming to the big moment. This evaluation process will help you recognize and capture ideas that don't burst forth onto the scene but rather appear quietly. It helps you know whether they are signposts on the road to breakthrough, or just gibberish.

Let's say you've had a potential breakthrough about what your team needs to do. You've realized you need to encourage more risk-taking while maintaining limits on those risks. Choose which hat you are going to put on, and then look at your ideas from that point of view. You can make your way along in any order.

You might first choose the red hat, the emotional one. You could ask yourself how the team is going to feel about being encouraged to take more risks. Will they be frightened? Feel pressured? Feel liberated? This makes you realize that how they feel will in part depend on how you present the issue.

Then you put on the black hat of the skeptic, the problem seeker, and you see the potential risks—the team going over budget, missing deadlines, building useless models all in the name of taking risks. It could turn into a situation in which people are just doing weird stuff to appear as if they're taking risks. Then, if you reprimand them, they'd feel confused and betrayed: you encouraged them to take risks and then punished them for doing it. You'd lose trust.

So you put on the white hat and look at the facts on the ground. How much time and budget can you allocate to risk? What areas should not be touched? This will help you create constraints.

You put on the green hat to think creatively about those constraints. What are reasonable limits and guidelines you could give the team ahead of time? You could limit how far anyone could go with a new idea. You could establish a system that all new ideas had to move through in order to slow down the process, with kill points along the way where new, risky ideas get assessed before they can move on.

Then you put on your yellow hat and look at the benefits of each of these new ideas. How might they play out successfully?

You could put your red hat on again, the emotional one, and look at how these new guidelines might be received by your team; then put on the black hat again and see how this might go sideways.

It's then time to put on the blue hat, the process one, to make sure that you are still on topic and on point.

You can cycle through these different hats, these different perspectives, as many times as is helpful.

The next step is to bring the breakthrough to people who "wear" different hats. So you find a red hat person, someone who is good at seeing how things affect other people, someone with a high emotional quotient (EQ), and you present the situation and your possible solutions to get his red hat feedback.

Then you find a black hat person, someone who is a good critical thinker and skeptic. You run your stuff by her and see what issues she points out. You get black hat feedback.

You continue through the other hats, collecting feedback from different people in very specific, directed ways that help you sift your idea.

To evaluate your breakthroughs, to know which are worth pursuing, which need further iterations, and what's still lacking, it is absolutely critical for you to get feedback from others.

One of the startups at StartX came up with an app that could track your movements via your smartphone and then construct a narrative of your day, your week, or your month for you. This app was not what the startup founders had gotten accepted into StartX to work on and they weren't sure if they should move forward with it.

This was a perfect opportunity to use de Bono's Six Thinking Hats. Judah identified six people in the incubator who were all naturals at one of the thinking hat perspectives. First he brought in the white hat, the one good at the facts on the ground. She helped the team lay out their idea in clear and concise language. Then he brought in a person good at yellow hat thinking, best-case scenarios, and optimism, and the team shared their white hat pitch. The yellow hat person spun out a number of possible ways this app could be world changing. Parents could make a record of their children's lives before they have memories. Children could watch narratives of their parents when their parents were teenagers. Politicians could be held accountable. Researchers could study troves of data about human behavior.

Then he brought in the green hat person, the creative thinker. This person wondered if the app could be used to track pets' days, or what would happen if you created a mesh network of narratives so you could see the interweaving experience of a group of friends or an entire junior high class. What could it teach us about our behaviors as a group of people?

At this point the founders were getting very excited. But then Judah brought in the black hat person, the one who was good at being skeptical. The black hat thinker pointed out that the technology wasn't ready to track that many interweaving stories. And besides, why would anyone pay for this? They'd expect it to be free. And so how would you sell ads on it?

The fun wasn't over yet. Next came the red hat thinker, the emotional one. The red hat thinker shuddered a bit. He felt it was creepy, like being followed all the time. And if you turned it on and then off and then on again there'd be gaps in your narrative that made it seem like you were hiding something. Very 1984.

But all was not lost. Judah brought in a blue hat thinker, someone who asked the founders what their big picture was, what the essence of the app was. With that question the green hat, the creative thinker, was brought back in. They traded ideas back and forth and realized that they had assumed the app would track individuals in their daily lives. But it could be used for research. Research had come up before but had been forgotten. It could be used for patients, for diagnoses, for any number of targeted applications where the user was willing and happy for the help.

The developers hit a number of bumps in the road along the way. We helped them with their breakthrough resilience. One day they met a fellow entrepreneur working in medical technology. As they spoke they realized that most medical technology was focused on biometrics, heart rate, sweat, and oxygenation. But the ins and outs of your activity, the narrative of your day, and how that might affect your health was blue ocean territory. They merged their companies and are in the midst of a round of getting funding.

Getting feedback is something that Professor Alex "Sandy" Pentland, director of the MIT Science and Human Dynamics labs, and Olivia's favorite scientist, strongly recommends you do in person. "When things matter," he told us, "you need 'rich' channels: nuanced, interactive channels that allow for serendipity and spontaneity. And [you need] the immediacy of face-to-face interactions, when both people can be talking at once, getting excited and talking over one another. You need to be able to get the feel of an idea."[1]

This is why MIT does not have campuses in any other location in the world: they want their people to interact face-to-face. (Yes, it is often pointed out the irony that the "nerdiest university in the world" is the one that insists on physical interaction.)

Pentland, who also helped create and direct the MIT Media Lab, recommends that you seek feedback from one person at a time, not from a group that will blitz you with feedback. "Think of Minsky and all those other 'lone geniuses,'" he says. "Yes, they're slightly odd, and curious about everything. And they get superexcited, and tend to talk about whatever the latest thing that excited them was, with everybody. But they talk to people serially. The thing they bring to person A gets modified by A's feedback, and what they get as a result is what they bring to person B, so they keep testing and validating their concepts, and the concepts build together into a story."

Pentland is describing mode switching of a different kind. Instead of switching between our EN and our DN, Pentland has us switching between talking to people and retreating back to our heads to ponder.

And this kind of mode switching hints at a paradox at the heart of how we have breakthroughs. On the one hand we need to be alone for the innovation to come to us. Story after story tells of people being alone when they have their moment of insight. An insight tends to be a quiet, internal event. But on the other hand, we need to be immersed in a flow of ideas. We need to hear what other people are thinking and doing. We need to take in lots of different things.

Pentland's group has performed the most advanced research on idea flow within groups and organizations, and his book is highly recommended to any executive tasked with innovation. (You'll find them listed in the resources section of this book.) He speaks of bees who pollinate every flower they come across. At every flower, they pick up the best pollen, and bring it to the next one.

A helpful tip to keep in mind: some flowers have a lot more pollen than others. When you are looking to talk to people about your breakthrough idea, talk to a diversity of people. But also look for people with as multifaceted a background as possible. Former Manpower CEO David Arkless is a good example: he's worked in senior positions inside multinational corporations, he's worked outside of them as a consultant, he's worked on getting more investment opportunities inside China, and on teaching marginalized youth in the Middle East and North Africa the skills needed to join the world economy.

Have a Crew

Many breakthroughs come from people who have a trusted crew they run their ideas by. As we've seen, Einstein had his Olympia Academy. J.R.R. Tolkien and C. S. Lewis used to read their drafts of *The Lord of the Rings* and *The Chronicles of Narnia* to each other. Nathaniel Hawthorne and Herman Melville were good friends and wrote many letters to one another about their work.

It is important to have a crew, a group of people you trust and who understand what it is you are working on. This crew makes you feel safe sharing your thoughts and, ideally, asks you questions that help clarify your ideas or push you forward into new areas.

When Keith Richards first listened to his opening eight bars of "Satisfaction" he was unimpressed. Mick Jagger described it this way: "It sounded like a folk song when we first started working on it and Keith didn't like it much, he didn't want it to be a single, he didn't think it would do very well. I think Keith thought it was a bit basic. I don't think he really listened to it properly. He was too close to it and just felt it was a silly kind of riff."[2]

Richards didn't see the breakthrough potential of his song. It took his bandmates to help him see it and refine it. Similarly, the first attempt at recording the song didn't go well. It took a second session to get it right. Your crew can act as a backup net to catch the butterflies that you don't see or that get away.

Judah was having a conversation with Andreas Ramos, who has been an engineer in Silicon Valley for over twenty years. He was telling a story about a side project his cubiclemate was working on in the mid-1990s. The cubiclemate was talking about his idea and Ramos and a third man started shooting ideas back and forth and decided they'd help write the code for their coworker Craig and his list. Yes, that was the foundation of Craigslist.

Biomimic Your Brain

So how do you build your trusted crew? Who should be in it? For starters, anyone who seems to excel at one or two of the Six Thinking Hat styles. But there's a deeper question. What skills should you gather in the room to increase the chances of a breakthrough?

When viewed from the point of view of design, Nature is a master class, and your brain is a design that has been iterated, tested, adapted, and iterated again for millions of years. If architects can learn how to save energy from termite castles, and engineers can learn about aerodynamics from a kingfisher's beak, think about what you could accomplish by biomimicking the brain's breakthrough council.

Mimicking the way your DN works, here are other qualities and personality types to look for in your crew or your team:

QUALITIES:

Empathy: You're looking for people who are skilled at taking other perspectives and have a natural ability to feel how others might respond to a new idea. You want the people others go to when they're having a hard time.

Contextual associations: You want people who have worked in different industries, people who have dual majors in subjects like math and poetry, or French and economics. You need people who have a deep hobby in something apart from their job, like computer programmers who practice Tai Chi or executives who paint.

Memory: Historians could be good for this, or people interested in history. People who worked on previously successful breakthroughs in a similar space are helpful, as is anyone who has been there before and is reflective about his experience.

PERSONALITY TYPES:

Mavens: You want someone on your crew who has her finger on the pulse of the market, the company, the culture. You want someone who knows what is expected to happen in five years and is already up on the thing that will be huge in six months. This person can gauge your breakthrough and give thoughts about whether or not it is new enough, different enough, and is pointing in the same direction as the cultural arrow.

Makers: You want the mechanical engineers, the designers, the builders, the people who will draw and build mock-ups and get very concrete about an idea. You need to stay grounded in reality and in what is feasible.

Theorists: You need people who have a deep knowledge of the subject even if they've never tried building something but have only studied it. Theorists can often offer deep pattern recognition and new insights that those only concerned with applying their idea might miss. This means including people who might be a little older.

Generalists: These people have a wide range of knowledge and as such they are very good at acquiring new information. They learn new things and integrate them and connect them to other things. They can be very helpful just listening to topics they don't know about. Their lack of knowledge leaves them open to helpful connections and insights.

There are two more steps you can take to biomimic the brain's breakthrough process with your teams. The first is the addition of a catalyst.

When you're off-task, not only does the power reroute to your genius lounge, but your hippocampus, your memory-maker, starts to build memories out of all the new things you've learned. Your hippocampus has an odd quirk: as it forms the new memories it takes pieces of them, shards of information, and tosses them into your genius lounge. This is why it is important to keep gathering new information. These new bits of information act as catalysts for your genius lounge.

So it can be a good idea to add a catalyst to your genius council crew.

Putting It into Practice: Catalysts for Your Genius Lounge

- Adding a new and/or random person

- Moving to or working in a new location

- Setting a ridiculous goal for an hour, like collecting all the orange Post-it pads in the office

- Reading a page or two from a book

- Watching a scene from a movie, or the whole movie

- Sharing specific stories (your worst vacation, your best day of school)

- Researching the history of anything—a building, a movement, a country, cave art

---

The other thing you can do to biomimic the brain's system is deputize someone, probably the leader already, but deputize them still to play the role of the EN. Here's what that entails:

You nominate the person.

Everyone agrees.

The EN announces the problem, focusing the team, even if everyone knows what the issue is.

The EN steps back and lets the team begin.

The EN steps in to point out a particularly intriguing idea or suggest a direction, then steps back again.

This dance continues. The deputized EN acts as a guide for the genius council and makes sure you don't go down too many rabbit holes.

Critique Your Breakthrough

Tom Chi is a legendary innovator in Silicon Valley. This is how he runs a brainstorming session. We found his set of rules ideally suited for testing out your breakthrough with your trusted crew. It also is structured enough to allow you to invite others into the process.

1. Start by having everyone state the things that work about the breakthrough. Write those on a board. Pick a goal, say fifteen things that work.

2. Don't write them in a list. Write them all over the board. No list, no prioritizing, no top, and no bottom.

3. Draw a picture beside the idea. Pictures turn on a different part of the brain, the nonverbal part.

As Chi told us, "You are taking something that is usually linear or sequential and verbal and making it something nonlinear, parallel and visual."[3]

This next part is important.

4. Tell everyone to do their best not to judge anything. Try to stay open minded. Do not voice opinions. Try not to let your ego become attached to any of the ideas on the board.

Chi suggests you spend thirty minutes to reach your goal of fifteen things that are working. And then you need to create a transitional moment.

5. Take two minutes of silence. Tell everyone to look at the board, take it all in, and let things start to connect.

The silence and the looking at the board are a way to use the EN to direct the DN's genius lounge to start connecting things, and to give it space to do so. You are creating a ritual to slide everyone into their associative state.

6. Have people draw the connections they see among the things that are working. Have them up at the board drawing lines. You want people to see the connections. Use different colored markers for the different connections. (The board starts to look like a spider web. That's okay. It will slow down naturally.)

7. Ask people to tell little stories about the connections they see, saying how these things are connected. The stories encourage people to build on one another.

8. Clusters will begin to emerge, groups of connected ideas. Once you have six, eight, ten clusters, ask people how they feel about them. Ask them to rate the clusters on a scale of 1 to 10.

9. Only look at clusters that rank at 7 or above.

This process allows you and your trusted crew to go through your breakthrough and see all the possibilities in it, or see that it just doesn't work. Or see that parts of it work but parts are missing or need more thought.

Build a Constraint Box

Thomas Edison did not invent the lightbulb. The first patent for a lightbulb was taken out in England in 1841. But Edison did create the first *commercially viable* lightbulb forty years later. And he didn't do it alone. Francis Robbins Upton was a Princeton graduate who was suggested to Edison by the German scientist Hermann von Helmholtz. The self-taught Edison was suspicious of university types but he hired Upton and set him to work on the lightbulb.

In order to find the right material to be a filament Upton built a constraint box. One constraint was that the filament have a high resistance. This meant it wouldn't take a lot of energy. The second constraint was that the filament glowed at a low heat. This meant it would be useful at a low energy point. The third constraint was that it give off enough light. The fourth constraint was that the filament last long enough to make the lightbulb economically sensible.

Once he had built the constraint box, Upton and his team made an exhaustive list of all the materials that met these criteria. They then tried each one until they reached carbonized bamboo, a filament that lasted for 1,200 hours.

While Upton used his constraint box to find his breakthrough, they can also be helpful to evaluate the output of your genius mode. Judah gave this tool to a team of researchers at Genentech. They were complaining about how difficult it is to work with federal regulations, so Judah had them lay out all the regulations they had to deal with. He used the regulations to build a constraint box. They formed the walls of the box.

The constraint box clearly defined the space the researchers could work in. It also focused their energy, so that they accepted the regulations rather than banged their heads against them, and used them to define the scope of their work.

Then Judah asked the researchers to share all their assumptions and he wrote them all down. Then he called them out one at a time and asked the whole group, "Is this true?" Doing it out loud as a group led to a number of assumptions being challenged and then taken away. The energy in the room increased as the team started to feel more confident.

Although drug research is a long and complex path, the team is still using the constraint box and assumption challenge today.

It can help to make this whole process visual by drawing it.

- Think of all the constraints that stand between you and the breakthrough you seek. Let's say there are eight constraints.

- Draw a big cube. Make sure it has a big, empty center.
- Draw eight squares around the edge of the cube.
- Write one of the constraints inside each of the squares.

You now have a constraint box and that big, empty center is your solution space. It is important to make the center big and empty so that you see it as a space of opportunity rather than confinement.

You can do one of two things with the box. You can take your breakthrough and see if it fits inside the constraints, or you can use it to set the conditions and then go and let your mind wander.

Now, outside of that box, on the edges of the paper, start to write down all your assumptions. Write everything you assume about your constraints and about the breakthrough you need. By writing them down, you see them and get to ask yourself if your assumptions are true. You get to test and push on them. If one of them is wrong and you get to remove a constraint, you suddenly have an opening in your constraint box. That opening is a space for a breakthrough to sneak in.

But more important, the constraint box sets the stage for your DN to create a breakthrough. It sets parameters around your problem and then, by laying out the assumptions, offers places for your DN to test out possible breakthroughs.

Try It

In order to see if it is a breakthrough, try it, play it out. Too often we sit with our breakthroughs and do not put them out into the world to field-test them. Go ahead. Test them. Do them. Take action. That's why there's mode switching. The breakthrough is not a breakthrough if you've just thought of it in your DN. You have to do something with it, put it into the world with your EN. If you've caught a butterfly, you need to make sure it can fly.

KEY TAKEAWAYS

- Once you've finished your research, gathered your data, and discovered new ideas, it's time to evaluate.
- Edward de Bono's Six Thinking Hats is a good tool for this analysis. We highly recommend his book *Six Thinking Hats*.

- Feedback from others about your ideas is critical. They will provide you with new insights, as well as identify your potential blind spots.
- Build a crew. Surround yourself with other people who can assist you. They will give you feedback, supplement your knowledge, make critical connections for you, and even help you execute your breakthroughs.
- Biomimic your brain by mapping your team members to the brain regions that create breakthroughs. Remember to add a catalyst and deputize someone to play the role of the EN.
- Use Tom Chi's critique method of brainstorming in a more open way. Get as many ideas up on the board as you can, find the connections, invite quiet, create narratives, create clusters of ideas and rank them.
- Create a constraint box by writing out all your constraints in the form of a box. The big, open center of the box will define your breakthrough space.
- Put your idea into the world and see what happens.

Part Two

The Blockers

Chapter 7

The Spiders of Fear

A Powerful Butterfly Repellent

HAVE YOU EVER felt a rush when imagining vivid negative scenarios? Let's say you're walking down the street and you feel your phone buzz in your pocket. You pull it out and see you have a text from your boss or colleague saying: Please stop by my desk when you get back from lunch. We need to clean up your presentation for next week. You feel a wave of dread start in your gut and move through your whole body. You grow cold and hot at the same time.

Oh my god, you think, *I totally screwed up the presentation. I knew I hadn't gotten it right.* As you walk to the office, you look back over the past week to find all the signs that you had indeed failed. There was that look your coworker Josh gave you at lunch. And that comment Amy made about needing to burn the midnight oil. That was directed at you, you now realize, because the presentation was missing the mark. Now you've gotten yourself to a place where not only is your presentation no good, but everyone else knows it.

I'm going to be fired. It's going to be impossible to find another job in this city. I'm going to have to move, take the kids out of school. Sell the house in a down market and lose my shirt.

This train of negative fantasies is called catastrophizing: interpreting mundane events as major threats. The fear it creates is one of the greatest inhibitors of our breakthrough butterflies.

Part of why we catastrophize is to emotionally prepare ourselves for the worst. You weren't being crazy; all the above scenarios could have happened—it's not as if you were worried about aliens coming to Earth. Everything you described has indeed happened to other people and could happen to you. But there was no foundation for them: all the things you imagined after reading the text message were pure conjecture, directed toward catastrophe not from real evidence, but rather from your emotional reaction.

This reaction may have served you in the past to prepare you for terrible things. And there is a part of you that enjoys catastrophizing: there's a rush of adrenaline and other neurochemicals as the fight-or-flight response kicks in. And paradoxically, catastrophizing can make you feel safer: *At least I won't be caught off-guard. At least I can prepare.*

We have a deep-rooted instinct to envision the worst because this tendency has, in the past, kept us alive. Mother Nature "wants" us to catastrophize because although a happy outlook might have led to a happier life, it also likely led to a much shorter one. The nervous system, which ensures our survival, was developed from jellyfish onward to figure out, essentially, "Can I eat this, or is it going to eat me?"

Now, if you miss out on eating something that's not a big deal; there will be other things to eat. However, if you miss the signal that this is something that will eat you, well, that's a problem of existential proportions. Those human beings who did not panic at the sound of a twig snapping? They weren't our ancestors—they were dinner. And so we evolved to have a bias toward negative information, a strange attraction to catastrophizing, in a manner similar to our predilection for fat and sugar.

But just like fat or sugar, while catastrophizing may once have been useful, now it just serves to shut down our brain.[1] Worse yet, because of neuroplasticity, the more you use those negative mental pathways, the deeper the groove gets, thus the easier it becomes to fall into it in the future. Welcome to the negativity bias: the tendency to give far more attention to negative details than positive ones.

In addition to the negativity bias, we also have a confirmation bias, which is our tendency to selectively retain information that confirms our preexisting notions. Unfortunately, with a negative bias in place, we tend to reconfirm our negative expectations.

Negative things produce more neural activity than equally intense positive things. We are quicker to recognize the negative in our world. We recognize angry faces more quickly and easily than happy faces. We even learn faster from pain than pleasure.

The amygdala, the fire alarm of your brain, uses two thirds of its neurons to look for the negative. These negative things get stored into memory almost immediately, a library of things to watch out for. Positive things need to be held in awareness for twelve seconds to transfer to longer-term memory. (This is why gratitude, meditation, and loving-kindness are necessary: we need to focus on the good for our brain to be able to truly remember it.) As Rick Hanson puts it, your "brain is like Velcro for negative experiences but Teflon for positive ones."[2]

From our survival instinct's perspective, failure can lead directly to death: misjudge the speed of the saber-toothed tiger and you die. Miss the crack of a branch announcing a falling tree and you die.

Failure can also indirectly lead to death via loss of status: there's a reason we have the expression "the lion's share of the meat." The lower on the totem pole, the fewer resources the individual receives, and someone who falls so low he or she is outcast from the tribe would certainly die. Both our own instincts and conventional wisdom seem to give us these two messages:

1. Failure is bad. If you're failing, you're doing something wrong. If you do something wrong, you should be punished. Punishment is shameful, so you must avoid failure at all costs. Failure is shameful, and if you fail, you are a loser and the group will shun you.

2. Failure is avoidable. If you're failing, you're doing something wrong. You should be able to avoid failure by doing everything right.

What we'll see in the following chapters is that both the fear of failure and the experience of failure are unavoidable. So you need to get good at handling them, especially because they can block the breakthrough process. This chapter covers *fear* of failure; the next chapter will teach you how to handle the actual *experience* of failure itself.

The goal of this chapter is to understand why we have this fear of failure—where it comes from—and what to do about it. You'll see how the fear of failure affects both our minds and our bodies. You'll learn about the most common manifestations of the fear of failure: the impostor syndrome, the inner critic, and the perfectionist. And you'll learn how to handle them so they no longer block your breakthroughs.

It's Unavoidable

Fear is an unavoidable part of the breakthrough process, whether you're seeking an intentional breakthrough or experiencing an unintentional breakthrough. The only difference is *when* fear shows up, and what this fear is directed toward.

For intentional breakthroughs, it shows up before the breakthrough. You want the breakthrough because you think the consequences will be good. So you don't fear the consequences of implementation as much (though things certainly could go wrong in the implementation phase). What you fear are the consequences of the quest itself. What if you fail to achieve the breakthrough you are seeking? What if it turns out you've wasted time, money, and effort "for nothing"?

The thing is, we *have* to accept the possibility of failure and deal with that fear. Intentional breakthroughs such as business or science innovation breakthroughs require the willingness to fail, to accept that what you're trying to achieve may not work out. If you're not willing to fail, you'll only do things guaranteed to succeed. Guaranteed success can only occur with things that have been done before, and therefore, by definition, aren't innovative. If you're not willing to risk failure, you won't innovate.

Most successful innovation breakthroughs were the result of countless iterations—which means countless consecutive failures. Or as Adam Berman, executive director of the University of California, Berkeley Haas School of Business Institute for Business Innovation puts it: "Innovation is evolutionary rather than revolutionary."[3]

For intentional breakthroughs, the fear you experience is the fear of not reaching that breakthrough. This fear of failure can prevent you from attempting all the things you'll need to do to succeed.

For unintentional breakthroughs, the fear comes after the break-through, but is just as toxic as it is for intentional breakthroughs. Unintentional breakthroughs aren't always welcome, and are often good in the long term but highly unpleasant in the short term—such as the sudden realization that "Oh! I need a divorce."

The unintentional breakthrough may seem to come out of the blue. It's actually, as we've seen, the result of a lengthy process, just not a conscious one. In this case, there was no need for you to deliberately "attempt" anything or "try things out" as you must for an intentional breakthrough. So you won't experience the fear of not getting to the breakthrough. You might be experimenting on your way to the break-through, but you won't be aware you're doing so.

We may worry: "What if this breakthrough turns out to be wrong? What if I rely on it and then end up looking like an idiot? Even if it's right, what will be the consequences of following it? Or what if I have the breakthrough and it's a legitimate breakthrough but I'm so broken I can't change? If I try to have a personal breakthrough and I fail, does that mean that I am stuck like this forever?" And so forth.

Whereas intentional breakthroughs raise the fear of not attaining a breakthrough, unintentional breakthroughs raise the fear of implementing a breakthrough.

Whether before or after a breakthrough, you *will* encounter fear: it's an integral part of the path. So you might as well learn how to overcome it, because otherwise, it could paralyze you. For intentional breakthroughs, fear could prevent you from attempting a breakthrough, thus preventing you from achieving one. For unintentional break-throughs, it could prevent you from implementing your breakthrough, thus rendering it useless.

It's a Real Breakthrough Blocker

Have you ever cried during a sad movie? Consciously, you know it's just a movie. You realize those are actors who are delighted to pretend they're dying heroically in exchange for a nice paycheck. Yet your brain sees what is happening on the screen and your tear ducts start flooding whether you like it or not. There's a reason they're called "tearjerkers."

In fact, you don't even need a movie screen to experience this effect: you can do it yourself. Close your eyes. (Well, close them after reading this.)

Imagine standing on a beach where the sand is too hot for comfort.

Imagine digging your feet down to the cooler sand beneath. Feel the relief.

Imagine being handed a margarita, taking the slice of lemon off the top, and biting into it. Feel the sour taste on your tongue. Do you feel your taste buds salivating in response?

Now imagine you're in a classroom. Imagine you're at the chalkboard, dragging your fingernails across it.

Sorry we made you cringe. There was no chalkboard, there was no lemon, and unless you're reading this on a beach, there was no sand either. And yet your mind produced very real physical reactions in response to completely imaginary events.

So what happens when you're feeling anxious about an upcoming performance review? You're focusing on everything you think could go wrong—and all of a sudden, your palms get sweaty and your pulse starts racing. Why? You're not in the performance review, after all! But because our brain doesn't distinguish between imagination and reality very well, when you imagine something, it will often send real, physical commands, as if the situation were real.[4]

When you imagine failing, these imaginary scenarios have the capacity to generate a real neural response, the activation of the threat response.[5] Even if the failure hasn't actually happened, the simple fear of failure can generate the fight-or-flight response.

The effects of this automatic response are well known. When a zebra is chased by a lion, stress hormones cause its body to increase heart rate and oxygenation, and shunt resources away from momentarily superfluous functions such as digestion, which is why a zebra chased by a lion immediately "lightens his load" while running away.[6]

In the same way, when stressed, the human body shoots stress hormones such as adrenaline and cortisol through our veins and directs all its resources toward crucial fighting or fleeing functions:

elevated heart and breathing rates, muscle reaction, acuity of vision and hearing, and so forth.

As Dr. Esther Sternberg, author of several books on the physiology of stress, explains, "The physiological stress response is actually designed to be an asset. It speeds the heart rate and diverts blood away from the gut and to the muscles so we can run away. It constricts the pupils of our eyes so we can focus on our attacker. It dilates the bronchi of the lungs to increase blood oxygenation, and converts energy stored in the liver into fuel for strength and stamina."[7] It's designed to help us survive.

Your body stops worrying about living ten more years, and instead reacts to survive ten more minutes. "Nonurgent" functions such as muscle repair, digestion, and the immune system shut down for you, just as they do for the zebra. And your "superfluous" functions—such as cognitive reasoning—also shut down. In other words, because it's not critical to survival, rational thinking gets shut down when the fight-or-flight response is activated.*

The physiological stress response was designed for short bursts. It evolved to put us in a powerful state in which most of our resources are narrowly focused on survival for a very short time. We were never supposed to stay in such a heightened state for very long.

If a zebra chased by a big cat on the African savannah manages to escape, it eventually slows down, stops, sits down, and then starts to shake intensely. We might interpret this as fear. In fact, the shaking helps the zebra release itself from the hold of its stress hormones, because it instinctively knows it is safe. When the zebra stands up again, it has returned to its earlier relaxed physiological state, with no residual stress in its body.

The reason the fight-or-flight system is so powerful is because it is built with direct neuron-to-neuron contact. This means that the neurons communicate *electrically* with one another, skipping the slower process of neurochemicals crossing the synaptic gap. Basically, your rational functions send instructions via horse-drawn carriage while your fight-or-flight system uses FedEx.

Negativity exists to make you act, to either fix the problem or get

---

* This might explain why so many project managers make bad decisions when something they are responsible for is off-track.

out of the situation. We evolved feelings like fear or anxiety partially to get us to *do something*.

There are times when the discomfort of intense fear is highly appropriate. If you're in life-threatening danger, then you want your body pooling all of its resources to ensure your immediate survival. However, in the civilized, modern world, few situations call for a full fight-or-flight response. In other cases, our instinctive reactions actually work against us.

How Fear Affects Your Mind

Think about a time you've become paralyzed in the middle of an exam, or even worse, on stage. You're like a deer in the headlights, frozen, heart racing, palms sweaty. You're trying to remember what you're supposed to do, but your mind is blank. Your higher cognitive functions have ceased operations.

Heightened stress triggers the mind to declare a state of emergency. In response your mind turns off what it deems to be unnecessary functions. Unfortunately, that means the body is reducing our cognitive abilities just when we may need them most. It's hard to remember this in the midst of an anxiety attack, but rest assured that this reaction is an entirely normal one intended for your well-being.

Philippe Goldin, director of Stanford's Clinically Applied Affective Neuroscience lab, told us: "The threat response can hijack attention; making us revert to very simplistic mental algorithms and habitual, automatic solutions."[8] David Rock, founder of the NeuroLeadership Institute, explains: "The threat response impairs analytic thinking, creative insight, and problem solving."[9]

The kinds of fear we are talking about here manifest as social inhibition in the form of the impostor syndrome and the inner critic, and as perfectionism and its close cousin, maximizing.

Social inhibition is, essentially, the fear of "what others would think." This fear of looking stupid or being judged are the flip side of our social awareness. Social inhibition is absolutely useful; it's the part of us that makes us "civilized," but it has its drawbacks. Insights can only happen in the wake of quieting your frontal lobes, and that is where your inhibitions live.

The problem with these inhibitions is that they can lead us to repress thoughts and ideas that could lead to great breakthroughs. In some cases, diminished social inhibition caused by the degeneration of the prefrontal lobes led people to a fountain of creativity—painting, art, and so forth. People who'd never had an artistic bone in their body suddenly became prolific artists.[10]

Social inhibition is likely the single biggest blocker you will encounter on your road to achieving or implementing breakthroughs. Does this mean you should voluntarily damage your frontal lobes? Of course not. You might have heard of the case of Phineas Gage, whose frontal lobes were damaged by a railroad accident in 1848. In the aftermath of the accident, he became "fitful, irreverent, indulging at times in the grossest profanity (which was not previously his custom)."[11] The man was "gross, profane, coarse, and vulgar, to such a degree that his society was intolerable."[12] We need our frontal lobes to function in society.

But it's certainly true that finding ways to put the frontal lobes "to sleep" is an age-old search for creatives. The saying "Write drunk, edit sober" captures it perfectly, and embodies the whole process of breakthrough thinking.

Write drunk: Drinking quiets the frontal lobes, the social-inhibition part of our brain, the monitor. You quiet the EN and you let the DN run wild to generate a burst of breakthrough thinking.

Edit sober: Then you bring the EN back online to sift, evaluate, and prioritize. This is the phase of convergent thinking, critical thinking.

Social inhibition shows up in our brains in the prefrontal cortex, and in our minds as the impostor syndrome and the inner critic.

The Impostor Syndrome

The impostor syndrome is experienced when successful and competent people believe they don't know as much as they should and live in constant fear of being exposed as a fraud. It is that deep certainty that most of us feel at some time in our life, that *we are just not good enough.*

Since the impostor syndrome was first identified, research has indicated that more than 70 percent of the population has had this feeling at one time or another.[13]

The impostor syndrome is also an obstacle to breakthrough thinking. If you believe that you don't really know what you are doing and spend mental energy fearing others will find you out, how can you possibly believe you will see something no one else has seen before? Can you imagine Thomas Edison thinking to himself, *I'm no inventor,* or Steve Jobs plagued by thoughts like, *Who am I to design computers?*

And yet, counterintuitive as it may seem, the impostor syndrome is most prevalent among high performers. When we speak about it at Harvard, Yale, Stanford, or MIT, the room goes so silent that one could hear a pin drop. When students discover this feeling has a name, and they aren't alone in experiencing it, we see them exhale in relief. Michael Uslan still gets that feeling occasionally when he's in the studio. "I still have this background feeling that one of the security guards might come in and throw me out," he told us.

The impostor syndrome can be a great motivating tool, getting us to work harder than anyone else. But at what cost? First, part of your brain is always occupied with it—arguing with it, trying to push it back, hiding away from it. Second, if there are not "enough" successes according to whatever arbitrary measure your brain has decided on, it activates the sympathetic nervous system and deactivates your creative capacities. Third, worst of all, it can prevent you from taking the risks you need to take to reach breakthrough innovation.

Today we finally have effective tools to handle the impostor syndrome. But just knowing the universality of such feelings can help us neutralize their effect and reduce their power. By reading this section, you've already taken the first step.

The basis of the impostor syndrome is having the impression of yourself as not competent for this job, this activity, this position—in our case, as not capable of creating breakthroughs.

This image, this impression of yourself, is technically known as a *self-image*. A self-image, in plain terms, is who we think we are: our personality, our capabilities, etc.[14]

Once people have developed an image of themselves, there is a strong tendency for that image to be maintained by a bias in what they pay attention to, what they remember, and what they are prepared to accept as true about themselves. In other words, the self-image becomes self-perpetuating.

The most effective way to handle (or even dismantle) the impostor syndrome is to change your self-image.

Before going any further, here are two shortcuts you can try to change the playing field so that the impostor syndrome simply no longer applies.

Shortcut #1: Change the Label

Try simply changing the name of what you aspire to be, and see if there is another term that fits more easily with your current self-image. Olivia, for example, doesn't consider herself to be creative. Resourceful, yes. Ingenious, yes. Those words feel comfortable. But she's not comfortable calling herself "creative," because creativity is not in her self-image. To her, "creative" belongs to those other people who have a design sensibility, to artists, to people who do creative things (like music, art, and theater). Creativity feels intangible, elusive, something she can't see the contours of. But with the self-image of someone who is "ingenious and resourceful," she achieves the same creativity.

Shortcut #2: Flip the Scenario

Ask yourself which elements of your experience (or lack thereof), personality, or background does the impostor syndrome use to make you feel like a fraud. Take each of these in turn, and flip them around:

"I'm too young for this job" becomes "My youth is a huge advantage because . . ." Do you have a better grasp of new technology? A better understanding of the customer base? A greater willingness to take risks, to try new things?

"I've never worked in this industry before. I'm not an industry expert" becomes "The fact that I'm not an industry expert is a huge advantage because they already have industry experts falling from the rafters. They don't need one more. What I can bring is a wealth of new perspectives and different experiences, and I can bring everything I've learned outside this industry to bear on the problems we're facing here." And so forth . . .

"At Microsoft," explains Kevin Sauer, "the imposter syndrome has taken on a life of its own. One of our most famous technologists wrote a blog about being a phony and it is referenced all the time internally.[15] It is almost so 'hip' to be a phony that it isn't."

Three of the brain's limitations will come in handy to change a self-image that's holding you back. The brain doesn't have a great sense of:

- Scale: A series of little things can be just as difficult to handle as one big thing. Our brain isn't naturally adept at prioritizing, and for once you can make it work in your favor. This is the science of "small wins." Dr. Teresa Amabile, professor and director of research at Harvard Business School, to whom we owe so many discoveries in the field of individual and team creativity and productivity, organizational innovation, and the psychology of everyday work life, found that even small wins could have a tremendous impact on people's inner state. "Many of the progress events our research participants reported represented only minor steps forward. Yet they often evoked outsize positive reactions."[16]

- Time: A vivid event that happened thirty years ago can feel "as if it were yesterday." It's the vividness and ease of recall that matter here, rather than how recently the event occurred.

- The difference between imagination and reality, as we've mentioned earlier.[17]

Now we will show you how you can use each of these limitations in your favor, to change your self-image step-by-step.

Step 1: Define Your Goal

What new self-image do you want? Meditation teacher Tara Brach, author of the wonderful *Radical Acceptance,* asks, "Who would you be if you didn't believe you were fundamentally flawed?"[18] What self-image do you need to achieve your goal? Maybe you want to see yourself as a risk-taker. Perhaps you'd like to see yourself as creative.

Step 2: Gather Past Evidence

Look back into your past and find at least five acts of creativity, five ways you've been creative. These could be big acts of creativity (that time when I found a solution for the whole project) or small ones (I found a way to get around the traffic jam this morning). It's quantity rather than quality that matters here. Remember you can also try replacing "creative" with "resourceful" or "ingenious."

Step 3: Put the Evidence on Display

Ellen Langer of Harvard University and her colleagues enlisted the help of two groups of elderly men in 1981.[19] The men, who were in their seventies and eighties, were sequestered far away from the world in a monastery in New Hampshire. When each group arrived at the monastery they encountered a world with the clock turned back. They were surrounded by things from the 1950s, a black-and-white television, an old-time radio, even copies of the *Saturday Evening Post.* They listened to a radio broadcast of the 1959 Preakness Stakes. They watched the 1959 movie *Anatomy of a Murder.* They even talked about the political issues of that era, such as the space race or Nikita Khrushchev.

Both groups stayed for one week, though not at the same time. There was only one difference between the two groups of men. The first group were told to pretend they were once again young men. The second group were told to simply reminisce about being young men.

Prior to and following the experiment, both groups of men underwent extensive cognitive and physical tests. After one week in the monastery both groups showed improvement in strength, hearing, vision, posture, and even flexibility, their fingers more agile and less curled by arthritis. They scored better on intelligence tests too. But the group of men who actually pretended they were young men showed significantly more improvement than the group that only reminisced. Their bodies actually seemed younger.

"Wherever you put the mind, the body will follow," Langer concluded. By the end of the monastery study Langer was playing touch football with these men. The canes they had used to walk now lay at the side of the field. "It is not primarily our physical selves that limit us," she explains, "but rather our mindset about our physical limits."

In order for this technique to be effective, you need to truly surround yourself with the evidence of a new self-image. In addition to
these lists of past creative acts, you can also post photos around the
room of you doing creative or crazy stuff—anything that shows you
being socially disinhibited!

Step 4: Embrace Your New Self-Image

Though many of us assume that our behaviors flow from our beliefs
and attitudes, in social psychology it is understood that most often our
behaviors are what change and form our attitudes, not vice versa. This
cognitive dissonance theory suggests that our behaviors have a stronger influence on our attitudes than our attitudes on our behaviors.

"The way that people change their self-image is to act," Robert
Cialdini, preeminent psychologist and author of the landmark book
Influence: The Psychology of Persuasion, told us.[20] "One strategy is to un-
dertake a systematic program of action that fits with the self-image
they aspire to."

If you start behaving in creative ways, even if the new behaviors
don't feel natural at first, your attitudes and beliefs will follow in order
to reduce your internal cognitive dissonance ("Gee, I must be creative
after all"). This is a more effective way to change our self-image than
self–pep talk ("I am creative, and can do something creative").

The Science of Small Wins

Remember, research has shown that small wins have enormous power,
and as Charles Duhigg describes it, "an influence disproportionate to
the accomplishments of the victories themselves."[21] Small wins fuel
transformative changes by convincing people that bigger achievements
are within their reach. And what that means for you is to start with
small steps, steps so small they seem ludicrously easy. That helps you
build success momentum.

Duhigg added, "'Small wins are a steady application of a small
advantage,' one Cornell professor wrote in 1984. 'Once a small win has
been accomplished, forces are set in motion that favor another small
win.' Small wins fuel transformative changes by leveraging tiny

advantages into patterns that convince people that bigger achievements are within reach."

B. J. Fogg, founder of the Stanford Persuasive Technology Lab, told us, "For about six months, I've been obsessed with 'success momentum,' the feeling you get when you succeed over and over. When you manage to change small things in your life, you feel a growing sense of satisfaction and control."[22]

It seems our brains aren't very good at distinguishing big successes from small successes. Your successes don't need to be big things, like cleaning your entire home. Just wiping out the bathroom sink, he explained, can help create success momentum if—and this is key—you feel you succeeded.

As Fogg explained, small successes are easier to get than big ones, so you can stack up many small successes within a few minutes. And you can have dozens during any given morning. Small successes (not big ones) are the fastest, simplest way to build success momentum.

When Fogg knows he's going to have a hard day, he told us that he "does a series of small wins to build momentum, increase confidence and resiliency." He especially favors tidying the house. It's also useful to combat procrastination: when B. J. finds himself procrastinating, he gives himself a window during which he can do "small win" activities.

Here's how small wins can help create a new self-image: If you have lost touch with your inner creative genius, start with tiny creative acts, such as making up nicknames for your plants or daily objects—Philip the photocopier, for instance. Then start to invent a backstory for each of them. Philip is from Minnesota, loves football (Go Blue!), and so on. Accumulating a lot of small wins can bulk up to a big win and a new self-image.

Putting It into Practice: Changing Your Self-image

- Define your goal. What self-image do you want?

- Gather past evidence. Look into the past and write out five ways you've been creative.

- Put the evidence on display. Pin them up on the wall or use a Post-it. Do this every night for ten days. On the last evening, read all the items at once. See how you feel about your self-image now.

- Embrace your new self-image. Take advantage of the science of small wins and build up many "small successes."

The Inner Critic

The inner critic is that nasty voice inside your head telling you that you have done this and that wrong, or that you are a failure, or any other of the infinite varieties on this theme our inner critics come up with. It is especially dangerous since it is most apt to launch the sympathetic nervous system, and so prevent us from even attempting anything.

A good way to know whether the inner critic is operating within you is to pay attention to how often you hear the word "should" in your own mind. You should have left earlier, or perhaps, You should be exercising daily. The inner critic causes you to, as they say, "should all over yourself."

Since internal attacks are perceived by our mind in ways very similar to those a real, physical attack would be perceived, they can generate the automatic physical reaction we met in the previous section, the threat or fight-or-flight response.

Professional basketball and football players often trash-talk to cause an opposing player to doubt his own abilities. Michael Jordan was famous for this. Unfortunately many of us trash-talk ourselves. We self-criticize, doubt our own abilities, and turn on our threat response. This can have a negative effect on our ability to perform.

As Dr. Philippe Goldin put it, "When people call in sick, their lack of productivity is obvious. But a more insidious hindrance to productivity happens when people are consumed by negative thoughts throughout the day. Internal self-criticism can severely limit innovation and creativity."[23] Though people may be physically present, they're really locked in a duel with their inner critic, unable to move forward. And because that mental absenteeism isn't visible, it can go unaddressed.

Self-criticism is one of the most common obstacles to great performance in any field. We have come to consider self-criticism and self-doubt the "silent killers" of business. So many executives suffer from it, yet so few dare speak out about it.

Over the years, we have heard everyone from junior associates to the most senior executives confess that much of their workday is spent in battle with negativity, an army of inner critics pointing out disappointments, forecasting failure, beating the drum of despair. In some cases, they (and we) were amazed they accomplished anything at all. One executive told us a full 80 percent of his day was spent fighting his inner critic.

The Inner Critic and Body Language

This kind of negativity doesn't just affect our actual performance, it also affects how others perceive us.

Let's say you're in a conversation. You say something, then immediately think, *Oh, that was a stupid thing to say.* What's going to happen to your face? You may wince at the thought and your expression may tense. Because we can't control our body language, any negativity in our mind will eventually manifest on our face.

No matter how brief that negative expression, the person facing you is going to spot it. And all they know is that while you were looking at them and listening to them, a negative expression crossed your face. Naturally they'll assume that expression was a reaction to them—what they said or did, or what you think about them. This is how internal negativity affects your body language and your performance.

People know their self-doubt and self-criticism doesn't help them, yet they can't let it go. Recognizing and acknowledging its purpose ("My body is responding because it's trying to keep me safe") or finding self-compassion ("Of course I'm reacting this way—this is scary") can help break the cycle.

Here's how the inner critic can hinder your breakthroughs. Let's say you're considering trying a new way of running meetings.

Your brain, with its ingrained negative bias, starts to imagine the possible failures. Immediately, you imagine others' reactions to your failure. Feelings of shame and fear rise up. You want to shut down, run away, hide, and certainly not try this experiment in real life.

But what actually happened here? The experience is in fact our own internal discomfort created by our inner critic's verdict on others' judgment. The good news is that everything we've just described happens entirely inside our heads. Let's see how to change this internal experience.

Knowing how to handle the inner critic is essential to unleashing your breakthrough potential. Unfortunately, our first reflex when under attack is to try to argue with the inner critic. And this is where practices like cognitive behavioral therapy, excellent in getting us to detach from thoughts and get some perspective, can get us into trouble.

Trying to suppress the thought would make things worse. But you can learn to *dance* with your shadow; you can learn to *handle* your inner critic. With practice, by using techniques such as the ones you'll learn here, you can achieve some distance from internal negativity, and maybe even get to a place where the inner critic's voice evokes in you only a smile or a chuckle. We promise.

Find Your "Everybody"

Dr. Martha Beck, who says that she has become extremely intimate with her inner critic through three Harvard degrees (including a PhD in sociology), explains that "everybody's Everybody is composed of just a few key people. Our social nature makes us long to fit in with a larger group, but it's difficult to hold the tastes and opinions of more than five or six individuals in your mind. So the resourceful social self creates a kind of shorthand: it picks up a few people's attitudes, emblazons them on your brain, and extrapolates this image until it covers the entire

known universe. The vague compilation of folks you call Everybody is
what psychologists term 'the generalized other.'"[24]

The tool that Beck recommends to detach from this limiting "everybody" in your mind is the most effective we've seen. Here's how it
works: find all the statements about creativity, innovation, and breakthroughs that you would like to believe about yourself and that could
objectively be considered true.

For instance:

- *I have an amazingly capable brain.* We guarantee that you do. Your
  brain processes millions of bits of information every second, without your even thinking about it.
- *I'm highly creative by nature.* Look around the room at the lists
  you've put up on the walls. Think of the adventures you created for
  your daily objects.

. . . and so forth.

For each of these statements, make two columns:

	People who have told you that this (or something like it) *is* true	People who have told you this (or something like it) *is not* true
I have an amazingly capable brain.	Mary, Jeff	Sam, Fernando
I am highly creative.	My first-grade teacher (Yes, this counts.)	
. . . and so forth.		

Fill in as many blanks as you can, and it's perfectly all right if the
same name comes up several times. The important thing is that you
are not allowed to generalize; you must use specific people.

Look over the columns of names you've written down, and answer
the following questions:

1. Whom do you like more? (People on the left or people on the right?)
2. Whom do you respect more? (People on the left or people on the right?)
3. Which people have the happier, more fulfilling lives? (People on the left or people on the right?)
4. Which people have more stable, intimate relationships? (People on the left or people on the right?)
5. If you had a baby and were forced to leave your child to be raised by other people, whom would you choose? (People on the left or people on right?)
6. Which individuals most deserve to have their opinions ignored, belittled, and discounted? (People on the left or people on the right?)
7. *Why in the name of all that's holy would you give any credence to the people on the right?*

Create a New "Everybody"

Because of our innate deference to authority, that encouraging, positive "everybody" is most powerful when composed of people you admire.[25] You could pick people who were tremendously successful after a long string of failures, like Lincoln, or people who enjoyed tremendous success while failing two times out of three, like Babe Ruth.[26] You could, for example, put up a photo of Babe Ruth on the wall with a caption that reads:

> Failed 6 times out of 10.
> Greatest player of all time.

Cheesy? Perhaps. Effective? Absolutely.

In fact, famous athletes are a great source of imperfection examples: Michael Jordan had a 50 percent failure rate for free throws; and Pelé and Diego Maradona, two of the greatest soccer players of all time, when playing in World Cup games, had a failure rate of *95 percent!* That's right, 95 percent of the shots they took did not result in a goal.

If you prefer non-sports examples, Tom Hanks has been known to say that of the hundred-plus movies he's made, "seven or eight were good, a dozen more are decent, and the rest are godawful."[27] And this is one of Hollywood's most successful actors.

If you prefer business authority figures, here's legendary inventor James Dyson on using failure to drive success:[28] "I made 5,127 prototypes of my vacuum before I got it right. There were 5,126 failures. But I learned from each one. That's how I came up with a solution." Dyson spent fifteen years creating 5,126 versions that failed before he made one that worked. The payoff was a multibillion-dollar company and a personal net worth estimated at $1.6 billion.

Steven is a very successful entrepreneur. He sold his first company when he was twenty-two years old and his second when he was thirty-two. Both of them had revolved around data storage. Deciding to embark on his third start-up, Steven decided to reach a little further than he had before. He had always enjoyed drawing and wanted to meld his love of art with his love of technology. He had seen a demonstration once where a man wearing sensors on his fingers was able to draw on a specialized screen. The cool part was the man was standing ten feet away from the screen. Steven was hooked.

But he had recently run into two roadblocks. The technology was proving difficult to master and, more important, investors were not impressed with the potential. They just didn't think people would pay for it. Steven had had such an easy time with his two previous companies. Their financial upside was clear. They made products with a clear use for businesses. He didn't have to do much selling. But now he was faced with serious doubts about his product. And what was worse, he really believed in this one with all his heart. He loved this product. He wanted to use it himself.

Clearly Steven needed help with his pitch, but before he could get near that part he needed to regain his emotional momentum. He was feeling like he had failed and it took the wind from his sails. He was beginning to lose hope.

Judah asked Steven to meet him in Emeryville, California, on the east side of San Francisco Bay. He and Steven began to walk.

As they did, Judah told him a story and timed their walk very carefully in his mind. He talked about a young animator working at Disney in the early 1980s. The young man had seen the movie *Tron* and became very excited about the potential of computer animation in movies. He made a short animated film using a computer and showed it to his boss at Disney. His boss asked how much it cost. The young man was eager to tell him that it cost no more than traditional animation. His boss said he wasn't interested. The only reason to use a computer was if it was cheaper. But the young man wouldn't take no for an answer. So you know what his boss did? He fired him. The young man was John Lasseter, cofounder of Pixar Animation Studios.

And as Judah finished the story he turned the corner and at the end of the block was the brick-and-iron gateway to the Pixar Studios campus. There was no need to give a pep talk or to say never give up. Steven was bouncing with excitement, realizing he was following in excellent footsteps.

The Perfectionist

Perfectionism can show up as a background feeling that you're never doing enough, that you're so far behind on everything, or that you're not on top of everything like you "should" be. The perfectionist makes you focus on all you haven't done, on all the ways you fall short, rather than all the ways in which you are doing well.

You think of all those books you "should" read, all these exercises you "should" do, and so forth. It's a litany of "shoulds"—just like the inner critic, the perfectionist causes you to "should all over yourself." However, unlike the inner critic, the perfectionist tends to focus on the goals and activities in which it thinks you're falling short, rather than on your value as a human being. It focuses on what you're doing rather than who you are.

Perfectionism can be related to social inhibition, or it can be separate. Some people seek perfection not because of what others would say, but for its own sake. Some artists are perfectionists just for art's sake.

There are elements of control and hubris in perfectionism: no one will ever read all the books. *No one* will ever know *all* the information.

And even if someone could know all the information, they couldn't know what it all means and how it all connects. Like it or not, we are limited in our capacity.

As shame researcher Brené Brown explains in *The Gifts of Imperfection*, perfectionism is addictive because when, as we go through life, we invariably do experience shame or judgment for some reason or other, we believe it's because we weren't perfect enough. And rather than questioning the faulty logic of perfectionism, we try even harder. Essentially, the self-blame lets us keep the aspiration of being perfect.

Perfectionistic thinking assumes that there is a perfect goal to be reached. Perfectionism is marching toward that predetermined goal, with only one acceptable outcome. That march does not allow the downtime that the default network needs, nor does it allow the open-mindedness to see all the new things on the periphery that will lead to a breakthrough.

Breakthrough thinking is recognizing that we're actually on a journey, engaged in a process. You may end up creating or stumbling upon something you didn't set out to. Keep reminding yourself that the journey is not a straight line; very often you end up at a different goal than you started toward, and that doesn't mean it's a failure.

Here are a few tools to handle your inner perfectionist. Though each one might not vanquish the perfectionist on its own, they'll definitely give you some breathing space, and when all done together are quite powerful.

- Remember that if it's rare, it's precious. Philatelists love "flawed" stamps. In fact, most of the most valuable stamps in the world are flawed. The Swedish Three Skilling Banco, Yellow Color Error, 1855 (it was supposed to be blue green) most recently sold for $2.3 million. The Post Office Mauritius, 1847 ("post office" was printed on the stamp instead of "post paid") went for $3.8 million. It's the flaw that makes them unique, thus valuable, to the tune of several million dollars. Whenever the perfectionist rears its ugly head, try reminding yourself that whatever action you have taken, whatever "mistake" was made, it is completely and forever unique. There will never again be this sequence of events. This may help to give you a different perspective on imperfections, because our brain's automatic reaction is to assume that anything that's rare is precious, and therefore to be treasured.[29]

- Post photos of people you admire with an imperfection-encouraging sentence below, a quote you make up. Yes, the first time you type it and read it, it may feel ridiculous. But within about a week, it will start to feel real. For example, try having an authority figure encouraging you to "only reach 70 percent of perfect. No more."[30]

- If you've figured out whom you got the perfection mandate from, write a letter, from them to you, about the downsides of perfectionism. This letter should also contain their apology for telling you to be perfect and their encouragement for you to be imperfect from now on. Definitely put up his or her photo surrounded with quotes you create to this effect.

In the next chapter, you will get a failure blueprint, directions on "how to fail right." Your inner perfectionist will be reassured that it is following a blueprint perfectly—it just so happened the blueprint calls for failure.

The Maximizer

Closely tied to perfectionism, the maximizer gives you the desire, the drive, and sometimes even the compulsion to make "the best" decision. It's less about making a perfect decision, in the absolute, Platonic-ideal sense, and more about making the best possible decision, in a relative sense, in comparison to others. It's about getting the most out of a situation.[31]

In a sense, perfectionism is more idealistic because it is measured against an internal standard of perfection, whereas maximizing is measured against an external standard: Will someone make a better choice than I will? Was there a better choice available? Will a better choice eventually come along?

The maximizer is rarely caused by social inhibition, but rather by our own internal drive to get the best from the situation. In this sense, it is more closely correlated with greed.

Though it is less personally destructive than the inner critic or the impostor syndrome, the maximizer can still greatly hinder your ability to achieve breakthroughs. Yes, this focus on maximizing does lead you to make marginally better choices. And within a certain range, it is a good tool for success. But it can easily go overboard, and you can find yourself spending an hour on the exact wording for your e-mail or social media post or on choosing the best brand of laundry detergent.

Worse yet, leading authority Barry Schwartz has found through years of research that the maximizer also leads you to: [32]

- be less satisfied with your decision
- get less happiness out of that decision and its outcome
- be less happy in life in general

How do you put the maximizer on a leash? Schwartz has several suggestions, such as setting a predetermined, arbitrary limit to the amount of maximizing you allow yourself—limiting the amount of research you do to choose a product, or the amount of time you spend figuring out the best route, and so forth.

Unfortunately, arbitrary limits don't work very well for strong maximizers. For those people, an arbitrary limit feels morally wrong, almost sacrilegious. If this feels like you, what you can try instead is to deputize your maximization.

For example, you could make an agreement with yourself that for any product you're considering buying, if you can find a review in a consumer report Web site, you'll go with their recommendation. These organizations specialize precisely on the comparison and evaluation needed to make the best possible choice (the essence of maximizing). The tests they put things through are intense, extensive, and comprehensive, and deciding that you want to keep reading further reviews (especially from amateurs if you're just surfing the Web) is just plain irrational. Make an agreement that you will accept the amount of research and comparison the consumer reports Web sites have done as good enough.

One of our clients deputized her health choices regarding to any new health information that comes out to a few of her friends who she describes as "health nuts." "They are willing to spend hours poring over science articles, cross-referencing studies, and keeping up with the latest research with a passion and commitment that I could never match. So I'm quite happy to simply ask them for their conclusions and recommendations and go with that!"

Handling Fear: Quick Fixes

So now you know what happens when the sympathetic nervous system is activated, and what a threat that is to breakthrough creativity. You've learned a variety of tools to help prevent its activation. But what can you do once it is activated?

To calm the sympathetic nervous system, you need to activate its counterpart, the *para*sympathetic nervous system. The parasympathetic nervous system, as psychologist Rick Hanson explains, is more fundamental to life than the sympathetic nervous system (the fight-or-flight response).

If your sympathetic system were surgically disconnected—as it was in years past as a last-resort treatment for hypertension—you would remain alive and pretty much yourself, though unable to cope well with commuter traffic, root for the home team, or have an orgasm. But if your PNS were disconnected, you would quickly die.

Fortunately, we have several tools with which to access and activate the parasympathetic nervous system. The mind can turn stress on, but it can also turn it off. Here are some quick fixes if you're feeling that you are in a less than creative state:

- Check your breathing. When we're feeling stressed, anxious, or in another active-SNS state, our breathing is usually rapid and shallow. Use the body's effect on the mind by taking deep, slow breaths. As you now know, your actions influence your beliefs; if you breathe as if you were calm, you'll feel much calmer.

- Change your body's position. As Stanford's Deborah Gruenfeld found, people who assume expansive poses (taking up more space) experience a measurable physiological shift. In one experiment, assertiveness- and energy-promoting hormones rose by 19 percent, while anxiety hormones fell by 25 percent. Assuming a strong, confident physical posture will make you genuinely *feel* more confident and more powerful. As you feel more powerful, your body language will adapt accordingly. This in turn gives you yet another biochemical boost, and the cycle builds upon itself.[32] All you have to do is get the cycle going, and if you keep practicing, confident body language will become second nature.

- Imagine getting a great hug from someone you love for twenty seconds. Of course, you may not have twenty seconds, but when you do, this is remarkably effective.

- Name your feelings. Try simply naming the feelings you're experiencing—anxiety, fear, shame, whatever they might be, don't worry about getting the "right" or "best" label—and adding "and it's okay" or even "and it's welcome." For instance, "I'm feeling fear, and it's okay."

- Yawn. Yes, really! Yawning activates the parasympathetic nervous system and relaxes our body. This is why you'll often see athletes yawn before a competition.

Relaxation

Harvard professor of medicine Dr. Herbert Benson is truly the pioneer for Western medicine on how to activate the parasympathetic nervous system at will, through a procedure now known as the Relaxation Response.[34]

In one of his recent studies, he showed that the mind can control genetic activity through the Relaxation Response. Three groups of meditators were studied: novices, short-term meditators (fewer than ten years), and long-term meditators (ten years or more). In this cross-sectional study, blood samples from all participants were analyzed to determine the expression of more than twenty-two thousand genes on measures of inflammation and cell lifespan.[35]

The Relaxation Response (RR) was observed to turn genes on or off, to amplify or decrease their effect. Eight weeks of RR on novices produced the same results (affecting the same genes in the same way) but to a lesser degree. The probability of this occurring by chance was one in ten billion.

Furthermore, the RR increased the effect of cognitive restructuring: when the mind is quieter, it is more receptive to new facts coming in. The protocol described next is therefore an excellent preamble to any visualization or mental rehearsal exercise.

Putting It into Practice: The Relaxation Response

Step 1: Pick a focus word, phrase, image, or use your breath as an object of focus.

Step 2: Find a quiet place and sit calmly in a comfortable position.

Step 3: Close your eyes.

Step 4: Progressively relax all your muscles.

Step 5: Breathe slowly and naturally. As you exhale, repeat or picture silently your focus word or phrase, or simply focus on your breathing rhythm.

Step 6: Assume a passive attitude. When other thoughts appear, simply think *Oh well,* and return to your focus.

Step 7: Continue with this exercise for an average of twelve to fifteen minutes.

Step 8: Practice this technique at least once daily.

Oxytocin is another surefire way to quiet the sympathetic nervous system and activate the calming parasympathetic nervous system. Paul Zak, author of *The Moral Molecule* and expert on the topic of oxytocin, was one of our key science advisers for this book. Among other things, his research showed that certain activities reliably cause people's brains to release oxytocin. He gave us a list of his favorites.

Putting It into Practice: Paul Zak's Favorite Oxytocin Triggers

- Give someone a hug. Aim for eight hugs a day!
- Try compassion meditation. (We'll cover this next section.)
- Dance.
- Soak in a hot tub.

- Surprise someone with a gift.

- Pet a dog.

- Take a hike with a friend.

- Write a note of thanks to a teacher or mentor.

Thanks to neuroplasticity, all of the oxytocin-releasing techniques in this exercise not only make you feel good in the moment, they also build your oxcytocin-producing brain muscles. And although "oxytocin is a purely social molecule, i.e., it requires a positive social stimulus for release," as Zak told us, this social stimulus need not be real: the right imagined social stimulus would produce some of the same effects.

Gratitude

Gratitude can be both a state of mind and a feeling, and there are practices and processes that can help you reach a state of mind or a state of heart, a feeling, of gratitude. Some of us *think* our way into gratitude; some of us *feel* our way into gratitude.

Why is gratitude good for the breakthrough experience? Because it releases oxytocin. A lot of difficult feelings will come up on the road to breakthrough. Gratitude, and the oxytocin it releases, is a really good remedy for most of them. Oxytocin will wash away stress chemicals in your brain.

Research is clear that gratitude helps us live longer, and be healthier[36] and even happier.[37] By helping us think of things we already have—whether material items, experiences, or cherished relationships—gratitude acts as an antidote to negative feelings. Not only is it good for health and happiness, it's also good for your social connections, friendships, and family relationships. It will even increase your level of charisma. Truly.[38]

Gratitude is a really important tool. But few of us can easily get into a space of gratitude for long periods of time. Human beings are instinctively wired for hedonic adaptation: we tend to take our blessings for granted.[39]

And even with good intentions, there's a catch-22: telling yourself that you "should" be grateful is often counterproductive, as it only makes you feel guilty. If someone tells you "you should be grateful," it's far more likely to bring up resentment than gratitude.

Just like resolving to read all the books on your nightstand by the end of the month, or trying to read *War and Peace* in one go, it can be daunting to try to be grateful for your whole life all at once. Instead, just as you would start with one chapter, or the shortest book, pick a small part of your life and be grateful for that.

Pick something, right now, anything that you could be grateful for: your ability to see, a nice piece of art on the wall, or a fantastic sunset. If gratitude feels cheesy, you can use the word "fortunate." "I am fortunate because I can walk." It doesn't have to be something profound; small positive things can have a significant impact on our brain.

This is one of the few cases where comparison can really help, if you use it right. If you're having trouble accessing gratitude, try comparing your situation with others who are less fortunate. But don't make the mistake of choosing an extreme example right off the bat.

We know someone who unfortunately has the reflex of comparing his situation with the worst possible one he can possibly imagine: the victims of the Darfur genocide. This creates an immediate sense of guilt that he "should" be going around in a constant state of gratitude, 24/7, because his situation is so much better.

This kind of comparison doesn't help. Yes, it is absolutely important to stay aware of what's happening in the world, and to do everything we can to stop the horrors that are unfolding. But when you're just starting out learning to feel gratitude, that gap can be too huge and backfire or be counterproductive.

Instead, start close to home. We evolved in small tribes, and in many respects that's how our brains still operate. You know how they say "a man feels rich when he earns more than his neighbor or brother-in-law"? Same concept.

Scan your body from head to toe and find a few things to be grateful for. Could be as simple as your ability to see, hear, or breathe. You think I'm kidding? There are many people for whom every single breath is a struggle.

Think of one small luxury you have that many others around you do not. Do you have keys in your pocket, or anywhere near you, right now? Listen to George Hill's extraordinary, well-told memories of being homeless for twelve years.[40] "Now, every time it rains and I have keys in my pocket, I have a joy of life that you cannot believe." It is so very, very easy to fall through the cracks of the system. The loss of a job, an accident or illness leading to hospital bills you cannot repay—and before you know it, you too are "one of them."

Perhaps the healthiest object of comparison to elicit gratitude in you is your former self. In addition to getting you to focus on your blessings, this gives you a sense of progression, of upward movement, that in itself is a wonderfully solidifying feeling.

Think back to high school. For the 2 percent of you who enjoyed high school, this exercise will not work. But it will be of interest for the other 98 percent of us. Remember some of your difficult moments: Perhaps the sense of doom you felt as you came to class totally unprepared for the calculus, chemistry, or history test. Perhaps the general feeling of awkwardness that is the all-encompassing experience of being fourteen, fifteen, or sixteen years old. Perhaps the deep surety that this uncool, misunderstood hell was going to be your life *forever*.

How different is your life today? How much better is your life? Be thankful for your independence, for owning your own car, for not living with your parents, for your good friends, for a spouse who loves you. Take a moment and feel gratitude for these changes, changes in your environment, and changes in yourself.

Looking back to how we were in the past to see how much we've grown gives us perspective on all the good things currently in our lives—the perspective we need to truly feel gratitude for what we have.

You could have a running list of accomplishments on a sticky note on your computer to help you realize how far you've come. Every month, or even every week, choose one accomplishment to bask in. It costs you nothing, and it rewires your brain in very advantageous ways.

For most of his childhood, David did not have a lot of friends. "I remember delivering to my parents the list they had requested of friends to invite to my Bar Mitzvah. There were three names on the list. It was a very lonely way to go through life."

By his own accord, the reason David didn't have many friends is that he wasn't always the most emotionally or socially attuned person.

"That's putting it very kindly," he corrected. "Some would say I was just completely oblivious to other people's feelings."

Nowadays, David still doesn't host many parties, and when he does, they're for a very small group. But it's not because he doesn't have any friends. Quite the opposite: he has too many friends, and as an introvert inviting them all to one party would be exhausting.

When David has to decide between two or three things he's been invited to do over a weekend, he thinks back to his lonelier years and feels gratitude for his current social life.

Have you ever noticed how most of us tend to focus on the things in our life that are going wrong—all the messes we see from the inside— yet we tend to compare this with all the things that seem to be going right in others' lives—as seen from the outside? That's not a fair comparison: we're comparing our insides with someone else's outside.

But we can make this work to our advantage by viewing our life through a third-party lens. Of all the gratitude tools, this is one of our favorites. To complete this exercise, you will need to sit down with a few minutes to spare. It is best to have a pen and some paper available. Writing accesses different parts of our brain and affects our beliefs in ways that other modes of expression do not.[41] The act of committing things to writing has been shown to be critical both in changing a person's mind[42] and in making imagined stories feel more real.[43]

Write about your life as though an outside person was describing it. Focus on all of your positive aspects as a human.

Write about your occupation and the people you are surrounded by in your workplace. Give a description of some of your most meaningful personal relationships and consider the good things these people would say about you. Find positive things that have happened today no matter the size or significance.

Take the time to write down this narrative. Just thinking about it won't be as effective.

For daily practice, we highly recommend the gratitude journals from Intelligent Change. You'll find the link in the resources section of this book.

One of Olivia's favorite clients decided to try the gratitude tools with his entire family. Initially, they were skeptical. "I thought it was a little goofy, like Thanksgiving when we all go around the table and talk about what we are giving thanks for that year," his wife said.

Robert was glad his family was joining him for the journey be-cause it gave him the discipline to keep at it.

The results, he is happy to report, were dramatic. Now, before any of the family members complain about something, they'll pause to first say out loud why they are grateful. This experience has helped them develop more appreciation for what's going well in their lives, and re-frame negative experiences as positive ones.

Putting It into Practice: Morning Gratitude

The next time you wake up in the morning, try this exercise to access gratitude.

You're waking up in the morning. First, you breathe. Think about that: you are breathing. Countless geological miracles had to happen in order for you to breathe. Just the right mixture of gases had to be present to make life possible. And, for that mat-ter, you just happen to be living on a planet that is exactly the right distance from our star, not too close, not too far, just right for humans to live comfortably. Any closer and it would be like Venus, far too hot for life to exist; any farther out and it would be like Mars, just too cold for life to survive.

And then, as Bill Bryson puts it: "Consider the fact that for 3.8 billion years [going right back to the first microbes on Earth] . . . every one of your forebears on both sides has been . . . healthy enough to reproduce, and sufficiently blessed by fate and circumstances to live long enough to do so."[44]

Not one of your pertinent ancestors was squashed, devoured, drowned, starved, stranded, stuck, untimely wounded, or other-wise deflected from their life's quest of delivering a tiny charge of genetic material to the right partner at the right moment in order to perpetuate the only possible sequence of hereditary combinations that could result—eventually, astoundingly—in you.

Now, you open your eyes. Think of the miracle, of all the little rods and cones that allow you to see. Think of the incredibly complex mechanical systems that must work in order for you to be able to move, to get out of bed.

Your bed. That's another thing to be grateful for. As is your bedroom. You have a roof over your head. And if you flip a switch to turn on the light, think of all that's come before you, to make electricity not just possible, but incredibly convenient. You make a small movement, and suddenly there is light. For most of human history, right up until the last two hundred years or so, such a power was considered to be absolutely godly.

Are you heading to the bathroom? Turning a tap? That's pure, clean water coming out. More than 700 million people in this world do not have access to clean water—that's one in nine people. You have not just access, but easy access to clean water. Plenty of clean water. As much as you like. But wait—it's not just clean water. You have the luxury of hot water. Without boiling it, without building a fire—all you have to do is turn a tap. Think of all the feats of engineering that have been necessary for that to happen.

And all this, even before your first cup of coffee. Can you imagine the number of things that have happened to make breakfast possible? All the people, processes, systems that were slowly, ever so slowly built over the years? All the innovations that have taken place in order for the food and drink you desire to so conveniently be waiting for you in your kitchen?

Did you open the refrigerator to get some milk? That's a refrigerator you've got there, my friend. A miracle of modern technology. Speak to anyone from before 1913 and they would simply not believe you. You are so rich that you can afford your very own personal electric cooling chamber? With light?

In fact, before 1834, what you are taking for granted in your kitchen would've seemed as magical as teleportation seems to us. Think of it: having a refrigerator in your kitchen would seem to the vast majority of humans in history like having a personal teleportation portal inside your home.

All this to be grateful for. Awed and amazed by. And you still haven't sat down for breakfast.

Self-forgiveness and Self-compassion

The creativity needed for breakthroughs cannot flourish in a self-critical brain. Research has demonstrated time and again that fear of judgment, whether from others or from oneself, impairs creativity. Interestingly, *self*-criticism was particularly harmful to creativity.[45]

What's the antidote to self-judgment and self-criticism? Self-forgiveness. Though it might sound like "fluff," it's actually a cornerstone of the training of people whose performance lives and dies by hard numbers: athletes.

"Athletes who get injured often blame themselves for getting injured," Dr. JoAnn Dahlkoetter, a sports psychologist who has coached five Olympic gold medalists and the author of *Your Performing Edge*, explained. "That blame, shame, and guilt slows down the healing. This is where self-forgiveness is so important."[46]

As you know, skillfully handling failure means both rebounding from and learning from each failure. To do this, you have to be able to stay in a productive mental state. This isn't easy, because our natural tendency when failure hits is to beat ourselves up.

In the course of researching this book, we discovered that the self-compassion techniques used to quiet the inner critic when aiming for charisma are just as effective to quiet the inner critic on the road to breakthroughs. What follows is adapted from Olivia's first book, *The Charisma Myth*.

Self-forgiveness, though uncomfortable for many of us, is an essential practice for breakthrough thinking. Without self-compassion, you can kill the breakthrough experience before it begins.

First, let's distinguish three key concepts:

- Self-confidence is our belief in our ability to do or to learn how to do something.

- Self-esteem is how much we approve of or value ourselves. It's often a comparison-based evaluation (whether measured against other people or against our own internal standards for approval).

- Self-compassion is how much warmth we can have for ourselves, especially when we're going through a difficult experience.

It's quite possible for people to have high self-confidence but low self-esteem or self-compassion. These people may consider themselves competent, masterful even, but that does not translate into liking themselves. These people can be exceedingly hard on themselves when they don't succeed.

Behavioral science research indicates that it may be healthier to focus on self-compassion than on self-esteem, because the latter is based on self-evaluation and social comparison.[47] Self-esteem is more of a roller coaster, contingent on how we believe we compare to others. It also tends to correlate with narcissism. Self-compassion, in contrast, is based on self-acceptance, and "self-compassion does all the good things that self-esteem was supposed to do," says Wharton professor of management and psychology Adam Grant.*

Individuals who score high on self-compassion scales display greater emotional resilience and fewer negative reactions to life's difficulties, such as receiving unflattering feedback.[48] Higher self-compassion correlates to a greater sense of personal responsibility for the outcome of events; it helps predict levels of accountability. People who score high on self-compassion also have a lower tendency for denial. This makes sense: personal mistakes would generate less self-criticism, so people would be more willing to admit to them.

In many cultures people often associate the term "self-compassion" with self-indulgence or self-pity. Surprisingly, the opposite is true: solid behavioral science research shows that the higher one's level of self-compassion, the lower one's level of self-pity.[49]

You can think of the difference between the two this way: self-compassion is feeling that what happened to you is unfortunate, whereas self-pity is feeling that what happened to you is unfair. Self-pity can lead to resentment or bitterness, and to feeling more isolated and alienated. In contrast, self-compassion often leads to increased feelings of connectedness.

Another assumption we often hear is: "But if I stop beating myself up, won't I lose the motivation to keep growing? My inner critic, never satisfied, always telling me I can do better, that's what drives me to success! I don't want to lose that!"

People find motivation and drive in different ways. To motivate

---

* Aside from being the youngest tenured and five-time highest-rated professor at the Wharton School, Grant is the author of two *New York Times* best-selling books that we highly recommend (see the resources section), and is legendary for his generosity in time, guidance, and active help.

themselves when facing a challenge, many are driven by a voice in their head, a critical voice they react to, trying to prove it wrong, quiet it, challenge it, or run from it. Such people often tell us that they're afraid that if they lose this self-critical part of themselves, they will lose their drive. For some people, this is true. Some people push themselves to their breakthroughs by being in a relationship with their critical part. That's okay.

If you are one of these people, then by all means stay in a relationship with this aspect of yourself. Let it continue to drive you forward into unknown lands and breakthrough ideas. The thing to be mindful of is that you are critical of your ideas and processes rather than of yourself.

Should you be so confident about this idea? Is it a good idea? Is it truly a breakthrough? Might you do a little more research or experimenting to be sure it's truly a breakthrough? Do some more associative thinking? Rather than destroying your confidence, a constructive critical voice pushes back on any tendency you have to sit back and say "that's good enough."

However, for some people the internal critic attacks and destroys their self-confidence and willingness to try new things. For some people, that critical voice is paralyzing and often kills interesting thoughts before they've even begun. That critical part can, in some people, take the energy needed for breakthrough thinking and redirect it to finding ever more things to criticize about the self. For those people, the inner critical voice is an obstacle to breakthrough thinking, not a motivator.

No one is immune from the paralyzing force of the inner critic. We will all face times when a series of things will go wrong, "just one damn thing after another," all in a row, and our fortitude will be tested. At such times, tools like self-forgiveness and self-compassion can be saving graces.

Self-compassion delivers an impressive array of benefits: decreased anxiety, depression, and self-criticism; improved relationships and greater feelings of social connectedness and satisfaction with life; increased ability to handle negative events; and even improved immune system functioning.[50]

Sounds great, doesn't it? Unfortunately, self-compassion isn't taught in school. In fact, in today's culture it sounds indulgent and unjustified, and can feel very alien. Many of us don't have a very clear idea of what it is to begin with.

Kristin Neff, one of compassion's foremost researchers, defines self-compassion as a three-step process: First, realizing that we're experiencing difficulties. Second, responding with kindness and understanding toward ourselves when we are suffering or feel inadequate, rather than being harshly self-critical. Third, realizing that whatever we're going through is commonly experienced by all human beings, and remembering that everyone goes through difficult times like these.

When things go wrong in our lives, it's easy to assume that other people are having an easier time. Recognizing instead that everyone at some point has had or will have the very experience you're having now can help you feel like part of the larger human experience rather than isolated and alienated.

When our inner critic starts pointing out our misdeeds and imperfections, it will often make us feel that everyone else is doing better, that we're the only ones who are this flawed. Self-criticism is much stronger when our suffering seems due to our own perceived failures and inadequacies than when it seems due to external circumstances. This is when self-compassion is the most precious.

One incredibly powerful self-compassion practice we know is a millennia-old Buddhist one called Metta, which roughly translates as "loving-kindness." Metta is the deliberate practice of developing kind intentions toward all beings.

When the brains of dedicated Metta practitioners were examined and tested by neuroscientists, significant differences came to light. Not only did they emit deeper brain waves, they also bounced back from stress scenarios much faster, and they showed particular enhancement in the left frontal lobe of their cortices, the "happy region" of the brain.[51]

You may remember that earlier we wrote that it is often effective to quiet the inhibiting frontal lobes to increase the likelihood of a breakthrough. Why then are we suggesting a practice to strengthen the frontal lobes?

By making us happier and more loving towards ourselves, the practice of Metta quiets our inner critic. When our inner critic is quieter, we are more likely to achieve a breakthrough. So while Metta enhances our frontal lobes, it also changes them, making them less prone to inhibit our thinking.

Another interesting part of this is that while the act of meditating shuts down the DN, meditation actually strengthens the brain regions—and the connections between them—that make up the DN. So you probably won't have a breakthrough while meditating, but meditating *will* strengthen your DN and make it more likely that you'll have one when you're wandering and you enter the breakthrough state of mind.

Metta is a wonderful way to counter your inner critic's attacks, and with its many benefits, it is also effective at boosting charisma. This is, however, a highly uncomfortable practice for many of us. When Olivia started it, it was more than uncomfortable—it was downright awkward. Even if it feels weird for you, too, do it anyway.

First, a Metta warm-up adapted from Neff's work. Pick someone for whom you have tremendous affection. In fact, it could be a person, a pet, or even a stuffed animal. Now imagine the two of you as a unit, facing the world together. And now, see if you can wish this unit well: "May we be happy. May we be safe from harm." Use whatever words feel comfortable for you.

The visualization below will guide you through a customized form of Metta step-by-step. It has been crafted to take advantage of two instinctive human tendencies: our absorption of images and our respect for authority. If you'd prefer to hear Olivia guide you through this exercise, you'll find a recording online at www.TheButterfly.net. Throughout this exercise, you may notice a certain rhythm created by the repetitions. That is indeed their purpose; just be willing to give it a try.

Putting It into Practice: Metta

- Sit comfortably, close your eyes, and take two or three deep breaths. As you inhale, imagine drawing in masses of clean air toward the top of your head; then let it whoosh through you from head to toe as you exhale, washing all concerns away.

- Think of any occasion in your life when you performed a good deed, however great or small. Just one good action—one moment of truth, generosity, or courage. Focus on that memory for a moment.

- Now think of one being, whether present or past, mythical or actual—Jesus, Buddha, Mother Teresa, the Dalai Lama—who could have great affection for you. This could be a person, a pet, or even a stuffed animal.

- Picture this being in your mind. Imagine their warmth, their kindness and compassion. See it in their eyes and face. Feel their warmth radiating toward you, enveloping you.

- See yourself through their eyes with warmth, kindness, and compassion. Feel them giving you complete forgiveness for everything your inner critic says is wrong. You are completely and absolutely forgiven. You have a clean slate.

- Feel them giving you wholehearted acceptance. You are accepted as you are, right now, at this stage of growth, imperfections and all.

Putting It into Practice: Acceptance Manifesto

You are perfect. At this stage of development, you are perfect.

At this stage of growth, you are perfect.

At this stage of perfection, you are perfect.

With everything that's in your head and heart, you are perfect.

With all your imperfections, you are perfect.

For this phase of growth, you are perfect.

You are fully approved just the way you are, at this stage of development, right now.

After going through the Metta exercise, our clients often report a physical sense of relief, their shoulders sagging during the forgiveness visualization, and then warmth rising during the self-approval process. Many people feel warmth in their solar plexus region. Some describe a kind of "exquisite ache," or feeling "very tender." No matter what you experience, if you are feeling anything, it means it's working.

Even when the experience itself doesn't "feel" like it's working, Metta is worth doing because of the spillover effect it produces. Often, though the exercise itself feels disconcerting, you will notice throughout the rest of the day that you are more present, connecting better with others, and better able to absorb and enjoy the good moments in your life. As self-compassion researcher and author of *The Mindful Path to Self-Compassion* Christopher Germer puts it: "A moment of self-compassion like this can change your entire day. A string of such moments can change the course of your life."[52]

You can use Metta visualization anytime you experience an attack of the internal critic. As Germer suggests, you can think of self-compassion as standing up to self-harm the same way you'd stand up to something threatening a loved one.

Researchers who started experimenting with these kinds of visualizations with highly self-critical people reported "significant reductions in depression, anxiety, self-criticism, shame, and inferiority," while noting a "significant increase in feelings of warmth and reassurance for the self."[53]

Now that you know how to handle the *fear* of failure, let's look at how to handle the experience of failure itself.

KEY TAKEAWAYS

- Fear and anxiety are major inhibitors of breakthroughs.
- Catastrophizing only serves to strengthen our negativity bias and shut us down to breakthroughs.
- Failure is unavoidable and natural. We must learn to handle our fear of it.
- With intentional breakthroughs, fear appears on the road to breakthrough, focused on failure; with unintentional breakthroughs, fear occurs after the breakthrough, focused on implementation.
- Common manifestations of the fear of failure are:
  - The impostor syndrome: the fear that you will be exposed as a fraud. Solution: create a new self-image and support it with concrete evidence.
  - The inner critic: the voice in your head beating you up. Solution: find out who you actually mean when you tell yourself "everybody" does this, then create a new "everybody" to think of instead.
  - The perfectionist: the feeling that you're never good enough, never doing enough. Solution: know that mistakes are precious and that others like your imperfection.
  - The maximizer: the drive to do better than everyone else, to do more. Solution: place limits on how far you are willing to go.
- Fear is best handled with relaxation, gratitude, self-forgiveness, and self-compassion.

Chapter 8

The Failure Wasps

Letting Go of Shame

SO WHAT, EXACTLY, is it that we fear? Of course, we fear the actual consequences of failure, whether tangible or intangible, whether they are in the form of money, time, effort, or reputation, among other things. But we also fear the experience itself.

And it's no wonder: for many of us, the internal experience of failure is one of shame, dismay, disappointment, or even despair. Understandably, this isn't something we look forward to. This is where *failure skills* come in. Failure skills ensure that you stay in a learning mode, the right psychological state to learn everything there is to learn from this failure and to rebound fast so you can try again.

Many of the sports psychologists and coaches we interviewed consider failure as a mini-trauma. Dr. Wes Sime, a sport psychologist with two PhDs, in sports science and peak performance psychology, told us: "Athletes actually suffer microtraumas: the embarrassment of having 'blown it' in front of an audience; possibly the embarrassment and shame of having let your team down." And then there's the potential blow to your earning power, loss of future sponsorships, and so forth.

Failure comes in different flavors. The four categories below represent a descending order of knowledge and control. For instance, category #1 means you had full knowledge and full control. Category #2 means you had imperfect knowledge but full control. And so forth.

For most of us, the hardest in order are #1, then #2, then #3, then #4. Some people take them all equally hard. Some tools are better suited for some cases than others. But it's worth trying all of them.

```
                                    #1 Knowingly ──▶ Inner Critic ──▶ Self-compassion/
                                    (I knew better)                   Self-forgiveness
              INTERNAL CAUSE ──
              (I/we failed)     ╲
                                    #2 Unknowingly ──────────────▶ Impostor
                                    (I did the best I could        Syndrome
                                    with what I knew)                 │
FAILURE ──                                                            │
                                                                      ▼
                                    #3 "Acts of God" ─────────▶ Responsibility
                                    (earthquake)                Transfer
              EXTERNAL CAUSE ──
              (something       ╲
              happened to us)      #4 Acts of Others ───────▶ Resentment
                                   (theft, new regulation)    Letters
```

You may need different remedies. Self-generated failure may need self-forgiveness. Externally generated failure may need the "resentment letter" technique.

This chapter will give you the tools you need to become more resilient to failure. Resiliency to failure is a subset of the broader category of resiliency to hardship. Failure is a form of hardship, one of many that we can experience. If you are resilient to failure, you are less affected by it and bounce back faster. This has a bonus effect: since you know you've got the skills to handle failure and are now more resilient to it, you'll be less afraid of it.

Reframing, or The Baby in the Backseat

Imagine that it's 9 P.M. on a Monday evening, after a long and tedious day at work, and you're finally driving home as darkness sets in. It's your significant other's birthday, and you've been planning the evening for months. Despite your tiredness, you're smiling as you look forward to the evening, happily anticipating spending some quality time together.

Suddenly, a large red sedan comes screeching into your lane out of nowhere. With your heart pounding and your hands gripping the steering wheel, you slam on the brakes. Not only did the driver cut you off, he's now swerved out of your lane, making the car to your right screech its tires. "What an idiot! Reckless driver!" you think as anger surges through your veins.

Your physical response to this encounter is the very definition of the fight-or-flight response. It causes your heart rate to increase as your muscles tighten. Your body is overcome with stress-induced hormones, overrun with the stress and anger that this event has generated. You cannot bring these emotions home with you. Unfortunately, you have only a few minutes to recover from this experience, and the powerful impression it has left on your mind will not subside easily.

Once the fight-or-flight response is aroused, it's hard to quiet down. Anger is a difficult emotion to flush out of our system, which is why an unpleasant traffic encounter in the morning can stay on our minds for hours and sometimes all day.

If you aimed to simply suppress the anger, you would be paying a high price. When people are induced into a negative emotional state and then asked to suppress negative emotions, their internal negative experience often remains unchanged and they sustain elevated stress responses in their brain and cardiovascular system.[1] Emotion suppression works as poorly as thought suppression.

But what if you happened to learn that this apparently reckless driver, who was driving so erratically, was actually a distraught mother whose baby was choking in the backseat? She was desperately trying to pull over into the breakdown lane, while reaching back to save her baby's life.

Would that immediately reduce your anger?

For most people it does.

If you decide to change your perception of events (this is technically called cognitive reappraisal, but we prefer to call it reframing), you will effectively decrease your brain's stress levels. Researchers using fMRI machines at Stanford concluded that deciding to change beliefs was a "far more effective and healthier solution than attempting to repress or ignore emotions."[2]

We rarely know for certain what motivates a person's actions, so why not choose the explanation that is most helpful to us? Create a version of events that gets you into the mental states you need for breakthrough thinking. Though it may sound outlandish at first, choosing to reframe your perspective is actually the smartest and most rational thing to do.

Let's say you're going to check on the sales of a new product you've just offered, and the results are dismal. If you go into a spiral of self-criticism and self-doubt, you know what happens: you're no longer in a rational learning mode, so you won't be able to accurately parse out reasons and consequences, causes and effects.

Reframing means simply switching the frame through which you view an experience or an event. It's changing your mind about the way you describe an experience.

Cognitive reframing is a rational, logic-based argument: "Here's why it's not as bad as you think." *Social proof* reframing, in contrast, does not need any logic; it says, "This happens to a lot of people" or even better yet, "This admired figure had this experience too."

Here's a great example of cognitive reframing. One of our collaborators told us: "My husband likes to buy and resell art for side money. His mentor, an expert in the field, advised my husband not to look at a bad purchase decision as a loss or deficit, but to consider it tuition, since this trade is not one you can go to school to learn. So he views his botched purchases as a tuition of sorts that he would have had to pay had he chosen art as a full-time career. And considering the current rate of college tuition, he has lots of room for error (aka learning)."

This is a fantastic reframe: don't see the outcome as a possible failure, but rather as *guaranteed learning*. And that learning will lead either to a pivot or to the end of the road. Imagine that, when the outcome happens and it's not the one you were hoping for, it's like a pinball machine saying, "Congratulations, you've learned something and you get to play again!" In this frame, the end of the road (success) is actually the less attractive option, because you don't get to play again!

Sometimes our clients ask us: "How do we balance the hope that our efforts will achieve successful innovation with the probability that each attempt will fail? It can't be right to assume failure, because motivation then becomes an issue."

We tell them: See each attempt as guaranteed learning. No matter what happens, you'll learn. You'll learn, as Edison did, countless ways to not invent the lightbulb. The answer is to see learning as the ultimate prize. You may have heard of the "growth mindset," also called the "learning stance."[3]

Take a longer-term view of your efforts. You are not looking to succeed at this one thing right in front of you. You are looking to succeed at making yourself a fantastic innovator. In this mental frame, nothing is a step backward, because you are always learning something new. Sometimes all you learn is "don't do that again." But that's still a step forward.

Let's say you're Edison working on finding a commercially viable lightbulb. And let's say, for the sake of argument, that there are 10,000 possible filaments. You manage to narrow that down to 1,600 by selecting only materials with high resistance at low energies. Now the testing begins. The chances are that each test will fail. But a learning stance, a growth mindset, looks at each failure and says, "I am now one step closer to finding the right one." You obtained guaranteed learning.

When Elon Musk's SpaceX attempted to land a rocket back on a barge in the ocean so it could be reused, the landing failed. But even though the landing didn't end in success, the fact that the rocket hit the barge at all is extremely encouraging. As Musk puts it, this "failure" "bodes well for the future."[4] You can do this too: see the failure as "guaranteed learning," and therefore something that bodes well for the future. It helps maintain emotional momentum.

Astro Teller recommends that instead of seeing what you put out into the world as a final product, imagine that you're saying to the world: "What do you think? How can we make this better?" As he told us, "It's much better to find out now what we missed than to find out years from now, with an incredible amount of additional expense and emotional investment."[5]

In some cases, a great way to get yourself into a "willing to fail" mindset is to see whatever you are doing as an experiment, something you're just trying once, with no commitment to follow through, and to phrase it to yourself as "it's interesting and I'm curious." For example, if you're trying a new behavior and someone comments on it, you can simply say, "It's a social experiment," and perhaps even mention an article about it, which distances the potentially embarrassment-triggering part of the experiment from your social identity.

Creativity expert Tina Seelig likes this saying: "Genius is the ability to make the most mistakes in the shortest period of time."[6] As she explains, each of those mistakes provides experimental data and an opportunity to learn something new. She, too, suggests changing our vocabulary from "failures" to "data," to enhance your (and others') willingness to experiment.

In her wonderful book *inGenius,* which we highly recommend to anyone interested in creativity, she explains that master inventors appreciate unexpected outcomes such as failures, because each one teaches them something important on the road to a breakthrough idea. They believe it's up to each of us to mine our failures for valuable information and insights. The key is seeing the process of trial and error as a series of experiments on the way to a success.

Take a hint from Silicon Valley and don't call it a failure, call it a *pivot.* Feel how different the word sounds and feels. Changing the language is one of the many ways they destigmatize failure; another way is to glorify it. Venture capitalist Randy Komisar says, "Silicon Valley recognizes that failure is an unavoidable part of the search for success."[7]

Detaching

In order to handle failure well, you need to learn how to detach from the thoughts and emotions it can evoke. The key to detaching? Realizing that: *just because it's in your head doesn't mean it's true.* Just because it *feels* true doesn't mean it *is* true.

Negative thoughts have power over you because you believe that what your brain is giving you is an accurate portrait of reality. This, however, is not true. Your brain often looks at the world through a distorted lens.

In one well-known study, Harvard researchers asked the participants to watch a short video in which two groups of people passed around a basketball. They were asked to count the number of passes made by one of the teams. Partway through the video, a woman walked onto the court wearing a full gorilla suit.

After watching the video, the participants were asked if they saw anything out of the ordinary take place. In most groups more than half missed the gorilla even though it had waved its arms at the camera![8]

We know what you're thinking, you'd do better? Let's see:

Take a look around the room you're in. Notice everything that's black.

Now you're looking at this page again. Good. Keep your eyes here. Without looking up, try to name everything you saw that was red.

Go ahead. We'll wait.

. . .

Okay, take a look around again.

Now do you see a lot of things that are red?

Interesting, right?

So why did this happen? Our brains have a lot to do. There is limited space dedicated to conscious attention. This constrains the amount of information we can be aware of at any one time. If the visual world is an ocean of information, then at any one time we only consciously perceive a small creek. The ocean would overwhelm us.

So our brains focus on information they consider relevant. Our brains make choices about what to pay attention to. Those choices mean we miss things, and that means our brains do not provide us with an accurate representation of reality. Our worldviews are incomplete.

Most of the time our brains make good choices and we draw a fairly accurate portrait of reality. But there are times when our minds distort reality. Often this distortion skews negative because our brains, in an effort to keep us safe, finds negative elements the most relevant. It's the negativity bias we talked about in the previous chapter.

Diane is a young project manager in charge of the biggest project of her career. Shortly after the project begins, she gets a call from Sarah, her point of contact with the client. Sarah tells her, "I think you're incredible at your job. I've been raving about you and your excellent work for the past year. My boss doesn't seem to get it. My best guess is he just wasn't impressed when you guys first met, and he hasn't gotten a chance to change his mind. That being said, I'd like you, Diane, to be in charge of all our company's projects. Your work is so good, I'm sure my boss will be wowed when he sees it. I want you to present your work at the company's next management meeting."

Sarah said many positive things about Diane—that she's incredible at her job, does excellent work, that she's being put in charge of all the projects. But what Diane's brain finds most relevant is the one negative piece: Sarah's boss wasn't impressed with her. If you've ever found yourself stuck on the one negative piece of information you heard in a conversation, you know how devastating it can be to your confidence.

The mind evolved to worry about everything that could potentially go wrong. In this sense, the mind is like the Jewish mother who sends you a telegram saying, "Start worrying. Details to follow." Or as psychologist Steven Hayes put it, "Hello, this is your mind speaking. Do you realize you need to worry?"[9]

Detaching is essential for handling the inner critic. Rather than being *the* voice in your head, it becomes one of many, which we all have. To maximize detaching, you can even give the inner critic a name and character—call it Oscar the Grouch or Dennis the Menace, and see it as a childlike cartoon character.

When you find yourself stuck on a negative piece of information and spiraling down, remind yourself that your perception of reality is more than likely off. If negative information was put in front of it, your brain will focus on it, following its negativity bias. It is likely declaring the negative elements relevant and omitting some positives entirely.

Putting It into Practice: Fear No More

The techniques below are designed to help you quiet the effects of negative thoughts. Notice which ones work best for you, and practice until they become a reflex.

- Don't give your thoughts the benefit of the doubt. Sure, they're yours. But that doesn't mean they're accurate. Start from the notion that you probably missed a lot of things and there are positive elements waiting to be noticed.

- Imagine your thoughts like graffiti on a wall.

- Name what you are experiencing: anger, anxiety, self-criticism. Naming what you are experiencing can help you neutralize it.

- Make it less personal. Don't say, "I'm feeling ashamed." Instead say, "There is shame being felt." Take a step back. Observe the experience like an anthropologist observing a ritual. Imagine that you're a scientist observing a phenomenon: "Fascinating. There are self-critical thoughts happening."

- Imagine looking at the Earth from space. Now come closer, see your country, your neighborhood, your house. Here you are, this one person, having this experience on this planet right now.

- Imagine your negative thoughts are a podcast. Take off your headphones, set your music player aside.

- Lay out what it would look like if everything you're worried about happens, if everything that can go wrong does. Now notice that you survived this scenario.

- Remember all the times before when you felt a similar negativity or anxiety. You didn't think you'd make it through then. And yet you did.

The skill is in knowing how to *handle* the negative thoughts, rather than trying to suppress them or argue with them.

Steven Hayes and his colleagues asked a group of subjects to not think of yellow Jeeps for a few minutes. Some subjects described the immediate appearance of yellow Jeeps. Other were able to suppress the thought for a short time, but the yellow Jeeps roared into their brains. The participants were thinking about yellow Jeeps for days and sometimes weeks afterward.

Because trying to suppress a self-critical thought only makes it more central to your thinking, it's a far better strategy to aim to neutralize it.

Destigmatizing an experience means reducing its power by simply understanding that it's normal, common, and nothing to be ashamed of. By doing so, you lift the stigma of shame off the experience, which is critical, because when in shame, you can't think straight.

Our minds' natural tendency when encountering failure is to

imagine the absolute worst-case scenario. With social proof, you can understand that "everyone" or "most people" go through this experience.

The way we react to failure is actually very similar to the way we react to grief. Grief is the feeling of something precious irretrievably lost; failure is a loss of something you presumably cared a lot about. The best way to understand grief is through a sequence known as the Kübler-Ross model.

1. Denial: "This cannot have happened." "There must be a mistake."
2. Anger: When the individual recognizes that denial cannot continue, he becomes frustrated. "How the #$%! can this have happened?" "Who screwed up?"
3. Bargaining: "There must be a way to make this un-happen. Maybe if we . . ."
4. Depression: "It really happened." "We failed. We suck. We might as well give up."
5. Acceptance: "Okay, we failed. Now what?" Acceptance is the last stage before moving on.

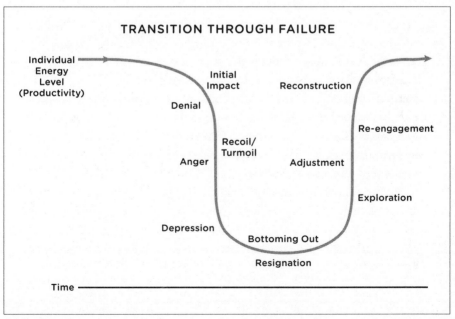

TRANSITION THROUGH FAILURE

Individual Energy Level (Productivity)

Initial Impact

Denial

Reconstruction

Re-engagement

Recoil/ Turmoil

Anger

Adjustment

Exploration

Depression

Bottoming Out

Resignation

Time

© Adam Klein

We can't avoid this dip in happiness, productivity, and creativity, but we can reduce its depth and duration by accepting it rather than fighting against it. As Shawn Achor told us: "The more you accept the inevitable post-failure productivity dip, the faster you'll move through it."[10]

Dr. JoAnn Dahlkoetter told us: "It is absolutely critical to go through the stages of grief, to process those stages of anger, sadness, and so forth. Grief, when ignored, can lead to depression." Dahlkoetter remarked that very few teams or organizations take the time to grieve when a project fails. Instead, they try to move right on, as if the failure hadn't had any emotional impact. "Unfortunately, repressing feelings just makes things worse," she told us.

You need a mourning process: whether it's a business opportunity or a gold medal that was lost, it's important to take the time to grieve, to mourn the failure before you try to learn from it. You'll be tempted to skip right past these uncomfortable feelings. Our instinct, whenever we feel discomfort, is to grab onto the first thing we think will make the discomfort go away. In this case, wanting to avoid the blues of mourning the failure, and knowing that being in a productive mode feels better, presents us with a big temptation to go straight from acknowledging the failure to analyzing it.[11]

But don't. Grieving a failure is a different process from analyzing it. Grieving a failure is an emotional process, one of acceptance. "This happened." We move through the grief not by asking why this happened or figuring out how it could have been prevented. Yes, after the grief, you will analyze the failure and learn from it, but that analysis is an intellectual process, not an emotional one.

"This is a particularly common trap for type As, who might tend to view grief/mourning failure as weakness—and I speak from personal experience," explains technologist and entrepreneur Safi Bahcall.*

So how does one grieve for a failure? Depending on the emotional impact of the particular failure, it could be as simple as taking a few

---

* Our dear friend Safi Bahcall knows whereof he speaks: son of a prominent physicist father and astrophysicist mother, he received his BA in physics from Harvard, his physics PhD from Stanford, and as if that weren't enough, after a stint at consulting giant McKinsey he cofounded two successive pharmaceutical companies, receiving accolades and awards along the way. The fact that he's also one of the nicest people you'll ever meet is borderline ridiculous.

moments to acknowledge the disappointment, all the way to a full-blown mourning process. Dr. Dahlkoetter recommends to her athletes, as we do with our clients, that they write down their thoughts and feelings. They need to express their anger, whether it's at themselves or at someone else (for instance, a relay teammate who dropped the baton).

Here are some ways she helps Olympians handle failure:

- Put things in perspective. Look back ten years from now. How much will it matter then?
- Focus on behavior, not outcome. Find something they did right. Did they keep good form, for example?
- When we fail, we're often asking negative questions, usually starting with "Why?"—including "Why am I an idiot?" That fires up the inner critic. Positive questions start with "What" or "How." What can I learn from this experience? What's good about what just happened? How can I use this situation to my advantage? What's the next step? How can I keep moving forward? What tools and resources do I need to keep moving forward?

To get closure on a failure, neuroscientist Richard Wiseman suggests a three-step process we firmly approve of:

1. Write it down: pour out onto paper everything that's on your mind, everything that weighs on your heart. What happened, how you felt—this is a mental purge, or as some of our clients call it, a "vomit sprint."
2. Rip it up: with gusto and enthusiasm. Really get into the motions, hear the ripping, feel the tearing.
3. Burn it, if you can, and officially declare the failure closed.

Reframing Using Social Proof

Ever notice how when one person starts dancing, they look like a maniac, but when twenty people start dancing, we assume it's Improv Everywhere?

Another kind of reframing uses the aforementioned social proof principle: finding admired figures who have failed, are willing to fail again, and who, in fact, integrate failure as an expected part of their process. The fact that an admired authority figure approves of failure (or whichever experience you want to destigmatize) makes it "all right."

> Anyone who has never made a mistake has never tried anything new.
>
> —Albert Einstein

Try to find at least five examples of failure. The human brain thinks in triads (from Olympic medals to fairy tales, it's three medals, three princes, three bears), and it cannot immediately comprehend numbers greater than four.[12] Past that number, the mind turns the number into "a lot" or, in this case, "everybody."

You can pick these examples from anywhere. Celebrities and peers will hit the social proof lever; authority figures will hit the authority lever. For best results, include all the different ways we absorb information: radio and podcast interviews, YouTube videos, books, letters, e-mails—find in any of these media examples of people talking about their failures. You want to bathe in that environment so that your brain gets the impression that the world around you thinks in this manner.

For example, you could remind yourself that almost every successful innovative person, just like Edison, integrates failure as a necessary part of their process.[13] You could tell yourself that failure is such an inherent part of innovation that Edison distrusted innovation without failure. In fact, when he first listened to the playback of his recorded voice on his phonograph he was worried. "I was always afraid of things that worked the first time."

Safi Bahcall recalls a quote from golfer Michelle Wie's coach, who instructed her to repeat to herself whenever she missed a putt: "I've gotten that out of the way. Now I'm one step closer to becoming the best putter in the history of golf." "I often think of that quote when I screw up," says Bahcall.

As Andy Ouderkirk, corporate scientist at 3M, told us: "Self-doubt is a natural part of breakthrough innovation, and there is usually little affirmation from others early in the process. Understand that self-doubt suggests that you are indeed likely working on a breakthrough idea. If you have doubts, others probably do as well, which is probably why the opportunity for a breakthrough still exists. I've learned that inventions that create little skepticism at the onset almost never end up being very useful. The ones that were most challenged led to the largest businesses. I now put much more energy into the inventions that create skepticism!"[14]

You could one day learn to see that feeling of doubt as a reassuring one, a sign that you're on the right track. Doubt is a signpost on the road to something new, a natural part of the journey to a breakthrough. If no one had doubts, they'd all have done it already!

And, of course, you can combine social proof reframing with pure cognitive reframing. Edison is said to have failed ten thousand times on his way to inventing the commercially viable lightbulb. When asked how he could persevere through a thousand failures, he answered that he didn't see it as "a thousand failures."[15] Instead, he had simply found a thousand ways to *not* invent this lightbulb. Eventually, the commercial lightbulb was invented.

If this had been phrased as: "Edison determined, from a comprehensive search of materials and conditions in over ten thousand trials, an experimentally refined construction of the lightbulb," the perception of those unsuccessful trials changes instantly.

The rephrasing of ten thousand failures as ten thousand trials is cognitive reframe. The fact that this sentence was said by Edison? That's social proof.

A Special Note for Those of You Who Lead Teams and Organizations

This is where you play a critical role as leaders. Because as leaders, people turn to you to understand how they should feel about something. As leaders, you are by definition the alphas of your pack. People will look to you for cues as to how they should view events and react to situations.

If you can tell them what to expect, how their brain will react to failure, which emotions they might feel, and what pitfalls to watch out for, they won't be as unsettled when it happens.

Why was Edison able to stay confident and focused after his first failure? It was six years between the debacle of his voting machine and the success of his broadband telegraph. That's six years of concepts not working. Six years of failure. But to Edison's way of thinking, "If I find 10,000 ways something won't work, I haven't failed. I am not discouraged, because every wrong attempt discarded is a step forward."

Practice Failure

Under duress, we seldom rise to our level of expectation. Instead, we fall back to our level of training. This is why we train.

—Army motto

When you go to the gym, you don't immediately pick up the 300-pound barbells. You work your way up to them. Practice is trying out a new behavior in a low-stakes scenario, a safe environment; it is trying out a much smaller version of that behavior, a baby step. This is precisely what you need to do with failure: practice it in low-stakes, safe scenarios, to gradually increase your ability to handle it.

There are two kinds of practice: physical and mental. Physical practice is the one most people think of first: actually experiencing something in real life. Mental practice is going through whatever experience you're practicing—in your head.

We'll cover real-life, experiential practice first.

Experiential Practice

All the tools we cover in this section help you rewire your response to failure, but they play on different mechanisms to get there. Some modes of reframing, such as cognitive behavioral therapy, are purely a logical, cognitive assertion; the EN is at work here.

Others, such as social proof, are more emotional. It is an instinctive response to an observed social behavior, whether or not one understands any logic behind it. When a train stops and everyone gets out and starts going in the same direction, you will instinctively go with the flow, move with the herd. Social proof can work even when the behavior that is approved of doesn't make sense—such as when an admired or authority figure models an illogical behavior.

Now, there is a difference between failing in private and failing in public. There are, in fact, a few stages on that spectrum: being all alone, being with a small group of friends where you feel safe, being with strangers, and being the center of a large group. You don't want to start with karaoke right off the bat! Get to know your own personal reactions to failure in a safe environment, where you are practicing failure, so that they won't take you by surprise when a real failure happens.

We're going to cover a few different ways of practicing failure.

Sports

Sports are a fantastic way to practice failure, and thus build resiliency to failure. Smart companies recognize it and make the most of it. Google, for example, knows that their employees must experience frequent failures on the road to breakthrough innovation, so they specifically seek people with a high resiliency to failure.

One of the Google recruiters described interviewing a candidate who used to play professional baseball, and who told him: "I know how to fail. I've struck out a million times. Literally." He hired him on the spot. Another Google executive told us: "I have a few baseball players on my team. They're all successful."

Poker

Poker is a phenomenal training ground for handling failure. Poker players *have* to accept that they're going to lose a certain percentage of the time. World Series of Poker winner Annie Duke says, "It has to be okay to lose, because losing *will* happen," no matter how good you are.[16]

Poker can help you learn how to bounce back from a failure. "You can't analyze or ruminate in the moment; that's not the time for it. You *have* to snap out of it because the next hand is coming up, and if you're still angry at fate, others, or yourself, you're going to play the next hand poorly. Tell yourself that you'll put a pin in it and analyze it later."

Annie explained that in poker when you analyze your decision after the fact you are not looking at whether you won or lost. Whether you win any particular hand in poker is very random. There are just so many things you don't know. You analyze your decision to see whether you understood the odds and probable outcomes as well as you could have, and whether you made the right decision according to this understanding.

Cooking

Cooking is especially useful because you get to practice failure and creativity at the same time. Neuroscientist Marie Pasinski is a big fan of this kind of experiential practice, and recommends *The Blue Strawberry Cookbook*, a cookbook without recipes that encourages you to be innovative and experiment. Cooking is also where Olivia practices failure.

Olivia's kitchen often looks like a crime scene—after particularly creative experiments, there is food everywhere, including the walls. She firmly believes that the amount of creativity generated is in direct proportion to the amount of mess made, and the word most often heard in her kitchen is "Whoops!" She once decided to "improve" tzatziki, a Greek yogurt and dill dish, with oranges and salami. She insists that she was doing fine until she added the salami. Thankfully, Olivia's black Labrador is always happy to eat what might dismay a less open-minded eater.

Here are two failure practices for you to try at home. Pick whichever appeals to you more.

Limited resource cooking allows you to practice both divergent and convergent thinking.

- How could you make a dessert with just what you have in your kitchen right now? It doesn't have to be delicious, just edible and dessertlike. Seriously, take the time to think about it. Feel that struggle in your brain? That's neuroplasticity at work.

- Now open your fridge. What main course could you make with *only* what is in the fridge?

- And now, considering everything in your kitchen, could you make pancakes, or something that vaguely resembles pancakes? Let's say all you have is a few unripe bananas. Here's what you can do: roast the bananas in the oven until they're black outside to speed-ripen (this is like turbocharging ripening). Mash the bananas. Heat frying pan, and use the mashed bananas as you would pancake batter. Wait until it's well caramelized before flipping. Enjoy.

Deliberate failure cooking encourages you to deliberately do something "wrong" to gain possible new insights. For instance, baking cookies at the wrong temperature ended up giving us soft-baked cookies.

Eric Maisel gives this exercise: Make an omelet with three eggs, but drop the eggshells into the pan with the eggs. Carefully put the omelet on a plate. Look at it. You've made an omelet that is a failure. Or is it? Isn't it pretty interesting, with a funny pattern of crispy shells sticking out? Bet you've never seen an omelet like that before! Didn't you feel different, slightly taboo, as you dropped your eggshells in the pan, wondering what would happen? Won't you remember this omelet while you forget all of the boring normal ones you've made a hundred times?

Improvisational Theater

Improvisational theater, commonly known as "improv," has been discovered to be an excellent leadership tool in recent years. Young leaders at some of the best business schools take classes on improv to help them become more comfortable with going with the flow, working with what people give them, trusting in the process of collaboration.

The practice of improv is like performing a play while the entire cast is walking on tightropes. There are no lines, stories, or anything even rehearsed. The actors are given a concept or a situation, such as "at a dentist's office," and then they start making it up, improvising. It is not easy. You have to take your cues from the other actors, build on what they're doing, and add your own ideas to the mix, all while trying to tell a coherent, and often funny, story. Failure is inevitable and expected.

Throughout your failure practice, it's really important to focus on the behavior, not the outcome. Dahlkoetter phrases it this way: "Focus on *process* goals rather than *outcome* goals."

Olympic coach Charlie Brown explains: "Outcome goals or 'performance goals' compare you against someone else. They are useful as aspirational goals, but you can't control whether they happen or not. And you want to focus on what you *can* control. Performance goals compare you to a preset standard. The problem is that this assumes specific (optimal) conditions, and you don't control those, either."

Process goals focus on the things that are under your control, which could be behaviors or mental processes. Just as we've told you that we can't guarantee breakthrough, but we can tell you how to maximize your chances of getting there, process goals help you maximize your chances of success in whatever you are trying to achieve.

Mental Practice

Now that you have some tools for experiential practice, let's talk about mental practice. The effectiveness of mental practice has been extensively studied, and mental practice is now an absolute requirement for world-class athletic training. Every single one of the Olympic coaches we interviewed spent at least half the interview on mental practice, and one of them told us: "I doubt you could find any Olympian who doesn't incorporate mental practice into his or her training." In fact, one Olympian even said: "Once you get to a certain level, it's all in the mind."

When we say "practice failure," what we really mean is practice your response to failure. You can't control the circumstances, you can't control the outcome, but you can control your response to the outcome. And that means changing the way you view failure, which really means changing the way your brain reacts to failure, changing the failure-response wiring in your brain. Changing your mind is rewiring your mind; every time you change your mind you are literally changing a response wiring in your brain. Hello, neuroplasticity.

Mental practice, which is also called mental rehearsal or visualization, is an elite tool for all high performers, from athletes to musicians to the U.S. Army Special Forces. Mental rehearsal is one of the many ways to rewire one's brain. Any time you think a thought, you are either creating a new physical connection or strengthening an existing one. By rehearsing a different reaction to failure, you wire and then strengthen the circuits of the new reaction.

Dr. Wes Sime has worked with many Olympic athletes and their coaches. He told us of one dramatic example of the power of mental practice he encountered when he was working with a young acrobatic diver.

Sime told us the story of a diver who hit the board on his way down and hit the water so hard he fractured his cervical vertebrae. Out of physical training for six weeks while his bones mended, the diver practiced mental training. He imagined and went through the perfect dive. It was a relief for the diver to continue to practice without risk of further physical injury.

Using neurofeedback, Wes taught the diver to quiet his mind and achieve total focus on the task, to "stay in the zone," as athletes often say. Sime told us: "Neurofeedback turbocharges mental training, because it allows you to focus so deeply that the imagery sinks into your mind far deeper."

After six weeks of mental training, he was in a competition. Sime told us: "Diving is such a precision sport. Usually, in competition, we get five perfect dives, two or three respectable dives, and the rest is a wash. Yet here was this kid, after six weeks out of the water, his first time back after an injury, and *every single one* of his dives was perfect."

Here are a few guidelines on how to get the most out of visualization.

Live the moment.

When pole-vaulters practice mental rehearsal, they practice every step of their run, planting the pole, feeling the air rushing about them. Legendary swimmer Michael Phelps has practiced his strokes every single night just before bedtime since he was twelve years old. He would imagine the feel of the water on his skin, the air in his nostrils, the tension of his muscles, and the torsion of his body as he completed his flip turns.

For best results, make sure that your rehearsals are in *first person*—meaning that rather than seeing yourself from the outside, you see through your own eyes, breathe through your own lungs. Remember to make it as sensory rich as possible.

Focus on behaviors, not (just) outcomes.

We're sometimes asked: "When is it constructive visualization, and when is it just fantasy daydreaming, mental escapism?"

The difference between the two is somewhat akin to the difference between helpful critique and destructive criticism. They're both critical, but with very different aims: Helpful critique focuses on the behaviors, the elements that you *can* change or adapt to, and gives you a sense of progression. Destructive criticism, on the other hand, leaves you feeling defeated and discouraged. In the same way, constructive visualization is focused on a specific *behavior* that you want to perform at a specific time, rather than just the outcome you're hoping for.

If, for instance, you're rehearsing an upcoming presentation, don't just imagine the congratulations of your peers, the applause of the audience. Instead, focus on how you will feel at each stage of your presentation, how you will move, walk, talk, and breathe.

There are two exceptions, when you actually do want to spend time visualizing the outcome: to help you make yourself believe that the goal is actually possible, and to test how you feel about a possible outcome, to see if that's really the outcome you want.

Rehearse all possible scenarios.

It is absolutely critical that your mental practice doesn't just include imagining a win. You also need to imagine every possible thing that could go wrong, and your ideal behavior in that scenario. Dr Dahlkoetter told us: "Too many athletes spend all their time visualizing only the perfect outcome, which rarely happens." Instead, she has her athletes visualize several action plans in an if-then scenario ("if this happens, I'll do this"), covering as many contingencies as possible.

Matthew Brady was a U.S. Army Special Ops aviator, a helicopter pilot flying for the Army's elite Night Stalkers unit in Iraq and Afghanistan. Special Operations forces are the ones who volunteer to step into the most dangerous situations.

Brady explained, "When the Army asks: 'Who wants to go behind enemy lines? Oh—and we have no idea what's waiting for you and we probably won't be able to send support,' these are the guys who raise their hands."[17]

The team members would usually start with table-talk rehearsals—everyone sitting around a table and talking things through. They would "what if" the mission: what might happen, what might go wrong.

Then there were computer-based virtual simulations. Let's say Brady was going to fly a mission through a valley in Afghanistan. He would send the coordinates of where he was going back to Fort Campbell, and the "sims" teams there would build a computer-simulated virtual terrain and send it back to Matt.

They would load this simulation into the flight simulator,

essentially a box sitting on hydraulics containing the exact replica of a helicopter cockpit. The "windows" are screens showing a virtual reconstruction of the terrain in which the mission will take place.

Brady would virtually fly through the simulated valley and land on the same mountain peak half a dozen times in the hours before the actual mission. He would add variables to the mission, such as poor weather conditions. Thanks to these rehearsals, by the time he actually went on a mission, he felt as if he'd already flown the course multiple times. In many cases, he told us, these rehearsals saved his life.

Brady recalled one particular instance, flying into a remote part of the Hindu Kush Mountains in Afghanistan on a dark, moonless night. The pilots depended entirely on night vision goggles to be able to see anything. The two helicopters were going in to pick up a Special Forces team they had dropped off the night before, and take the team back to base. They were flying down a corridor of mountains, with 12,000-foot peaks on either side of them.

The lead helicopter aimed for the landing while Brady held back. The terrain was so rugged that, as the lead helicopter descended, an outcropping protruding from the side of the mountain pushed the hydraulic actuators in the rear of the helicopter through a fuel line and cut off fuel to the right engine. At 9,000 feet, they couldn't maintain altitude with just one engine, so with the engine cut they plummeted downwards. It was a huge explosion, and worse yet, the ammunition started going off.

Somehow, miraculously, no one was hurt. But the light from the explosion came barreling down the mountain corridor and blinded Brady and his copilot through their night vision goggles. "A massive fireball, on a zero illumination night, in the middle of a hallway of mountains, wearing night vision goggles, kinda looks like the Apocalypse, only brighter." Flying blind, Brady had to maintain a holding pattern at 9,000 feet.

"When you want to hold your position in a helicopter, it's more efficient to fly in a very small circle or a figure-eight pattern than to stay stationary because of the power required to perform a stationary high hover. At our altitude, it was not only more efficient, it was absolutely necessary. Had we tried to hold stationary, we would have dropped like a stone, and there was nowhere to land for about five or six miles." Altitude makes the air thin and the air pressure low. Helicopters can't hover in low-pressure air; the back rotor goes out and the helicopter goes into an uncontrollable spin.

Imagine trying to fly a helicopter in a figure-eight pattern, inside a narrow valley, with jagged rock on either side. And now imagine doing all that blindfolded, knowing that if you err even by a few yards, you will slam into the rock, crash, and die.

"So we performed a small figure-eight pattern while sorting through the possible 'what if' scenarios. This also allowed our night vision goggles, and our eyes, a chance to recalibrate when facing away from the fireball." It was only their rehearsal of flying through the terrain that made it possible.

"We didn't know what had happened. Were they shot down? Was it mechanical failure? Was the team compromised?" One thing they did know was that it was almost daylight, and in daylight you can be seen and shot at. They were running out of time: dawn meant you had to be out of there.

So they flew to an intermediate base about five miles back, landed, and "talked it through" all over again. They learned from intercepted Taliban radio chatter that, because the Army had been firing artillery into the surrounding mountains that night, the helicopter crash was assumed by the enemy to be just another shell.

Since the Taliban didn't know the team was on the mountain-top, Brady and his copilot decided they could afford to wait and come back the next night. In situations like these, Special Forces joke that the stranded team would just have to sit and roast marshmallows.

Brady flew back to the Bagram Airbase to "reset" his crews and equipment (prepare for the next flight). The next night, they successfully returned and picked up every member of the team. "Because we had flown virtually before, we felt we would be able to solve it. And we did. And it was because we had tried it before."

Playing out what-ifs, hypothetical scenarios, while your fel-low soldiers have just crash-landed and are stranded on a mountaintop in enemy territory might seem a little cold. But

Brady explained that's what helped him stay focused in the midst of overwhelming uncertainty. "We didn't think of it personally. We thought of it like a puzzle, more clinically. That helped us deal with it." This is where tools like detaching that we covered earlier can be useful.

While most of us will never fly night missions into the Afghan mountains or have virtual terrains created for us, we also won't be put in situations that might get us killed. That means we can rehearse by having actual experiences.

Learning

We saw in the previous chapter that to develop his breakthrough vacuum, James Dyson adopted the trial-and-error frame Edison used in his Menlo Park research lab. Dyson would build a prototype, test it, analyze why it failed, make corrections, then build another prototype. This makes complete sense—you know you should learn from your failures. But how? Though each failure (experiment! pivot!) is unique, here are a few guidelines that may be helpful.

Don't Beat Yourself Up

You learn from a failure when you analyze and critique the decisions, the process, or the behavior—but not the person who made those decisions or engaged in that behavior. As Brené Brown puts it, there is a huge difference between thinking "I've done something stupid" and thinking "I *am* stupid."

Tina Seelig recommends that the very first thing to do after a failure is to take a circus bow. "After a failure, just like a clown at a circus, throw your arms in the air and announce 'Ta-daaaa!' In this manner, you acknowledge the failure but in a positive way."

Ignore the Outcome (for Now)

"World-class poker players talk about the decisions they made, not the outcomes," says Annie Duke. These players know to focus on the things they can control, which are the decisions they made, rather than the outcome, which in poker is truly out of their hands.

What Duke means is that you shouldn't judge how good your decision was based on the outcome of that decision, because you don't actually control the outcome. In her case, she wants to know whether or not she'd calculated the odds correctly. If, for example, she had correctly assessed that she had a 70 percent chance of winning the pot if she stayed in the game, and ended up losing, she doesn't take that to mean she was wrong to stay in the game. Instead, she accepts that there was a 30 percent chance that she would lose. The outcome doesn't invalidate her reasoning. "In poker, it's never a hundred percent certain," she explains.

Learn to judge the success or failure not by the outcome, but by the quality of the decisions made. "You should only be as happy or sad as the quality of the experiment you ran," says Astro Teller, "independent of the outcome. If you ran a smart, thoughtful experiment but got a bad result, you still celebrate."

"When you lose a hand, hindsight bias makes it very easy to feel you were wrong. And when you get into that space, it can cause you to adjust your play in very bad ways." Annie told us that often, when you "called" and lost, you actually were right to call, and you have to embrace that you did all you could. "It was a good call whether I won the hand or not."

Look Around the Failure

Marie Curie discovered radium and polonium in the "imperfections," the dust surrounding two other elements that she was focusing on. Her Nobel Prize truly emerged from the dust, debris, and unwanted materials around the uranium minerals that she had set out to study.

She also changed the world of physics forever. Up until the late nineteenth century, the atom was still believed to be the smallest indivisible unit of matter. People thought atoms could not break apart. Henri Becquerel was starting to believe this was not true. But it was Marie Curie who blew the lid off the theory. Coming off William Roentgen's work with X-rays, Curie began working with the newly discovered phenomenon of radioactivity. Some elements gave off energy. The question was how. Curie was the first one to realize that it was a physical phenomenon, not a chemical one. Atoms were physically falling apart and releasing energy.

Curie conceived of an experiment to prove this and performed the experiment. As a nuclear chemist who works at Curie's original lab put it: "While many others were battling in the jungle of odd and unexplained phenomena, she was the first to climb to the top of a tall tree, look around, and shout 'Wrong jungle!' or rather 'This is not the jungle in which we thought we had landed!'"

Curie ushered in the age of atomic physics and quantum mechanics.

Get Feedback

Go see people whose opinion you respect: one or a few people in your field, such as mentors or colleagues, and a few outside of your field.

To avoid your feedback source being tainted by hindsight bias, you can use the poker mindset Annie Duke revealed earlier: "When world-class poker players talk to one another for help analyzing a play, you never hear them talk about the outcome. Instead, they lay out situations, all the factors they were aware of, and they ask for feedback on each of their decisions, turn by turn. It's not until they have gone through the entire chain of events and received feedback on each decision that they reveal the outcome."

You can do the same thing with the people you ask for feedback. Rather than starting with the outcome, describe the situation as you understood it, the variables, and what decisions you made at each point. Ask them what they would have done. Mention a few of the alternative options you've thought up and see what they say. And only when you've received feedback on each intermediary step and decision should you tell them how it ended up.

"If you win, it's not luck, it's included in the math. And if you lose, it was also included in the math, and you have to accept that, because losing will happen a certain percent of the time." There will be times, as Annie Duke explained, when you will have made every decision correctly and still lose or fail. That's the math.

Now that you're familiar with all the tools needed to handle failure, here's how they all come together in a blueprint:

Putting It into Practice: The Failure Blueprint

• Reframe failure—learn to see it as an essential part of the breakthrough process.

• Practice failure:

 ➤ Experientially: sports, poker, cooking, etc.

 ➤ Mentally: rehearsals and visualization.

• During failure, use self-forgiveness and self-compassion to quiet your fight-or-flight response.

• Learn from the failure:

 ➤ Don't beat yourself up.

 ➤ Ignore the outcome (for now).

 ➤ Deconstruct the process.

 ➤ Look around the failure.

 ➤ Go see other people.

 ➤ Write up your post-mortem.

• Knowing that there actually is a "right" way to fail helps talk back to:

 ➤ The inner critic: "We were following the Failure Blueprint."

 ➤ The impostor syndrome: "Maybe we're an impostor, but we have a blueprint to follow that will help us do things right."

 ➤ The perfectionist: "We're perfectly following the blueprint. It just so happens the blueprint calls for imperfection and failure."

 ➤ The maximizer: "This is the way to get the most out of the process."

KEY TAKEAWAYS

- The internal experience of failure is one of shame, dismay, disappointment, or even despair.
- Failure skills ensure you are always in learning mode so you can rebound and keep going.
- Reframing helps turn our failures into learning opportunities. There is cognitive reframing, which is rational and logical, and social proof reframing, reminding yourself that lots of people have been in the same situation.
- Detaching from the emotions and thoughts around failure helps create perspective.
- Learn to handle negative thoughts. Don't repress them, or they will grow stronger.
- We react to failure like we react to grief.
- Practice failure both mentally and physically.
- Visualization, or mental practice, is a powerful tool in controlling your response to failure.
- Learn to judge success and failure not by the outcome but by the quality of the decisions made.
- Get and give feedback to others.

Chapter 9

Icy Uncertainty

Accepting the Unknown

HAVE YOU EVER had the awful feeling that you're just waiting for the other shoe to drop, and finding sometimes that you'd rather have a negative outcome than be left in suspense?

Imagine that you've landed in a foreign country, halfway around the world. You're shuffling along in the customs line, feeling tired, grubby, jet-lagged, and very unfamiliar with your surroundings. When the immigration officer waves you up to his counter, you hand over your passport and try to muster as friendly a hello as you can.

The immigration officer takes a long look at you, then flips through the pages of your passport. He turns back to the front. He looks at the photo, looks at you, and back again. He reaches for the stamp, but as he does so, he glances at his computer screen and freezes. Then he closes your passport and says, "Wait here, please." You watch him walk off, your passport in his hand.

Now, you *know* you're not a terrorist, drug smuggler, or international art thief.* But still—your heart rate increases, adrenaline surges through your veins, and you suddenly feel wide awake and seriously anxious.

What happened?

Did the immigration officer see something on the screen? Had

---

* We hope.

you been flagged for some reason? Perhaps it's a mistake, maybe someone with a similar name. You wonder if you'll be detained for hours.

Your mind starts spinning all sorts of scenarios, and as you stand there the anxiety becomes so unbearable that you almost wish the immigration officer would reappear even with bad news, anything but this complete uncertainty.

Now imagine that the immigration officer, after looking at your passport, says, "I'm having a problem with my reader. Can you hold on while I go check this with my colleagues? It won't take more than a minute." In this case you might tune out, take out your phone, start playing Candy Crush, and wait patiently.

The only difference in these two scenarios? The level of uncertainty about what was going on and what was going to happen.

We all have different comfort levels when it comes to uncertainty. Each of us has a range, a comfort zone, below which things seem too predictable and life feels boring, and above which things feel unsettling, overwhelming, and confusing. At the extreme of the uncertainty spectrum, you get chaos—total unpredictability.

Interestingly, *Chaos* is the name of the vale from which the Titans, creators of the universe, arose. Does more uncertainty equal more creativity? Yes, in a way. In fact, as we're about to see, the ability to handle uncertainty is absolutely critical to the breakthrough process.

Uncertainty, just like failure, is an unavoidable part of life. In fact, considering the ever-increasing pace of business and technological advances, as well as ever-present unforeseeable economic upheavals, uncertainty will always be a part of our daily lives. As business guru Alan Weiss puts it, "The environment is changing on an hourly basis. This morning's strategy may not work by lunchtime."

The inability to tolerate uncertainty carries multiple costs, such as leading us to make premature decisions. Too often, people feel so uncomfortable being uncertain that they're willing to do anything to get themselves out of that state. They'll make a decision before all the elements are in place, or perhaps they'll kill projects too early because it felt too uncomfortable to let things unfold.

In fact, not being able to handle uncertainty is a real breakthrough blocker. The ability to handle uncertainty is particularly important for innovation breakthroughs. Just like with failure, if you're not willing to do things that have uncertain outcomes, you'll only do things that have a guarantee of success, which means things that are already known and, by definition, not innovative.

The very nature of breakthrough innovation is stepping into uncharted territory: we don't know where we are, where we're going, or how we're going to get there. Innovation requires allowing for a certain degree of uncertainty. In fact, uncertainty is so fundamental to innovation that most companies would see a measurable increase in innovation just by increasing people's comfort with uncertainty.

Discomfort with uncertainty can also catch us in sneakier ways. Sometimes, when you're experiencing more uncertainty than you're comfortable with, your verbal processor (often called the "confabulator" by neuroscientists) will construct a story or a reason in order to create a sense of certainty instead.

This story becomes a frame through which you see the rest of the experience, which can be limiting: the confabulator tempts us with a feeling of certainty, but its effect is a bit like putting blinders on a horse. You only see a narrow frame.

The frustrating thing about a breakthrough? Until it happens, you don't know how close you are. Until you break through the surface, not one ray of light—and then all of a sudden, illumination. But you have to be willing to stay with the process the whole way through, not knowing how long it will take for the breakthrough to appear.

Why Is It So Uncomfortable?

Uncertainty is uncomfortable for most of us. In fact, it is physically uncomfortable for the human brain: it registers in the brain just like pain, activating the amygdala in the same way.

Our natural discomfort with uncertainty is a legacy of our survival instincts. We tend to be more comfortable with what is familiar, since it obviously hasn't killed us yet. The unknown could be dangerous, and we'd better find out if it is. Though you were far from a life-threatening situation when you were left alone in the customs line, the uncertainty your brain experienced felt the same as the kind our ancestors evolved to avoid long ago.

We crave certainty because it gives us the (often illusory) feeling of control. And most of us *love* control. It makes us feel safe. Uncertainty, on the other hand, is often caused by something outside of our control. In fact, it almost always is unless the uncertainty is caused by indecision.

It's also particularly hard for us today because we are living in an age of answers. From the moment we start school, we are judged by and valued for how much we know, how many answers we get right. Having an answer provides certainty to a situation. Parents want to be able to answer their children's questions; teachers want to be able to answer their students' questions; scientists want to answer the riddles of nature. Nobody wants to stand up in front of others and say "I don't know."

But there is an interesting paradox in all of this. Although we get rewarded by society for knowing answers, for playing our role in establishing certainty, it's actually when people say "I don't know," when they step into not knowing and explore from there, that we move forward as a society.

Breakthroughs do not come from people who stand in the certainty of their answers, but from those who have the courage to stand in the uncertainty of their questions.

Those very answers that we use to score well on tests were discovered by people who were willing to stand in a place of not knowing. The breakthroughs that decode the world and give us answers only happen because of the people who are willing to withstand uncertainty without flinching and without blinking. They are willing to stand in uncertainty and ask why. Without that, we'd have no answers at all.

Answers and questions are two sides of the same coin. Our scientists, anthropologists, economists, philosophers, artists, mathematicians, and innovators have created our world of answers by having the heart and courage to live inside the questions.

In the nineteenth century, the British Empire owned half of all the oceangoing vessels in the world. It was an incredibly lucrative position to have in a world where oceans were the primary trade routes; but the British also had to contend with the uncertainties of piracy, war, and the forces of nature. To deal with pirates, they built the world's largest navy. To deal with lost ships, they became the insurance center of the world.[1]

The tools we're going to give you in this chapter serve essentially the same purpose—protection and insurance—on a psychological level. Some tools will help protect you from uncertainty. You'll learn how to limit uncertainty by "loading your certainty bucket," and how to reduce uncertainty by thinking like a poker player. You'll also learn how to practice uncertainty so you can be less affected by it and handle it better as time goes by. Other tools are like insurance. They help you neutralize uncertainty that has reached an overwhelming level and risks creating uncreative mental states.

You know why uncertainty can be uncomfortable and why it's important to handle it well. Let's look at a few tools and exercises to help you deal with it, perhaps even embrace it and make it work to your advantage.

Balance Uncertainty

Everyone has an uncertainty threshold, above which their mind goes into the fight-or-flight state. When we don't know where we are, where we're going, or how we're going to get there, our natural reaction is to activate our sympathetic nervous system, with all its unfortunate consequences.

We instinctively seek to remain below this uncertainty threshold. If your uncertainty-handling capabilities are maxed out and you're already handling all the uncertainty you can, you'll avoid adding any more uncertainty elsewhere. This might be disastrous if you're working on a breakthrough, since uncertainty is vital for creativity. That's why it's worth decreasing the uncertainty in areas where it's not necessary.

Imagine a scale with certainty in one bucket and uncertainty in the other. If you want to be able to handle a heavier uncertainty load, you need to equally load the certainty bucket to keep things in balance. What can you load it with?

Returning to Old Favorites

There is a special kind of agony in the process of writing a book. Few of us have ever made a substantial creative work that didn't have a series of difficult stages. Feelings of being lost, disoriented, overwhelmed, and afraid of the consequences are par for the course, and, paradoxically, often the sign that one is getting into interesting territory.

One author we know finds herself instinctively turning to well-known and well-loved books during her writing periods. What she is seeking in them is the certainty of an enjoyable experience; there is no uncertainty about what the experience of reading them will be like. The familiarity of the phrases themselves has a comforting effect.

During the writing of her most recent book, she read Jane Austen's *Pride and Prejudice* eight times, cover-to-cover. "There was a reassurance, grounding, and a comfort in reading the familiar phrases—every word perfect, every sentence a delight," she says.

Loading the Certainty Bucket

Gustave Flaubert's maxim was "Be regular and orderly in your life . . . so that you may be violent and original in your work."[2] This sentiment is echoed by a number of creatives; you would be surprised at how many well-known artists, novelists, or designers use strict routines, rituals, and schedules in all noncreative areas of their life.

Mason Currey, the aforementioned analyzer of the habits of nearly two hundred of the world's most prolific inventors and innovators over the ages, wrote: "A solid routine fosters a well-worn groove for one's mental energies and helps stave off the tyranny of moods."[3]

Many of the people Currey studied had established a standardized day from the moment they opened their eyes to the moment they went to sleep, seven days a week. Legendary choreographer Twyla Tharp, who has broken every ballet choreography rule in the book, wakes up at the same time, has the exact same breakfast, does the same gym workout, and so forth, through every single moment of her day until she heads to bed. Immanuel Kant went on daily walks that were so exact that people said you could set your watch to them.

Having so much predictability in 90 percent of their days allows people like Tharp to be wildly creative, going boldly into the uncertainty, in the 10 percent of their day when this creativity is key. If you want to handle uncertainty in breakthrough areas, you must minimize uncertainty everywhere else. By confining uncertainty to the areas where it is most useful, you can maintain a consistent performance in all areas of your life.

This is where routines and rituals* come in. These are some of the most effective tools you can use. They add predictability and reliability

---

* We are using both terms because although people tend to use them interchangeably, they are different. A routine is done without thinking; a ritual is done with intention.

to your life. They are grounding experiences you can count on, no matter what's going on. Their consistency is what makes them effective: they provide a kind of psychological bedrock, a way to load the certainty bucket and provide a counterweight to uncertainty.

Human habits have been under much scrutiny lately, and the science of habit formation is fascinating. You'll find several excellent books on the topic in the resources section of this book. B. J. Fogg, head of the Stanford Persuasive Technology Lab, creator of the Tiny Habits method, considers habit making a fundamental skill and one that should be taught in school, "especially in the age of scattered distraction we live in."

In addition, "Habits can permanently raise people's happiness baseline," happiness researcher Shawn Achor tell us. Even if you think you have no discipline at all, you have more than you think. Everyone has some routines that are good for them, such as brushing your teeth.

The Science of Habit Formation

If there's one thing we can learn from Mason Currey's research, it's that there really is no single ritual, routine, or habit that will lead to generating breakthroughs. The only two common threads are:

Chemicals: Alcohol, of course, but also every kind of drug one could possibly imagine. Olivia was shocked to discover how many world-famous mathematicians and scientists used amphetamines daily. ("Poets, yes, writers, artists, perhaps; but not scientists, not physicists, they're supposed to be *respectable* people!") Judah has spent enough time at Burning Man to have seen everyone, from priests to politicians, under a variety of influences.

Daily walks: walking every day is a great ritual and serves a dual purpose, loading the certainty bucket and giving you a good way to access your breakthrough experience.

Yes, ideally you'd want all your rituals to serve this dual purpose. But don't get caught in the trap of thinking that all of them must do so: that's your maximizer talking. Don't go chasing after "the best" rituals. If you do something, that's enough to make it worth it.

Ideally, your rituals would allow you some change of pace from the rest of your tasks. Performance researcher and author Tony Schwartz has found that our brains become easily fatigued: they need breaks to be able to refocus, create, and produce.

"When we don't give them the needed time to refuel," he told us, "they more or less start to shut down and ratchet up the crankiness until we *have* to listen. By then, we've often spent hours at work without really accomplishing a whole lot of actual work. When you don't give your brain a chance to refuel, you lose creativity, cognitive function, productivity, and you put yourself at risk of fear and anxiety."[4]

Aim to have your rituals give you a break from what you were doing. Your brain needs downtime; it can't stay at peak performance mode or any other steady state throughout the day. It needs to alternate from high-performance mode to low-performance mode, like a shark that needs to keep swimming to stay alive.

Even just thirty seconds of any ritual to clear your head—whatever works for you—can allow your brain to ramp down and thus get the oscillation it needs to avoid a crash. And yes, we understand how busy your days are, but don't tell us you can't take just thirty seconds at regular intervals throughout the day.

Here are some tips to help you form workable routines, rituals, and habits.

Start Small

Every single expert we interviewed about rituals was adamant about the importance of starting small. Fogg's Tiny Habits method teaches people habit formation by setting tiny goals to increase the likelihood of success.[5] Not only does this give you the "small wins" that add up to a real sense of confidence in your momentum, it also satisfies the basic human need for completion we no longer get from our 24/7 jobs.

Olympic coach Charlie Brown says that more than anything else, our confidence is based on whether or not we have achieved our goals. So set smart goals: small goals you know you can achieve and that will build your confidence.

Make your new habit easy. In fact, make it so easy it seems laughable. If your aim is to floss regularly, for example, Fogg recommends you start with the goal of flossing just one tooth. When you get to that stage, that's when you know you've made it easy enough. One of our clients, after a decade of meditation practice, decided to take a few months off. As with any other training or fitness program, it was all too easy to let things slip, and soon these few months became a year, then two.

She assumed she should immediately return to her previous level of practice: a full forty-five minutes of meditation every day. Somehow, there was always an "excellent reason" to delay until the next day. She finally, begrudgingly, realized that she'd have to start small. *Really* small. She began with just two minutes. "It's really hard to argue that you can't take two minutes in a whole day. From there, it was easier to tack on another minute—'Just another sixty seconds'—then five minutes, then ten, and so forth."

When Shawn started his research to determine which habits were most conducive to creating happiness, he ended up with an Excel spreadsheet fifteen habits long. "By day two, I was feeling overwhelmed, it was 2 P.M. and I hadn't gotten anything done other than those happiness things. By day three, I'd totally given up." Nowadays, he recommends choosing only *one* new habit at a time.

Get Specific

Translate target goals into specific behaviors. For instance, if you're aiming to exercise more, translate it into the necessary behaviors: go running every morning, get a trampoline, and so forth. "Rituals," Tony Schwartz told us, "need precision to be effective: be very specific about the time, place, and any other specific you can determine for the behavior you want to adopt."

Find a Trigger

What will prompt the behavior? Some behaviors are natural (waking up). Others you must design or determine (answering the phone). For our client, the right trigger turned out to be having her meditation space set up in such a way that she had to pass over it to get to her closet: it was impossible not to see it.

Set Incentives

Tim Ferriss, author of the wildly successful *The 4-Hour Workweek*, told us that "When seeking to create new habits, new rituals, or achieving new goals, people focus far too much on the mechanics when they should, instead, focus on the incentives. Figure out the *why*, and the *how* will take care of itself." As he explained it, the mechanics are very attractive because they seem like variables that can be endlessly tested with little effort.

For reinforcement, our meditating client used gold stars, but with a loss-aversion twist: she would give herself the gold star *before* she started the meditation, and if she didn't finish it, she had to take the gold star away.

Plan for Failure

Yes, really. Kelly McGonigal's research showed that predicting how and when you might be tempted to break your vow increases the chances that you will keep a resolution. When are you most likely to be tempted and give in? What is most likely to distract you from your focus? What justifications will your brain use to convince you to skip the new habit "just this once"? Imagine yourself in that situation, what it will feel like, and what you will be thinking. Look at how a typical willpower failure unfolds. Consider what specific actions would help. Then visualize success.

"Your rational self sets a course for you to follow, but often the tempted self decides to change course at the last minute when presented with the temptation," says McGonigal. "The result will ultimately be self-sabotage." In *The Willpower Instinct*, she quotes behavioral economist George Ainslie on this point: "Take steps to predict and constrain that self as if it were another person."[6] Study your tempted self; see what choices it makes and organize things so you have the best chance of success.

Don't Rely on Willpower

McGonigal describes willpower, which is also called self-control, as a muscle. When used, the muscle tires, and if you don't rest it, you can run yourself into exhaustion. In fact, exerting willpower physically fatigues us.[7] It is a finite resource, so be strategic about where and when you expend it.

What is absolutely critical to understand is that every single act of self-control depletes willpower, whether you're trying to stay calm, refuse a cookie, or sit through a boring meeting. Anytime you have to fight an impulse, filter out distractions, or make yourself do something difficult, you use a little more of your willpower. This includes even trivial things, such as choosing between twenty brands of laundry detergent. Whenever you have a decision to make, you're using up your willpower reserves.

When our willpower tank hits empty, we revert to the path of least resistance, or the default setting: that is, the way things are unless you expend energy to change them.[8]

A fantastic study from Eric Johnson and Daniel Goldstein of Columbia University's Center for Decision Sciences, published in the prestigious journal *Science* in 2003, revealed a striking difference among European countries with regard to the rates of organ donation consent.[9] The contrast was especially drastic between Germany (12 percent consent) and Austria (99.98 percent consent) or between Denmark (4.25 percent) and Sweden (85.9 percent).

Why would countries with very similar social and healthcare policies in other respects be so drastically divergent on this one issue? Because of one simple, small difference. In Sweden, you are presumed to agree to organ donation unless you check the box to opt out. In Denmark, you have to opt in: by default, you are presumed not to have consented to organ donation unless you take action to consent.

You'd think people would care pretty strongly about whether or not their organs will be removed from their body, but they don't. At least, not enough to express a preference. In the vast majority of cases, people let the default setting stand.

What you want to do is make it *easy* to go into the new behavior, and in fact, to make it so easy that it becomes the default. The classic example is putting your workout shoes and gym bag near the door.

Better yet, make it hard *not* to do it. If it's more effort not to do the behavior you hope will become a habit, that's ideal. Make the old behavior harder to do than the new one: one author dismantled his laptop to prevent his tempted self from surfing the Internet to procrastinate.

Another removed the computer's wireless card and destroyed its Ethernet port.

You'll have a much greater chance of success if you assume, when you're envisioning the new behavior, that the person in this situation is the most tired, grumpy, exhausted, hungry, sleepy version of yourself. Better yet, imagine a grumpy, tired kid. Stop trying to speak to the adult in you; the adult (cortex/neocortex) is fully on board. Instead, focus on the less rational, more primal brain parts, which are the ones that will resist the change.

Tim Ferriss says he has succeeded, and continues to succeed, *despite* himself rather than *because* of himself. Known for his extreme accomplishments in matters both physical (muscle mass, martial arts, tango) and psychological (speed-reading, language learning), Ferriss explains that most of his readers and viewers have a preconception of him as having a will of iron and the self-discipline of a monk. In fact, he says, "I enjoy frittering my time away as much as the next person. Self-discipline and willpower are very overrated."

Reduce Uncertainty: Think Like a Poker Player

For Annie Duke, the key attribute that separates the best poker players from the rest of the pack is that they embrace uncertainty. You can reduce uncertainty, she explains, but once you have the percent range, you know you'll only be right a certain amount of time. "It's about how tight can you get that range, and then accepting the fact that you can never know for sure."

Whether or not you realize it, you're always living in probability ranges. When professional poker players talk to one another, you'll often hear how that permeates the rest of their life.

When Duke's brother and brother-in-law (both professional poker players) heard that she was going out on a date, they discussed the odds of whether or not she and her date would get married: "I think it's two to one they're going to get married," said her brother-in-law.*

"We do this with anything," Duke reveals. "What's the probability a table frees up in the next five minutes? What's the probability

---

* The option got named the EBAD (the couple's initials) and is now a running family joke.

she's just a waitress? When you're a poker player, you're always thinking probabilistically."

Almost everything in Duke's life is expressed that way; it's just the way she thinks. When she buys a Christmas present, such as the coat she recently bought for her boyfriend, she includes the possibility that he might not like it. If that's the case, she wouldn't feel hurt, because she knows it was fifty-fifty. She was playing the odds, "setting a market" on the coat.

We strongly encourage you to read any of Annie's books, which you'll find in the resources section of this book, and to take her course. Executives who have to make decisions in uncertain conditions would greatly benefit from it.

Practice Uncertainty

Author Chris Germer explains that most people have a very low tolerance for distress. The moment they begin to feel uncomfortable, they look for anything to get rid of that feeling, quick! They try to find ways to soothe or distract themselves, some helpful and healthy, some not.

At other times, they instinctively go to battle against unpleasant emotions and try to suppress them, which unfortunately only makes matters worse. As we've seen, suppress grief, and chronic depression may develop. Struggling to fall asleep can keep you awake all night long. Waging a war against our internal feelings is completely counterproductive. There's great value in considering discomfort as a normal, unavoidable part of life. Everyone, no matter who they are, no matter what they do, will experience it. Often.

Accepting anxiety actually decreases anxiety, even in people with chronic anxiety disorders. Paradoxically, people with generalized anxiety disorder are freed from many of the limitations they'd been living with by accepting these limitations and the chronic anxiety rather than fighting against them.[10]

Meditation teacher Kenneth Folk recommends naming whatever emotion you are experiencing, then adding ". . . and it's okay." For instance, you would say, "I'm feeling really anxious right now, and it's okay." Try it—out loud, if at all possible. It really works. Tara Brach offers a variant on this theme, adding ". . . and my life is very blessed." As we've seen in the gratitude section, your life really is very blessed, and you can start a nice oxytocin brain wash by focusing on your innumerable blessings.

Just as we practiced failure, we can practice small steps of uncertainty day by day. You can build tiny uncertainty into your day, every day, by simply doing one thing different. This could be as simple as taking a different route to work, reading a different newspaper, putting on the other sock first.

Neuroscientist Marie Pasinski advocates that people "indulge in the new" by making small changes in their daily routine as a way to stimulate their brain and ultimately expand their intellectual horizons. "It's amazing to me how new experiences have a way of snowballing," Pasinski told us. "You stop at a new venue to buy your morning coffee and notice a flyer for a gallery opening. You go to the opening and run into an old friend who then invites you to join her book club. Never underestimate the power of a single action."[11]

Go to the Movies

Choose a mystery or thriller and make it a good one: check the reviews and blogs, or be old-fashioned and get a recommendation from a trusted friend. Ideally, come at it "blind"—know as little as possible what it's about. Watch the movie, but before the mystery is revealed, turn it off.

And now, just be still. Sit with whatever emotions, feelings, and sensations arise. You don't know what's going to happen. Do you feel unsettled, as if you had an itch you can't scratch? Do you have a desire to move, to eat, to drink, to talk to someone? How is your mind reacting? Are you playing out the possibilities in your head? Notice how your body is responding to the uncertainty. Where are most of the sensations located? What kind are they? Pressure, tightness, constriction, tingling?

It's really difficult to simply stay with whatever discomfort or difficulty you're experiencing at the moment. Sometimes it's the hardest and most courageous thing you can do, to just be with the feelings, thoughts, and sensations, and let the moment roll in. There is such a strong urge to run away from the experience of internal discomfort. Meditators sometimes joke, when speaking of difficult emotions, "Don't just do something, sit there!"

Or, as Franz Kafka put it: "You need not leave your room. Remain sitting at your table and listen. You need not even listen, simply wait, just learn to become quiet, and still, and solitary."[12] This is wonderful advice. Kafka, however, goes on to assure us: "The world will freely offer itself to you to be unmasked. It has no choice; it will roll in ecstasy at your feet." We wish.

Throughout this exercise, notice that none of your reactions have any effect on the outcome.

Go to a Game

You can also experience uncertainty, and get comfortable with it, while watching sports. Uncertainty is a big part of why sports are so enthralling to us when we watch them in real time: we don't know the outcome. Here, the uncertainty is exciting, and this is a great illustration of how uncertainty isn't always correlated with anxiety. Rather than being tied to anxious apprehension, it can be tied to eager anticipation.

If you've ever heard someone say "the suspense is killing me," that's because, as we've seen, uncertainty registers in the brain as pain. Even when it's in an overall pleasurable situation, we phrase it as something that hurts. Watching sports is a great way to experience uncertainty in a safe environment and to get comfortable with that sensation.

Choose any sport you like. Ideally, pick a game in which a playoff spot or championship is on the line, as that will heighten the experience. As the game or match progresses, delve into the sensations you are experiencing. Notice how the uncertainty feels in your body.

Notice how you feel when your team is winning as opposed to when your team is losing. How do the physical sensations change? How do your behaviors change? Do you get up and walk around a lot? Do you wish the game would be over already so you would just know and this discomfort in your body could settle? Do you find yourself parsing the tiniest detail about the players to try to gain insight into what will happen? Has the suspense, the uncertainty, grabbed your entire attention? The desire to settle uncertainty can do that.

And when the game is over, how do you feel? Elated your team won? Sad that they lost? Either way, pay attention to how it feels to have the uncertainty settled at last.

The purpose of these exercises is to help you detach from the sensations of uncertainty, to view them objectively, just as you would any other physical sensation, like hot or cold. This helps loosen the hold uncertainty has on you. Knowing the feelings, physical sensations, and behaviors you tend toward when coping with uncertainty can also alert you and help prevent a premature action. Sometimes, we don't realize that we're having trouble with uncertainty, and we'll take action before we realize that the decision is motivated not by rational considerations but by an unconscious desire to make the uncertainty end.

Neutralize Uncertainty: The Responsibility Transfer

The flip side of fear of uncertainty is the need for certainty. Imagine you're dealing with a difficult situation whose outcome is uncertain. You envision a variety of ways it could play out, and you strategize how to best deal with each. So far, so good. Once you've thought through each scenario, the rational, reasonable, logical thing to do would be to put the situation out of your mind and go about your day until action is actually required.

But how many of us have felt our minds going over the different outcomes again and again, rehashing the various plans we've made, replaying the possible scenarios, mentally rehearsing the upcoming conversations, not once or twice, but ad nauseam? And all this because we're unable to rest comfortably in the uncertainty. At what point do we declare this rehashing irrational?

How can we make the uncertainty less daunting, more comfortable? At heart, most compulsive habits, whether of thought or of behavior, are a way for people to feel safe and reassured, to feel they've done all they can to stave off the potential for failure.

When we're worried about an uncertain situation, what we're really worried about is whether things will work out all right. If we could instill in ourselves the belief that everything will work out well, for certain, we'd be much more comfortable with not knowing exactly how that'll happen.

One psychological tool Olivia developed over the years is called the responsibility transfer. It helps people get more comfortable with uncertainty and let go of their need for certainty, or rather find the certainty they need in more helpful ways. We give a modified version of this tool to all our clients, and many of them, from seasoned CEOs to starting students, report how effective it is.

Putting It into Practice:
The Responsibility Transfer

- Sit comfortably or lie down, relax, and close your eyes.

- Take two or three deep breaths. As you inhale, imagine drawing clean air toward the top of your head. As you exhale, let that air whoosh through you, washing away all worries and concerns.

- Pick an entity—God, Fate, the universe, whatever may best suit your beliefs—you can think of as benevolent.

- Imagine lifting the weight of everything you're concerned about—this meeting, this interaction, this day—off your shoulders and placing it on the shoulders of the entity you've chosen. They're in charge now.

- Visually lift it off your shoulders and feel the difference as you are now no longer responsible for the outcome of any of these things. Everything is taken care of. You can sit back, relax, and enjoy whatever good you can find along the way.

After doing the responsibility transfer, many clients report feeling lighter, or as if their chests opened up and expanded. If you don't feel any physical reaction or mental relief when you try this exercise, it may simply mean that uncertainty is not creating anxiety for you. If you do feel something happen, fantastic—you've performed a responsibility transfer.

The next time you feel yourself considering alternative outcomes to a situation, pay close attention. If your brain is going around in circles, obsessing about possible outcomes, try a responsibility transfer to alleviate some of the anxiety. Consider that there might be an all-powerful entity—the universe, God, Fate—and entrust it with all the worries on your mind.

Over time, many of our clients have found themselves returning to this technique so often that it becomes instinctive. With each practice, it becomes easier to visualize, to transfer their everyday worries and cares, and to enjoy the physiological effects of the transfer.

The reason this technique works is that, as you now know, when presented with a scenario, our brain's first reaction is to consider it as possible. William Bosl, former research scientist at the Harvard-MIT Health Sciences and Technology program, explains the implications of a recent fMRI study on belief, disbelief, and uncertainty as follows.[13]

"Our brains are wired first to understand, then to believe, and last to disbelieve. Since disbelief requires additional cognitive effort, we get the physiological effects first. And, though this belief may last only a brief moment, it's enough to produce an emotional and physical reassurance, which can change our thought patterns as well as help alleviate the uncomfortable feelings."[14]

In other words, visuals bypass our slower cognitive circuits and go straight to our brain's emotional centers, and our physiology responds well before cognitive disbelief kicks in. By then, we've already gotten the beneficial brain wash.

Uncertainty is not actually dispelled by the responsibility transfer; the outcome remains uncertain. Instead, it makes the uncertainty less uncomfortable. This distinction matters. People will go to great lengths to get rid of the anxiety produced by uncertainty, which can lead them to make premature decisions, to force bad outcomes, or to numb their anxiety with state-altering substances of various kinds.

The responsibility transfer, on the other hand, works without trying to negate uncertainty. Instead, it helps you to be less affected by it, drawing you out of the negative mental and physical states that often accompany a position of not knowing. So though the outcome of your situation may still be uncertain, you will no longer feel so anxious about it.

By presenting your mind with the possibility that responsibility has been transferred, you're putting to good use the wonderful placebo effect—the brain's inability to distinguish between imagination and reality. The placebo effect works even when we know we're self-deceiving, perhaps thanks to this natural cognitive delay in disbelief. A study conducted by the Harvard Medical School suggests that deception may not be necessary for the placebo effect to take hold; it may work its wonders even when people know full well that they're taking a placebo.[15]

KEY TAKEAWAYS

▪ Uncertainty is uncomfortable, but it's a necessary step in achieving maximal creativity and reaching breakthroughs. Avoiding uncertainty may reduce short-term anxiety, but it limits our potential, leading to premature decisions and missed opportunities.

▪ Uncertainty can be balanced with healthy habits, rituals, and routines in other areas of our life.

▪ When working to form a new, positive habit, start small. Define the target habit or routine specifically and find a trigger to spur consistency. Create incentives for yourself, but anticipate that some level of failure will accompany the process.

▪ Willpower isn't enough. When it comes to new habits, willpower is a finite (and easily depleted) resource. We cannot rely on it alone to achieve our new desired behavior. Create defaults to make your new routine easy.

▪ Practice uncertainty. There are ways to do this, including playing games like poker, naming and accepting the uncertainty verbally, or experiencing uncertainty in safe situations like at a movie or a sporting event.

▪ Use the responsibility transfer exercise to lessen the anxiety of uncertainty. Uncertainty will remain, but the discomfort will be reduced or even eliminated. Repeat the exercise as needed.

Chapter 10

The SuperTools

ORLÉANS, 1429. THE city has been under siege for five long months. The French army, still reeling from their crushing defeat at Agincourt, is demoralized, defeated, and by their own account, have lost all sense of initiative. England and France have been at war for ninety-two years. And Orléans is of such strategic importance that if it falls, the English regent is likely to succeed in conquering all of France. Things are bad—really bad. And that is when a sixteen-year-old illiterate peasant girl named Joan changed the course of history.

Young Joan of Arc was burning with such a strong sense of purpose to "kick the English out of France" that she left her father's farm in the small village of Domrémy and made her way through embattled territories to the French court of Chinon, where she gained an audience with the young French prince and convinced him to send her at the head of a mission to break the English siege of Orléans.

In the five months before Joan's arrival, the demoralized French army had only made a single attempt to free Orléans. With Joan carrying their banner into battle, they mounted three offensives in five days, and freed the city in nine. It was the first significant French success in fourteen years.

It is impossible to overstate just how extraordinary Joan's achievement was. In medieval Europe, for an unmarried peasant girl to reach the French court would already be remarkable. For her to gain an audience with the prince was astounding. But for her to convince the future king of France to send her at the head of his army is simply extraordinary.

Similarly, we cannot overstate the importance of a sense of purpose on the road to breakthroughs. Knowing that you are working for a higher purpose can be a source of strength when taking risks, trying again after a failure, or quieting the voices inside that are telling you to give up.

A sense of higher purpose is the first of three SuperTools we gathered in this chapter. There are some tools that are more like practices than tools that you can pull out at a moment's notice. Their effects are cumulative and more powerful over time. We've chosen to call these SuperTools because they not only activate your brain's genius mode, but also break down creativity blockers on a consistent basis.

SuperTool #1: A Sense of Higher Purpose

Now, you can have a sense of purpose that's not altruistic. A young sales associate who feels that his purpose in life is to climb the ladder to CEO no matter what it takes does have a purpose. It's just not one that will give him the breakthrough power that an altruistic purpose would have.

All great innovators we spoke to had a sense that their work was going to help all of humanity. They all seemed to share not only an immense curiosity but also a desire to make things better for everyone.

Alfred Nobel's brother was killed at one of the family's factories in an explosion involving nitroglycerin, a highly unstable compound. Nobel became determined to find a way to stabilize the substance. He did, and called it dynamite. And thus the Nobel Prize's founding father followed his own higher purpose all the way to breakthrough innovation.[1]

Purpose tends to be externally focused. It is something that we do in the world, to create a change, to help others, to make an impact. Purpose also tends to come with a goal. Gandhi wanted to free India from British rule. Joan of Arc wanted to free France, also from British rule. Jonas Salk, and many others, wanted to save children from the scourge of polio. This was purpose—a drive to take action to achieve a goal.

The sense of purpose created Silicon Valley. The men, and at the time only some women, inventing new technologies were often working for companies developing systems with the U.S. government.[2] They were trying to win the Cold War. In other words, there was a deep purpose to their work. Many of them had a core belief that what they were doing was necessary and right. This emotional grounding in purpose is often found where breakthrough innovation flourishes.

When you feel you're on a mission, working for a higher purpose, that this is your calling—what you've been born to do—then every one of your faculties will go on hyperspeed. You're lit with an inner fire, your brain is firing on all cylinders. This is why Steve Jobs cast himself as a prophet, and why charismatic leaders inspire measurably more breakthrough innovation.

Purpose Turns Your Work into a Mission

Feel the difference between "doing a project" and "being on a mission." Could Joan of Arc have inspired an army if she saw it as a "project"? The sense that you're on an important mission can help you do extraordinary things. Joan's burning sense of purpose spread like an emotional wave throughout the entire French army. They went from feeling like demoralized losers to feeling divinely inspired. Joan's sense of higher purpose turned a political war into a holy crusade.

Now, it doesn't have to be "your life's one true purpose." We're not asking you to be Joan of Arc. We're just saying that if you feel you're working toward a higher purpose, you'll have far more breakthroughs.

"I'm not a risk-taker by nature," says Meg Lowman, chief of science at the legendary California Academy of Sciences.[3] In fact, Meg was so shy that she used to throw up before presentations. But she had a passion for the undiscovered tree canopy of the Amazon jungle. And if she wanted to live that passion, she had to take risks. It was the only way.

The first risks were social—going into what was at that time strictly a man's world. Then the risks were physical—the safety equipment simply didn't exist at that time, and wouldn't for quite some time. Meg's passion for the canopy led her to sew herself a slingshot and design her own walkway. "I was bumping into physical constraints," she explains. "There were no tools. I was forced to invent."

Circumstances compelled her into self-reliance. So she took the risk and survived, and with each risk she survived, she became a bit more confident, and it became a bit easier to take the next risk.

A sense of purpose has many other benefits when it comes to breakthrough thinking, strengthening our resolve as we face down a number of daunting challenges. For instance, it makes you more resilient, more focused, and better able to handle stress and make decisions. It is a foundation to happiness—you'll probably even live longer. For instance:

- A sense of purpose helps navigate uncertainty. It gives you something solid to cling to even when all else seems uncertain. Though you may not know where you are in the process, or what's going to happen, you know what you're aiming for.

- A sense of purpose increases self-confidence. It also decreases the impostor syndrome and helps silence the inner critic. In fact, it's the single most effective tool we know after destigmatization. We often ask clients who are feeling nervous about giving a speech, What if you had the cure for cancer? What if it were your God-given mission to bring this message to the world? Would you still feel nervous?

- A sense of purpose makes you healthier. Having a strong sense of purpose in life may lower the likelihood of brain tissue damage in older adults, new research suggests. When annual psychological evaluations were stacked up against autopsy results, the research team determined that men and women characterized as having a strong sense of life purpose were 44 percent less likely to have suffered major brain tissue damage. "Having a sense of purpose," concluded one of the study coauthors, "will make a difference to your physical health."[4]

Purpose-Finding Questions

We'll cover several purpose-uncovering exercises, from quick questions to intense visualization. Though none of these are guaranteed to show you a purpose, they are all useful in helping you find the direction.

Make sure you're in a quiet spot where you can think uninterruptedly for a few minutes. Read the questions one by one, and take a break after each question to let your mind wander.

1. What would you like to see written on your tombstone?

2. When your life is over, how would you like the world to be different because you have lived?

3. Think of everything you are blessed with, every advantage you have—whether material or immaterial, whether money, time, knowledge, skills, or character traits. These gifts that have been given to you—how have you used them in the service of others?

Putting It into Practice: Finding a Purpose at Your 100th Birthday Gathering

- Sit or lie down, close your eyes, and set the scene. Where is your gathering being held? What day of the week, what time of day? What is the weather like? See the building where the gathering is being held. See people arriving. Who's coming? What are they wearing? Now move into the building and look around inside. Do you see flowers? If so, smell the flowers' scent heavy in the air. See people coming through the door, perhaps getting drinks at the bar or food at the buffet. Imagine, perhaps, that everyone is sitting around round tables filling the room. What kind of chairs are they sitting in? What do these chairs feel like?

- Someone taps on a glass to request attention, and announces that the toasts will begin. Think of the people you care most about or whose opinions matter most to you. What are they thinking? See them standing up one after another and delivering their message for you or their stories about you. What are they saying? Do they mention accomplishments? Regrets?

- Now think: What would you like them to have said? What accomplishments would you have liked them to mention, if any? What regrets do you have?

SuperTool #2: Altruism

Imagine you're in the middle of a really bad day. You had a big presentation but because of technical issues you couldn't get your slides up on the screen. You might have had time to fix the problem but you showed up late because your daughter woke up sick and threw up on you. Changing your clothes and waiting for your mother to get to the house to take care of your daughter left you no time. You made it through your presentation as best you could, then got back to your desk to find your project lead and design lead in a shouting match. After separating them you decide to call it a day.

You're in the elevator feeling sorry for yourself when it stops on the fifth floor. You're annoyed because you thought you were going to make it to the lobby without a stop and you really don't want to see anyone. A young woman makes her way into the elevator balancing six boxes in her arms. She tries to hit the button for parking level 2 when two of the boxes fall to the floor.

At first you're just annoyed. Then you grudgingly say, "I got it." You press the button she missed and then pick the two boxes up off the floor. The young woman smiles and says, "Thank you so much." Her thanks feels good. It's the first good thing to happen all day. So you offer to take a third box from her and help her to her car. The young woman, smile widens and she tells you how much she appreciates that. That people in this building tend to be a little cold to one another and that your kindness is refreshing and so helpful. As you help her to her car, the bad things in your day start to lighten.

On the way she tells you that she doesn't like her job, they don't pay well at all, and there's no one in the office near as nice as you are. As you place the last box in her trunk she thanks you for making her day.

Imagine a tool that can:

- Help you handle fear, the impostor syndrome, and the inner critic
- Help you handle failure and make you more resilient to failure
- Help you handle and navigate uncertainty
- Boost your breakthrough council and increase creativity
- Give your brain a great chemical wash

And as a bonus . . .

- Make you happier and healthier
- Increase your feelings of connectedness
- Decrease your feelings of isolation and the risk of depression
- And even make you more persuasive, more charismatic, more attractive, and give you more satisfaction in life

Welcome to the wonders of altruism. Sounds a bit far-fetched? We thought so too. While we were researching and writing this book, altruism kept coming up again and again. We were rather uncomfortable writing about altruism as one of the most powerful tools in a business book, and we have to admit that we even tried to find ways around it. Unfortunately, the evidence was overwhelming and backed by solid science. In fact, it showed up so often we finally decided to gather it all in one place.

Altruism, like a sense of purpose, truly is a SuperTool when it comes to fostering breakthrough innovation. If engaged in consistently, it provides insurance and protection against a number of major creativity blockers. For instance:

- Altruism provides a wonderful counterbalance to feelings of failure, impostor syndrome, and the inner critic ("At least I'm doing good"). Helping others tends to boost your own self-worth. It also helps foster self-compassion, makes it easier to forgive yourself (you know your intentions were the best, you were really trying), and brings up common humanity (a key part of self-compassion).

- Altruism helps you navigate uncertainty, first by providing some certainty ("At least I know for sure I'm working for the greater good"), and second by giving your brain a great oxytocin wash.

- Altruism gets you out of your own head (where most of the tailspins are happening) and more focused on the outside world. With this broader focus, you're more inclined to take the perspective of others, and that alone increases divergent thinking, the biggest measure of creativity.

Adam Grant told us that "the necessity of others is the mother of invention."[5] His research discovered that when people are in an altruistic mood, they naturally become more creative, and produce ideas and products that are judged to be more novel and useful by experts.

"Prosocial behavior," he told us, "makes you more open to others' ideas, more willing to help, more driven to make the world better, less focused on taking credit. It makes it easy for many voices to be heard in the room. It makes it easy for people to share their ideas."

Altruism increases creativity in many ways. First, by creating positive emotions, it gives your brain the chemical wash that cleans away bad things like stress and anxiety, replacing them with helpful neurochemicals that enable broader focus, divergent thinking, willingness to take risks, and all the other components of creativity and innovation breakthroughs.

And if that weren't enough . . .

- Altruism makes you healthier. "Altruism is good for our immune system," our science adviser Jon Lieff explained.

- Altruism makes you happier. In fact, altruism is "the biggest bang for your buck in terms of happiness," as Adam Grant puts it. It's also an equally powerful element of mental hygiene.

- Altruism makes you more persuasive and charismatic. How? It increases confidence. Knowing you're doing good gives you a feeling of efficacy, and that increases the power quotient of your level of charisma. Of course, it also increases your level of warmth. Can't get a date? Try altruism.

Last but not least, by increasing your self-confidence and enthusiasm, altruism increases your level of persuasiveness, thus your ability to move an idea through the organization and/or to make it happen.

Altruism in Practice

Altruism can be as simple as offering to give someone a ride home, holding a door open for a stranger, or letting someone go in front of you at the market if you see they only have an item or two. Perhaps you stay late to finish a project and let your coworker go home early to be with his newborn baby. Or you let the harried man who is clearly in a hurry go in front of you at airport security.

You can also perform a "random act of kindness," such as paying the toll for the car behind you or letting a car go in front of yours in a traffic jam. Here's why these random acts of kindness are useful: If you expect an external reward for altruism, you limit its effectiveness. But when you perform an anonymous act and can imagine whatever recognition, reward, or impact you want, you get the oxytocin boost that reciprocation would have given you.

It's worth noting that altruism won't yield its full benefits if it's motivated by guilt or performed with an expectation of reward. To ferret out whether or not you have a hidden expectation of reward, just ask yourself: If I know that I'll never get recognition for doing this, do I still want to do it?

For best results, Grant recommended that altruistic activities be tailored to the individual: "Either a cause they truly care about, or a use of their signature strength, or ideally both. We can learn a lot by observing our own past behaviors." Looking back on your life, think about times when you performed altruistic (or, as Grant would call them, prosocial) behaviors. Which ones did you enjoy the most? From which ones did you get feedback that you had impact?

"The mistake a lot of people make is that they try to be Mother Teresa or Gandhi. And that's not sustainable for most of us." In his research, Grant focused on doing a lot of five-minute favors, and paid attention to which ones energized him the most and which ones had the most impact. Interestingly, this brings to mind Mother Teresa's philosophy of "doing small things with great love."

If you want the most effective altruism, look into impact philanthropy.

Impact Philanthropy

Until fairly recently, most philanthropists gave without much of a strategy in mind. They gave because they felt obligated, or because they were giving back, or to enhance their reputation, or because an issue had affected them personally. While (mostly) well intentioned, this kind of philanthropy's effect has been spotty at best. But in recent decades there has been a big breakthrough in philanthropy called impact-focused philanthropy. The idea is to maximize social good by making the biggest difference with the capital donated. It's doing good strategically, not just emotionally.

"Our obsession is impact; we provide unrestricted money to organizations that have a scalable solution and a demonstrable ability to deliver," says Kevin Starr, director of the Mulago Foundation.[6]

The Mulago Foundation is a private foundation focused on high-impact philanthropy, and funds organizations that address the fundamental needs of the very poor. This is an area of particular passion for Olivia, who is a strong supporter of Mulago. "Frankly, it's the biggest bang for your philanthropic buck that I know of," she often says. Any organization in their portfolio has been rigorously evaluated or, in Olivia's words, "they do the thorough due diligence so you don't have to." Stroll through their portfolio, pick one organization whose work you like, and donate. You'll have a huge impact, and the satisfaction of knowing for certain you're having an impact.

Purpose + Altruism

If there's any magic formula, this is it.

Josh Balk vividly remembers the night of his first breakthrough. "I was watching a documentary about the food industry," he told us. "And then they started talking about the chickens."

Chickens live in stable social groups, Josh learned. They can recognize each other—and over a hundred other beings—by their facial features. They also converse with each other using twenty-four distinct vocalizations that communicate a wealth of information, such as whether a predator is traveling by air, land, or sea. They can identify images, remember objects hidden from view, play small musical instruments, solve problems, and even do simple math.

Watching this documentary was probably tripling the total amount of time Josh had spent in his entire life learning about chickens, but he found he couldn't tear himself away.

Chickens form bonds with each other, the documentary continued, and other species, including ours. They show a wide range of emotions, such as grief when mourning the loss off an offspring or of a being they had bonded with.

"Right at that moment, my dog walked into the living room, plopped down on the carpet, and laid his huge head upon my foot. And that's when it hit me. Why love my dog, but completely ignore the pain of these other animals who could very clearly feel pain just as acutely?" That day, Josh decided to dedicate the rest of his life to reducing animal suffering, and it's this sense of purpose that has driven him from breakthrough to breakthrough ever since.

As you may know, the standard egg-industry practice is for hens to be crammed four or more to a tiny cage. Each caged hen is provided less space than an iPad in which to live her entire life. She's unable to move more than a few inches and can't spread her wings. (Imagine spending more than a year in a cage so small you can't lift your arms. Ever.) Not surprisingly, the hens often go crazy from boredom and turn on each other, or even themselves, and that's why the factories slice off the beaks of female chicks.

After a year or two, the hens are ripped from their cages and stuffed inside a carbon dioxide box, where they suffocate to death. "This is what happens behind almost every carton of eggs you see in supermarkets," explains Josh.

The life of chickens in the egg industry is perhaps the one filled with the most suffering of any animal raised in food production. Shortly after hatching, male and female chicks are separated and thrown down separate chutes or onto separate conveyer belts that lead male chicks to a "macerating machine," where they are ground up alive. Since males can't lay eggs, they're useless in egg production, and they're a breed that's too small to be of use to the meat industry.

Chickens are the only farm animal excluded from the Humane Methods of Slaughter Act, so there are no real rules or regulations to govern how they are treated in a factory environment. Every year, more than 200 million baby chicks are ground up alive. "Most of us agree that torturing animals is wrong. Yet without realizing it, most of us give money every day to an industry that does exactly that," said an industry insider on condition of anonymity.

This is why for Josh, changing the way chickens are treated was a first priority.

He knew he couldn't tackle the farming industry head-on; the egg companies weren't going to change their practices just because he asked nicely. Realizing that these companies have no incentive to change their ways unless their customers demand it, Josh focused on the customers, like restaurant chains, grocery stores, and food manufacturers. And that's how Josh ended up traversing an ice-encrusted parking lot in Minneapolis on a cold winter day.

He was there to meet with about a dozen leaders at General Mills to try to convince them to stop purchasing eggs from caged hens.

Some members of the GM team conceded that the treatment of these hens was, indeed, barbaric, and that switching to cage-free eggs was the right thing to do. But since caged-hen eggs are cheaper, the caging of chickens for General Mills's eggs was to continue.

Josh left that meeting feeling defeated, feeling like he had failed. He'd been going around the country meeting with companies and too often hitting brick walls of rebuttals: too much money, too much effort, or simply too much change.

And that's when he had a second breakthrough. What if food companies didn't need eggs to make their products? What if we could make doing the right thing the cheaper and easier thing to do? If they couldn't afford to go cage free, why not replace eggs altogether with something that works just as well and is actually more affordable? What if it also made the products less expensive for customers, the taste more delicious, and the food safer?

Josh had been assuming that he had to fix the system from the inside. This constraint, he realized, didn't need to be there. The entrenched system inside food companies wouldn't change overnight, and in some cases wouldn't change at all. So rather than keep running into brick walls, he removed the constraint and decided on a flanking maneuver.

And that's how Josh Balk and his childhood friend Josh Tetrick created Hampton Creek. The company's first vision was to produce a plant-based replacement for egg ingredients used in end products like baked goods or dressings. But it was slow, waiting for companies that produce mayonnaise, dressing, cookies, cakes, and so on to test the replacement product and offer feedback, with no urgency about actually using them. "It was a frustrating time in the company's history," Josh admits.

And that's when "the Joshes," as they are known, had a breakthrough. Instead of waiting for manufacturers to use their product, why not turn Hampton Creek into a company that makes those products on its own?

That shift would turn Hampton Creek from a small ingredient company to what *Conscious Company* magazine called "the fastest growing food company in the world," selling products like mayo, dressings, cookie dough, and cookies at grocers across the country. In fact, one of their products garnered so much buzz it attracted the attention of one of the giants in the industry—and not in a good way.

In the industrial garage that functioned as the company's headquarters, Josh Tetrick was chatting with his team when a courier walked in and handed him a large white envelope. Ripping it open, Josh drew out a single sheet of paper: a legal notice informing Hampton Creek they were being sued by Unilever, one of the world's largest corporations.

Unilever claimed that Hampton Creek's Just Mayo was unfairly taking away market share from its iconic mayonnaise brands, Best Foods and Hellmann's. How was the fledgling company being "unfair" to the global giant? The lawsuit referenced an antiquated regulation, dating from the early twentieth century, requiring products labeled as "mayonnaise" to contain eggs. Of course Hampton Creek's Just Mayo was egg free. That was the whole point.

The first thing that the Joshes felt was despair. How could their start-up company with a few dozen employees stand up to a $137 billion multinational food empire with armies of lawyers? "Of course we were scared," Josh recalls. "Just fighting the lawsuit seemed like an unrealistic option; winning wasn't even in the realm of possibility."

But the thing about being driven by a sense of purpose is that it gives you persistence, courage, a drive to figure things out. Perhaps that's why eureka moments are a common theme in stories of social good, a reward for the determination, empathy, and boldness found in any ardent advocate. So the Joshes walked around and around their small San Francisco block, turning the situation to every angle they could consider. Their breakthrough came when they boldly turned it upside down. "What if, instead of being the worst thing that had ever happened to us, this lawsuit could be the best thing that ever happened to us?"

The regulation upon which Unilever was basing its lawsuit specifically applied to products labeled as "mayonnaise." Hampton Creek's product doesn't carry that label: it's called Just Mayo. Not only were the Joshes on the right side of the legal battle, they also realized that public opinion would be on their side too. Who would take the side of Goliath attacking a David just trying to make a kinder world?

The Joshes were right. Unilever was scolded by everyone from the *New York Times*, to the *Wall Street Journal*, to NPR, to the Associated

Press, and even David Letterman. The first week of coverage alone brought Hampton Creek $21 million of free media coverage.

Embarrassed by the media backlash, Unilever quietly dropped the lawsuit. Within two years, they came out with their own eggless mayonnaise.

Only five years after Josh's first breakthrough in the Minneapolis–St. Paul Airport, Hampton Creek has expanded to sell more than forty varieties of plant-based products, including cookies, cookie dough, pancakes, cakes, and cupcakes at tens of thousands of grocery locations across the U.S. and China. Bill Gates has predicted that it will be "one of the top three companies to forever change the food system."[7]

Where will your breakthroughs take you?

SuperTool #3: Meditation

"The word meditation describes a variety of deliberately mental activities," Jon Lieff explains. "Some define it as a type of concentration, others as a self-study of their own mental processes, and yet others as a method for transcending worry and concerns."

Meditation helps you increase mindfulness, which is critical for breakthroughs. What is mindfulness? Simply paying attention, moment by moment, to everything that is happening right now. George de Mestral noticed the burrs stuck to his clothes and his dog's fur after a walk. Looking at the burrs under a microscope, he noticed they were made up of tiny hooks. This eventually led him to the creation of Velcro. This is also an example of associative thinking and an early example of biomimicry.

The same is true of the pacemaker. A professor of electrical engineering at the University of Buffalo, Wilson Greatbatch was working on a device to record the rhythm of the heart when he pulled the wrong transistor out of a box. But he noticed the transistor emitted a steady, regular pulse, like a heartbeat. He figured this might be used to actually influence and steady a person's heartbeat.

Teflon is another good example. Roy Plunkett was working on a better refrigerator for DuPont in 1938. He placed a gas in canisters to wait overnight so he could continue with his experiment in the morning. But when he returned the canisters were empty. Yet they weighed the same. Cutting a canister open, he discovered it was coated with the slippery substance we know as Teflon. But think about how mindful he was. How observant. How easily he could have been annoyed and moved on.

Regular meditators have more gray matter in their prefrontal cortex, and over time their brains become finely tuned willpower machines. Better yet, meditation directly increases the horsepower of your brain's breakthrough council. A very recent study of a variety of meditation techniques showed increased connectivity in the areas related to memory, learning, and emotion.[8]

Another significant recent study showed that all the main meditation techniques result in increased folding of the cortex, that is, increased gyrification. Increased gyrus formation is thought to increase processing of information, so you could literally become smarter by meditating.[9]

Meditation is for the mind what a health and fitness program is for the body. It's a mental gym, training the mind. Neuroscientists found that when you ask your brain to meditate, it gets better not just at meditating, but at a wide range of self-control skills, including attention, stress management, impulse control, and self-awareness.

In other words, meditation is a lot like exercise. When the body is trained using exercise, it becomes healthy and fit, which then results in a whole host of well-documented physical benefits.

Similarly, when the mind is trained using meditation, it also becomes healthy and fit, which then results in a whole host of well-documented benefits including improved health, reduction in stress, better concentration, increased happiness, more satisfying relationships, and even enhanced resistance to the flu. In some studies, meditation was shown to be more effective than exercise both in decreasing negative emotions and anxiety increasing focus.[10]

Meditation will also turbocharge your sleep, helping you to get more from the same amount of sleep.[11] (This is the one thing that gets all start-up founders to suddenly pay attention!)

Meditation in Motion

For those of us who have trouble sitting still, you can start by using your own motion as an object of meditation. Some meditation traditions have official "walking periods" during their retreats. Some movement practices, such as Tai Chi, Qigong, or 5Rhythms, are designed to be meditative. You can use running to meditate, though we recommend that you run without any music.

You can, in fact, use *any* motion as an object of concentration. While doing the dishes, you can pay attention to the feeling of water splashing on your hands. Many teachers talk about the concept of mini-meditations: using simple things like handwashing, walking up stairs, or brushing your teeth as opportunities to practice mindfulness.

You can also focus on external motion. Watch a flame or a fire; it's a great way to start. There's a reason humanity has such a long tradition of fire gazing. You can also watch water or the rustling of tree branches in the wind.

Whichever form of meditation you choose, we can guarantee that your mind will wander away from your object of focus many, many times. Don't worry about how often that happens. Simply, gently, return to your object of concentration whenever you notice that your mind has wandered.

Letting go is an act in which you release your need to control the situation, you stop telling yourself how it should be. Some teachers describe this as a catch-and-release process in which you get caught, release yourself, over and over again.

Catch: "Why didn't I . . ."

Release: "Oh, there goes a thought about . . ."

Catch: "I really should . . ."

Release: "Just because a thought about . . . is floating through my mind doesn't mean I have to believe it."

. . . and so on.

You're not trying to quiet the mind, make it peaceful, make it happy. "Probably the most destructive myth about meditation is that it is a practice of quieting the mind," meditation teacher Isaak Brown told us. "Eventually, the mind will get quieter, yes, but I wish no one ever shared that because now all my clients feel like they're failing when their minds are chattering constantly when they meditate."

Just One Breath: "Don't Worry, Be Lazy"

Olivia's dear friend and Buddhist meditator Chade-Meng Tan, author of *How to Master Your Mind in 100 Minutes, Search Inside Yourself,* and *Joy on Demand,* offers in his books practical, concise, funny advice on reaching inner peace. Hang out with Meng and he will convince you that meditation does not have to be hard. In fact, it can actually be quite easy. What is the absolute minimum amount of meditation practice before there is any sort of benefit? His answer: "One breath. Here, try it right now. It doesn't get easier than this, I promise."

Putting It into Practice: Meng's Lazy Practice

You may close your eyes or keep them open. Take one slow, deep breath. For the duration of that one breath, give your full attention to your breath in a gentle way. Total and gentle attention on feeling your breath, that is all. If you prefer a more specific instruction, bring attention to the feeling in either your nose or the belly as you breathe.

"Simply taking one mindful breath, any time and in any circumstance, is beneficial," explains Meng. Taking slow, deep breaths stimulates the vagus nerve, which in turn activates the parasympathetic nervous system. That lowers stress, reduces your heart rate and blood pressure, and basically calms you down.

Like many other meditators and habit experts, Meng recommends finding a routine cue. He explains that you can use as a trigger the moment you wake up, the moment you lie down to bed at night, or you can add an hourly chime to your smartwatch or smartphone and get a mindful breath reminder once per waking hour.

"They are all great, I use all of them. The one cue I most highly recommend, however, is this: Every time you have to wait, take a mindful breath. I spend a lot of my time waiting, and I imagine you do too. I wait at traffic stops and at lunch queues. I wait at the airport, at the train station, and at the taxi stand. I wait for meetings to begin, for VIPs to arrive, for my computer to start up, for Web pages to load up. So much waiting. Every time I need to wait, I take one or more mindful breaths. This is a wonderful practice with many benefits."

Putting It into Practice: Creating a Habit of Taking Mindful Breaths

- Choose a cue, something that, when it occurs, activates the habit of taking a mindful breath. The cue we most highly recommend is any situation in which you have to wait.

- Whenever the cue occurs, take one slow, deep breath, and bring some amount of attention to that breath. For safety reasons (for example, if you're walking or driving), you may need to maintain the appropriate amount of attention on your surroundings as you pay some attention to your breath.

- If taking that mindful breath makes you feel any better, simply notice that. That will be the reward that reinforces the habit.

Chapter Summaries

Chapter 1: The Four Wings

A breakthrough is an idea that solves a problem or satisfies a need in an entirely new way. We identified four distinct styles of breakthroughs. Eureka breakthroughs are clear, sudden, and fully formed. They create great excitement as you know exactly what problem they will solve and how. Metaphorical breakthroughs come first as metaphors or analogies, sometimes as dreams, and require interpretation to understand what problem they are solving and how. Intuitive breakthroughs defy logic and explanation and tend to be more of a beginning, the start of progress down a longer path. Paradigm breakthroughs reveal a grand theory or explanation that is without any clear, immediate application. They arrive clear like a eureka breakthrough but with more awe and wonder than excitement. This is the most rare, but also most powerful type of breakthrough. Each person is prone to one or two styles. None is better than the other.

Chapter 2: The Chrysalis

Breakthroughs happen when we switch between two different but connected brain modes: the focused mode of the executive network, the EN, and the meandering mode of the default network, the DN. The EN is goal and action oriented. The DN is associative and non-linear. Switching between them in a disciplined way is what creates breakthroughs. The EN focuses and delivers the problem to the DN, also called the genius council, to work on at times when you are off-task. The EN and DN work together to notice the breakthrough. The hypnagogic and hynopompic states—the time as we fall asleep and wake up—are particularly fertile environments for breakthroughs.

Chapter 3: On the Hunt

Breakthroughs occur when we allow our minds to wander. Research shows that alternating between cognitively challenging work and activities with a low cognitive load enhances creativity. Walking is one of the best activities to induce breakthrough mind-wandering. Always have a way to capture your thoughts along the way. All walking helps; though outside is best, in the office or a treadmill are also very beneficial. Changing your environment can also spark breakthroughs. You can change your physical environment, but also your auditory, social, or psychological environments. And don't forget to set constraints, which can be financial constraints, time constraints, or creative constraints, which can produce unexpected breakthroughs. Likewise, removing constraints can also be productive.

Chapter 4: The Butterfly Process

Associative thinking, making associations between two seemingly unrelated ideas or subjects, is a key attribute of breakthrough thinking. One tool is the SEIQ, or seven essential innovation questions. These help guide you or your team through a process to create new associations. Another powerful tool that can allow you to associate two series of concepts is pattern recognition. Pattern recognition can help you see the underlying patterns and connections between two narratives, subjects, entities, roles, and so on, noting the similarities between them and discovering new applications.

Chapter 5: Cultivating Your Garden

Neuroplasticity is a major tool in our quest to achieve breakthroughs. Everyone's brain remains plastic throughout life. Though many of us are out of shape neurologically, we can still increase our plasticity. We increase our plasticity when we do new things, and learn and experience new things like new tastes, new sights, new sounds, new stories. Or we can play with Einstein-style thought experiments. Gathering large amounts of information helps our plasticity, and our genius councils will have more breakthroughs. Gather information from your area of expertise, from adjacent fields, and from far afield. Seek input from those in other fields. Also look to nature for lessons by using the field of biomimicry. And remember to keep notes in a central place for later reference. Consider a notebook, or an online app like Evernote, which allows you to sync notes to multiple devices (phone, laptop, desktop) simultaneously.

Chapter 6: What's in Your Net?

We looked at a number of ways to evaluate the breakthroughs in your net. Edward de Bono's Six Thinking Hats is a good tool for this analysis. Talk to other people about your idea. Create a crew, a trusted group of advisers. Biomimic your own brain to build that crew, making sure you cover the qualities needed: empathy, contextual association, and memory, and the types of people needed: mavens, makers, theorists, and generalists. Remember to add catalysts and an EN representative. We discussed Tom Chi's brainstorm critique method and the power of building a constraint box. Just try it. Put your idea to the test and see what happens.

Chapter 7: The Spiders of Fear

Fear is a major inhibitor of breakthroughs. We are hardwired to catastrophize and reinforce our negativity bias. We must learn to handle our fear and understand that failure is unavoidable. The fear that overwhelms our breakthrough abilities comes in one of four main forms. The impostor syndrome can be fought by defining your new self-image, gathering and displaying supporting evidence, and acting in a new way. The inner critic can be fought by finding who the "everybody" is you think you're less than and creating a new "everybody." The perfectionist can be fought by remembering mistakes are rare and thus precious, and by posting pictures around you of people you admire encouraging your imperfection. The maximizer can be fought by putting limits on its demands and expectations of you. To handle fear, be present to the experience of your body, yawn, relax, and make a practice of gratitude, self-forgiveness, and self-compassion.

Chapter 8: The Failure Wasps

The experience of failure is one of shame, dismay, disappointment, or even despair. But with failure skills we can stay in learning mode so we learn from failure and rebound fast. We can reframe our failures as learning opportunities with cognitive or social proof reframing. We can also detach from the emotions failure evokes: just because it's in your head doesn't mean it's true. Learn how to handle your thoughts, don't try to suppress them. Bouncing back from failure is similar to bouncing back from grief, the more you accept that the faster you'll move through it. Practicing failure helps you get used to the experience, whether in sports, poker, cooking, or improv. Remember to focus on the behavior, not the outcome. There are also mental practices, living the moment and rehearsing all possible outcomes. Learn to judge the outcome by the quality of the decisions made and learn from others about how they make decisions.

Chapter 9: Icy Uncertainty

Uncertainty is an unavoidable part of the breakthrough process. It is possible to balance your uncertainty by creating areas of more certainty. You can create steady routines, habits, and rituals. Start with small, easy, specific goals, with triggers to spur consistency—and plan to fail. You can also learn to think in probabilities, like a poker player. But though uncertainty can be contained within ranges, it can never be gotten rid of completely. Practicing uncertainty can be helpful: watch a movie or a sporting event and notice how the uncertainty of the outcome feels in your body and mind. The responsibility transfer can be used to help ease the pain and anxiety of uncertainty.

Chapter 10: The SuperTools

Knowing what higher purpose your project will serve and reminding yourself of it regularly helps minimize the worries and self-doubt that can interfere with breakthrough thinking. Small acts of altruism have a proven effect on happiness, health, and inventive thinking; just don't be fake about it. Meditating is the ultimate exercise for a stronger, healthier brain. Try it during the minutes of your day when you're waiting for things to start.

Key Exercises

Using Sleep to Access Genius Mode

The minutes just before and after sleep can be a fertile environment for breakthrough. Falling asleep allows us to access DN solutions in the hypnagogic state. Waking from sleep allows us to discover DN solutions through the hypnopompic state.

Falling Asleep: Accessing Your Hypnagogic State

How to enter the hypnagogic state:

- Clear the room of clutter and distractions.
- Have pen and paper, voice recorder, your phone on airplane mode and set to take notes, or . . .
- Dim the lights (or wear an eye mask).
- Ensure you're in a quiet place, or that only white noise is audible.
- Don't get too comfortable—no wearing pajamas or getting in bed.
- Try to find time at midday, or right after you've eaten, when you're just the right amount of tired.
- Set your alarm for ten to fifteen minutes.

- Take a moment to focus your brain on the problem, and then let it go. Relax and drift off.

Waking Up: Accessing the Hypnopompic State

How to access the hypnopompic state:

- Watch a documentary on something you know nothing about. Thinking about new narratives will trip new neural circuits and help your brain form new associations.
- Look through old photos. Your DN might find something valuable in a memory file that you'd forgotten years ago.
- Read a book from your adolescence. Old thoughts and feelings will come rushing in.
- Take a walk outside. You'll simultaneously oxygenate your brain, flip the script on your bedtime routine, and see and feel things more interesting than your bathroom.
- Choose a progressive alarm that starts out quietly and builds in volume. You don't want to be jolted awake, bypassing the liminal state you were trying to take advantage of. Nature sounds work well here.
- Have a recording device nearby, whether to write, type, or record your voice. The breakthroughs emerging from the hypnopompic state can be fleeting and ephemeral, so if you don't record them, they'll retreat from you as you wake up.

Mindless Activities We Recommend

To achieve true breakthroughs we must allow our minds to wander. Research shows that alternating between cognitively challenging work and activities with a low cognitive load enhances creativity.

Mindless activities we recommend:

- Doing puzzles or walking labyrinths
- Watching a movie you've already seen countless times
- Throwing a rubber ball against the wall
- Watching sunlight through the trees
- Staring out the window

- Running
- Washing dishes by hand
- Playing video games
- Folding laundry
- Cleaning a cluttered space
- Drawing, doodling, or using an adult coloring book
- Cooking a meal you've cooked many times before

Creative Walking

Walking has been shown to be one of the best activities to enhance creativity. It is a wonderful way to set the conditions for a breakthrough, but there is more to it than simply meandering along.

- Define your problem. The act of verbalizing what you're looking for can get you started on finding the answer.
- Review your raw material. Read over the latest information you've collected. Check all the random Post-it notes and slips of paper you've jotted notes on, or any digital equivalent.
- Set a goal. Are you going to walk till you break through the blockage, or just for a set period of time or to a destination?
- Pay attention. It's fine to space out a bit, but don't neglect the scenery entirely.
- Carry a notebook. Always have a way to record your thoughts on hand.
- Keep something in your hand like a coin, a stone, or a memento. Our hands send massive amounts of information to our brains and keeping those channels open keeps our brains in a more open, associative state.
- Stop and write it down. Don't enjoy the moment of insight so much you keep playing with it in your head. Few things are as frustrating as forgetting a brilliant thought.

Change Your Environment

This change can be to your physical environment, but it can also be a change to your auditory, social, or psychological environments.

Change Your Perspective

- Put up prisms, which combine the advantages of light, color, and motion.
- Bring nature indoors by filling your creative space with natural elements such as plants, rocks, a small fountain, natural light, etc.
- Climb a tree. Yes, we're serious. You probably haven't done it in some time, and that's exactly why you should do it. Seeing the world from a weird angle is surprisingly helpful in unlocking a new perspective.
- If you live in a city, go to the top of a tall building and look out. If your building has windows in public spaces, go up and look from there. Borrow a colleague's office that looks out a different side of the building than yours. Stare out the window with the new view and notice the differences. How are the streets laid out? What are the trees like? Where are the bodies of water? How would you have designed the city differently?

Change Your Physical Environment

- Right now, find five colors you enjoy around you.
- Touch textures till you find five you find enjoyable.
- Find five different hand movements. Go ahead, we'll wait. Just do different things with your hands.

Change Your Auditory Environment

- An app called Coffitivity recreates the ambient noise of a coffee shop. (The creators originally set out to test the effect of background noise on productivity levels.)
- If you're stuck doing repetitive work, binaural-beat tracks—which play slightly different frequencies into your right and left ear—can help you through the laborious implementation necessary to turn an insight into reality.
- Try electronic music, which features gradually building "narratives" of repeated base melodies.

- The chug-chugging of a train and the churning of a washing machine are incredibly soothing. You can find countless clips online.
- For a choice of ambient sounds try the Web site ASoftMurmur .com. It gives you choices that you can mix and match, like rain and thunder, or waves and wind, or waves and rain.

Change Your Psychological Environment

- Watch a documentary about a topic you'd consider "random." Try to find connections to what you are working on. How is this new world of bourbon distillers in rural Kentucky in any way similar to your project on marketing lip balm?
- Spend the day dressed like someone else. If you're usually a casual dresser, wear a suit. If you wear a suit every day, try wearing a sleeveless shirt and shorts. How do you feel different, knowing that you're being perceived differently? (Our clothes are an element of our psychological environment. Several studies have shown that participants' confidence levels were boosted by wearing a doctor's white lab coat.)
- For the next twenty minutes, give in to your first impulse. Just do whatever you feel like doing. Harder than you thought, right? We are constantly stopping ourselves from doing all kinds of things.

Seven Essential Innovation Questions

Use these by yourself or with your team to look at your problem or need from every angle and possibility. You can go down the list in order or jump around. Whenever you get stuck, just choose another direction from the list.

1. Look

Higher: Look at something from a 30,000-foot view.

Reverse: Look at something in reverse, from the back, from the other side.

Value: Look at something from the point of view of its value.

Kids: Look at something the way a kid might look at it.

Ignore: Look at something and ignore what you know to be true about it.

Holistic: Look at something from the point of view of the whole thing, from a systems point of view.

2. Use

Leverage: How could you use this to leverage something else?

Foundation: How could you use this to build the foundation for something?

Substitute: How could you use this in place of something else?

Aspect: How could you use an aspect of this in a new way?

Change: How could you use this to change something you're doing?

Apply: How could you apply this in a new way?

3. Move

Import: What new component could you bring in to make a change?

Rearrange: What could you rearrange to make a change?

Replace: What could you swap out and replace to make a change?

Remove: What could you remove to make a change?

Speed: What could you make go faster or slower to make a change?

Frequency: What could you have happen more or less often to make a change?

4. Interconnect

Power: What could you connect to create a more powerful idea?

Combine: What could you combine with to make something new?

Network: What could you network with to make something new?

Transparent: What could you expose to make something new?

Open: What could you open to the world to see something new emerge?

Partnership: What could you partner with to make something new?

5. Alter

Quality: What could you improve the quality of?

Design: What could you design differently?

Performance: How could you increase the performance ability?

Aesthetics: How could you change the look?

Experiential: How could you change the experience?

Standardize: How could you make it fit with other things?

6. Make

Processes: What new processes could you create?

Meaning: What new meaning could you create/infuse?

Harness: What could be harnessed to make something new?

Instantiate: What can you instantiate into something new?

Functions: What new functions can you create?

Specialize: What could you make more specialized and focused?

7. Imagine

Amplify: How can you imagine amplifying this?

Easier: How can you imagine making this easier to use, buy, sell, assemble?

Negatives: What are the negatives that you could fix?

Go: Imagine anything you can.

Sci-fi: Imagine a sci-fi solution or improvement.

Try: Try using IT in different ways to see what happens.

Plasticity Exercises

Experiment with Movement

- Use your nondominant hand for a variety of activities. Brush your teeth, use a fork, use the key to open your house, write your name. This is also a great exercise to experience what it's like to build new connections—you'll really feel neuroplasticity at work.

Experiment with Taste

- Go to a restaurant and order something you've never had there before. Really taste it. What's different about it? Your brain has to create new connections in order to build a structure to represent new flavors.
- Make a dish, but leave all the salt out of the recipe. Taste it. Notice how the lack of salt changes the flavor. Now add just a little. And taste. Then add a little bit more. Inch your way forward until you've added the perfect amount of salt.

Experiments with Sight

- Take a new route to work, the market, or home. Notice as many new things as you can. The next day, take the exact same route, but this time try to predict the landmarks you will see.
- Watch twenty minutes of a foreign film without subtitles. See what you can piece together about the plot. Are you watching facial expressions more? How well can you understand the emotional state of the characters even without their words? A few of our favorites are:

  - *Life Is Beautiful*
  - *Amelie*
  - *The House of Flying Daggers*

- Sit in a coffee shop while pretending to read this book, and watch the people around you. Don't worry, they'll be too focused on whatever they're doing to notice you. Look at their facial expressions. Look at how they hold their bodies. Are they moving fast or slow? Do they seem jumpy, nervous, neurotic? Now pick one person and imagine what his morning has been like. If he's on a computer, try to imagine what he is typing. Is it for work? Is he searching for a new home? Is he shopping? Writing an old flame? Building a narrative with a who, what, why, when, and how is great plasticity work.

Experiment with Sound

- Listen to music from another culture, whether Bollywood dance music, African blues, or traditional Afghani music. Lose yourself in completely different tempos. If you are home alone, try to dance. When you try to figure out how to move your body to an unfamiliar rhythm, you force your brain to translate new sounds into movement.

Plasticity Thought Experiments

- **Gravity:** Imagine that gravity stops working after 10 P.M. Now, what does the world look like? Are our beds on the ceiling? What does this do to the sports we play? How do we transport goods? Do people have parties in trees covered by nets? Is there a new business making those nets? Are there lawsuits when the nets fail and people go floating off all night? Are movies made where true love is found when these people float down in some random place in the morning? Do teenagers sabotage the nets to float off for adventure?
- **Social norms:** Let's say that you are allowed to kick someone if they truly annoy you. Now what does the world look like? How do you prove the person truly annoyed you? Are there special courts to determine whether you were truly annoyed? How hard are you allowed to kick someone? Are special shoes made that allow you to kick without leaving a mark? Is there a social peace movement to stop the kicking?
- **Age:** Imagine you just discovered that you are guaranteed to live to be 130 years old and remain in excellent physical health. You might notice an internal reaction, perhaps a fleeting thought of

"Wait, I thought I would live till . . ." It's natural to unconsciously set expectations. Did you know you had been using that age as a general barometer? Now try to imagine what your life would look like. How does that affect the decisions you make? Will you stay in your current career the whole time? Will you remain in your current marriage or relationship? How would society change if everyone were to live to 130? Would everyone be expected to have more than one marriage? How long would people wait to have children? Would everyone have to wait their turn to have children due to overpopulation from longer life spans? Would people auction off their right to have children to others?

- **Magic:** Maybe you've heard tales of cities that stand entirely on stilts with suspended walkways for sidewalks. Or a city that consists of nothing but plumbing, pipes, showerheads, bathtubs, and valves connected in a maze of metal devoid of any buildings. Other cities trade only in memories, and you can only buy things by sharing memories. Now you design one of these magical cities. What does it look like? How do the people interact in this city? What are the rules? Here's a way to increase your brain plasticity even more: Imagine you are in a scene, like a character in a highly realistic video game. You're walking down the street, opening doors, turning your head left and right to look at new things. Imagine putting your hand up to feel the wind. Walk down one of the main streets and hear the traffic.

Using the Six Hats to Evaluate Potential Breakthroughs

Find people who are naturally talented and have one or more of the thinking styles. Run your breakthrough idea by them and get their feedback. Try to have all six thinking styles represented.

The **blue** hat focuses on the process, managing time, keeping the big picture in mind.

The **white** hat focuses on facts on the ground, figures, metrics, the reality of the situation.

The **red** hat focuses on the emotional resonance of the situation and the solution, and how others might be impacted, including your empathy and fears.

The **green** hat focuses on creative thinking, new possibilities, new perspectives on the situation and the solution, and on refining new ideas.

The **black** hat has a skeptical outlook and considers risks, potential problems and obstacles of the solution, or weaknesses in the plan.

The **yellow** hat, on the other hand, is an optimistic outlook, positive thinking, a focus on the benefits and best-case scenarios of possible solutions.

Breakthrough Tools for Teams

When building your breakthrough crew or genius council, you want the following qualities in the room:

- **Empathy:** You're looking for people who are skilled at taking other perspectives and have a natural ability to feel how others might respond to a new idea. You want the people others go to when they're having a hard time.
- **Contextual associations:** You want people who have worked in different industries, people who have dual majors in subjects like math and poetry, or French and economics. You need people who have a deep hobby in something apart from their job, like computer programmers who practice Tai Chi or executives who paint.
- **Memory:** Historians could be good for this, or people interested in history. People who worked on previously successful breakthroughs in a similar space are helpful, as is anyone who has been there before and is reflective about his experience.

And you want the following personality types in the room:

- **Mavens:** You want someone on your crew who has her finger on the pulse of the market, the company, the culture. You want someone who knows what is expected to happen in five years and is already up on the thing that will be huge in six months. This person can gauge your breakthrough and give thoughts about whether or not it is new enough, different enough, and is pointing in the same direction as the cultural arrow.

- **Makers:** You want the mechanical engineers, the designers, the builders, the people who will draw and build mock-ups and get very concrete about an idea. You need to stay grounded in reality and in what is feasible.
- **Theorists:** You need people who have a deep knowledge of the subject even if they've never tried building something but have only studied it. Theorists can often offer deep pattern recognition and new insights that those only concerned with applying their idea might miss. This means including people who might be a little older.
- **Generalists:** These people have a wide range of knowledge and as such they are very good at acquiring new information. They learn new things and integrate them and connect them to other things. They can be very helpful just listening to topics they don't know about. Their lack of knowledge leaves them open to helpful connections and insights.

Tom Chi's Brainstorm

1. Start by having everyone state the things that work about the breakthrough. Write those on a board. Pick a goal, say fifteen things that work.
2. Don't write them in a list. Write them all over the board. No list, no prioritizing, no top, and no bottom.
3. Draw a picture beside the idea. Pictures turn on a different part of the brain, the nonverbal part.
4. Tell everyone to do their best not to judge anything. Try to stay open minded. Do not voice opinions. Try not to let your ego become attached to any of the ideas on the board.

Chi suggests you spend thirty minutes to reach your goal of fifteen things that are working. And then you need to create a transitional moment.

5. Take two minutes of silence. Tell everyone to look at the board, take it all in, and let things start to connect.

The silence and the looking at the board are a way to use the EN to direct the DN's genius lounge to start connecting things, and to give it space to do so. You are creating a ritual to slide everyone into their associative state.

6. Have people draw the connections they see among the things that are working. Have them up at the board drawing lines. You want people to see the connections. Use different colored markers for the different connections. (The board starts to look like a spider web. That's okay. It will slow down naturally.)
7. Ask people to tell little stories about the connections they see, saying how these things are connected. The stories encourage people to build on one another.
8. Clusters will begin to emerge, groups of connected ideas. Once you have six, eight, ten clusters, ask people how they feel about them. Ask them to rate the clusters on a scale of 1 to 10.
9. Only look at clusters that rank at 7 or above.

Changing Your Self-image

- Define your goal. What self-image do you want?
- Gather past evidence. Look into the past and write out five ways you've been creative.
- Put the evidence on display. Pin them up on the wall or use a Post-it. Do this every night for ten days. On the last evening, read all the items at once. See how you feel about your self-image now.
- Embrace your new self-image. Take advantage of the science of small wins and build up many "small successes."

Handling the Impostor Syndrome

Shortcut #1: Change the Label

Try simply changing the name of what you aspire to be, and see if there is another term that fits more easily with your current self-image.

Olivia, for example, doesn't consider herself to be creative. Resourceful, yes. Ingenious, yes. Those words feel comfortable. But she's not comfortable calling herself "creative," because creativity is not in her self-image. To her, "creative" belongs to those other people who have a design sensibility, to artists, to people who do creative things (like music, art, and theater). Creativity feels intangible, elusive, something she can't see the contours of. But with the self-image of someone who is "ingenious and resourceful," she achieves the same creativity.

Shortcut #2: Flip the Scenario

Ask yourself which elements of your experience (or lack thereof), personality, or background does the impostor syndrome use to make you feel like a fraud. Take each of these in turn, and flip them around.

"I'm too young for this job" becomes "My youth is a huge advantage because . . ." Do you have a better grasp of new technology? A better understanding of the customer base? A greater willingness to take risks, to try new things?

"I've never worked in this industry before. I'm not an industry expert" becomes "The fact that I'm not an industry expert is a huge advantage because they already have industry experts falling from the rafters. They don't need one more. What I can bring is a wealth of new perspectives and different experiences, and I can bring everything I've learned outside this industry to bear on the problems we're facing here." And so forth . . .

Handling Fear: Quick Fixes

Here are some quick fixes if you're feeling that you are in a less than creative state:

- Check your breathing. Use the body's effect on the mind by taking deep, slow breaths.
- Change your body's position. Assuming a strong, confident physical posture will make you genuinely *feel* more confident and more powerful. As you feel more powerful, your body language will adapt accordingly.

- Imagine getting a great hug from someone you love for twenty seconds.
- Name your feelings. Try simply naming the feelings you're experiencing—anxiety, fear, shame, and so on.
- Yawn. Yawning activates the parasympathetic nervous system and relaxes our body. This is why you'll often see athletes yawn before a competition.

The Relaxation Response

Step 1: Pick a focus word, phrase, image, or use your breath as an object of focus.

Step 2: Find a quiet place and sit calmly in a comfortable position.

Step 3: Close your eyes.

Step 4: Progressively relax all your muscles.

Step 5: Breathe slowly and naturally. As you exhale, repeat or picture silently your focus word or phrase, or simply focus on your breathing rhythm.

Step 6: Assume a passive attitude. When other thoughts appear, simply think *Oh well*, and return to your focus.

Step 7: Continue with this exercise for an average of twelve to fifteen minutes.

Step 8: Practice this technique at least once daily.

Paul Zak's Favorite Oxytocin Triggers

- Give someone a hug. Aim for eight hugs a day!
- Compassion meditation.
- Dance.
- Soak in a hot tub.
- Surprise someone with a gift.
- Pet a dog.
- Take a hike with a friend.
- Write a note of thanks to a teacher or mentor.

Write Your Own Biography

Write about your life as though an outside person was describing it. Focus on all of your positive aspects as a human. Write about your occupation and the people you are surrounded by in your workplace. Give a description of some of your most meaningful personal relationships and consider the good things these people would say about you. Find positive things that have happened today no matter the size or significance.

Take the time to write down this narrative. Just thinking about it won't be as effective.

Metta

- Sit comfortably, close your eyes, and take two or three deep breaths. As you inhale, imagine drawing in masses of clean air toward the top of your head; then let it whoosh through you from head to toe as you exhale, washing all concerns away.
- Think of any occasion in your life when you performed a good deed, however great or small. Just one good action—one moment of truth, generosity, or courage. Focus on that memory for a moment.
- Now think of one being, whether present or past, mythical or actual—Jesus, Buddha, Mother Teresa, the Dalai Lama—who could have great affection for you. This could be a person, a pet, or even a stuffed animal.
- Picture this being in your mind. Imagine their warmth, their kindness and compassion. See it in their eyes and face. Feel their warmth radiating toward you, enveloping you.
- See yourself through their eyes with warmth, kindness, and compassion. Feel them giving you complete forgiveness for everything your inner critic says is wrong. You are completely and absolutely forgiven. You have a clean slate.
- Feel them giving you wholehearted acceptance. You are accepted as you are, right now, at this stage of growth, imperfections and all.

Acceptance Manifesto

You are perfect. At this stage of development, you are perfect.

At this stage of growth, you are perfect.

At this stage of perfection, you are perfect.

With everything that's in your head and heart, you are perfect.

With all your imperfections, you are perfect.

For this phase of growth, you are perfect.

You are fully approved just the way you are, at this stage of development, right now.

Fear No More

The skill is in knowing how to handle the negative thoughts, rather than trying to suppress them or argue with them.

- Don't give your thoughts the benefit of the doubt. Sure, they're yours. But that doesn't mean they're accurate. Start from the notion that you probably missed a lot of things and there are positive elements waiting to be noticed.
- Imagine your thoughts like graffiti on a wall.
- Name what you are experiencing: anger, anxiety, self-criticism. Naming what you are experiencing can help you neutralize it.
- Make it less personal. Don't say, "I'm feeling ashamed." Instead say, "There is shame being felt." Take a step back. Observe the experience like an anthropologist observing a ritual. Imagine that you're a scientist observing a phenomenon: "Fascinating. There are self-critical thoughts happening."
- Imagine looking at the Earth from space. Now come closer, see your country, your neighborhood, your house. Here you are, this one person, having this experience on this planet right now.
- Imagine your negative thoughts are a podcast. Take off your headphones, set your music player aside.

- Lay out what it would look like if everything you're worried about happens, if everything that can go wrong does. Now notice that you survived that scenario.
- Remember all the times before when you felt a similar negativity or anxiety. You didn't think you'd make it through then. And yet you did.

Getting Closure on a Failure

To get closure on a failure, neuroscientist Richard Wiseman suggests a three-step process:

1. Write it down: pour out onto paper everything that's on your mind, everything that weighs on your heart. What happened, how you felt—this is a mental purge, or as some of our clients call it, a "vomit sprint."
2. Rip it up: with gusto and enthusiasm. Really get into the motions, hear the ripping, feel the tearing.
3. Burn it, if you can, and officially declare the failure closed.

The Failure Blueprint

- Reframe failure—learn to see it as an essential part of the breakthrough process.
- Practice failure:
    - ➤ Experientially: sports, poker, cooking, etc.
    - ➤ Mentally: rehearsals and visualization.
- During failure, use self-forgiveness and self-compassion to quiet your fight-or-flight response.
- Learn from the failure:
    - ➤ Don't beat yourself up.
    - ➤ Ignore the outcome (for now).
    - ➤ Deconstruct the process.
    - ➤ Look around the failure.
    - ➤ Go see other people.
    - ➤ Write up your post-mortem.
- Knowing that there actually is a "right" way to fail helps talk back to:

➤ The inner critic: "We were following the Failure Blueprint."

➤ The impostor syndrome: "Maybe we're an impostor, but we have a blueprint to follow that will help us do things right."

➤ The perfectionist: "We're perfectly following the blueprint. It just so happens the blueprint calls for imperfection and failure."

➤ The maximizer: "This is the way to get the most out of the process."

The Responsibility Transfer

• Sit comfortably or lie down, relax, and close your eyes.

• Take two or three deep breaths. As you inhale, imagine drawing clean air toward the top of your head. As you exhale, let that air whoosh through you, washing away all worries and concerns.

• Pick an entity—God, Fate, the universe, whatever may best suit your beliefs—you can think of as benevolent.

• Imagine lifting the weight of everything you're concerned about—this meeting, this interaction, this day—off your shoulders and placing it on the shoulders of the entity you've chosen. They're in charge now.

• Visually lift it off your shoulders and feel the difference as you are now no longer responsible for the outcome of any of these things. Everything is taken care of. You can sit back, relax, and enjoy whatever good you can find along the way.

Finding a Purpose at Your 100th Birthday Gathering

• Sit or lie down, close your eyes, and set the scene. Where is your gathering being held? What day of the week, what time of day? What is the weather like? See the building where the gathering is being held. See people arriving. Who's coming? What are they wearing? Now move into the building and look around inside. Do you see flowers? If so, smell the flowers' scent heavy in the air. See people coming through the door, perhaps getting drinks at the bar or food at the buffet. Imagine, perhaps, that everyone is sitting around round tables filling the room. What kind of chairs are they sitting in? What do these chairs feel like?

- Someone taps on a glass to request attention, and announces that the toasts will begin. Think of the people you care most about or whose opinions matter most to you. What are they thinking? See them standing up one after another and delivering their message for you or their stories about you. What are they saying? Do they mention accomplishments? Regrets?
- Now think: What would you like them to have said? What accomplishments would you have liked them to mention, if any? What regrets do you have?

Meng's Lazy Practice

You may close your eyes or keep them open. Take one slow, deep breath. For the duration of that one breath, give your full attention to your breath in a gentle way. Total and gentle attention on feeling your breath, that is all. If you prefer a more specific instruction, bring attention to the feeling in either your nose or the belly as you breathe.

Creating a Habit of Taking Mindful Breaths

- Choose a cue, something that, when it occurs, activates the habit of taking a mindful breath. The cue we most highly recommend is any situation in which you have to wait.
- Whenever the cue occurs, take one slow, deep breath, and bring some amount of attention to that breath. For safety reasons (for example, if you're walking or driving), you may need to maintain the appropriate amount of attention on your surroundings as you pay some attention to your breath.
- If taking that mindful breath makes you feel any better, simply notice that. That will be the reward that reinforces the habit.

Science Appendix

Neuroplasticity

Dr. Jon Lieff, our main science adviser on this book, graduated from Yale University with a degree in mathematics before going on to Harvard Medical School. He is a specialist in the interface of psychiatry, neurology, and medicine.

He explained that in order for you to have a thought, you need to build the physical structure of the thought. That means your brain has to build new neurotransmitter receptors to allow your neurons to connect to each other in a new way.

Imagine your neurons as a string of trapeze artists. To have a new thought, these trapeze artists have to connect to new trapeze artists. But all the trapezists have differently shaped hands. So in order to swing from one and get caught by another, they need to grow new hands—a new, specially shaped set of hands that can connect with the new trapeze artist. This is how your ability to think works. To create new thoughts, your neurons have to build new hands to grab each other with. How does your brain do that?

We've all heard of DNA, the double helix of our genes. But not many of us remember RNA. RNA is shaped like a single helix with nucleotides running its length. Some RNA is "messenger RNA," or mRNA, which sends instructions to a different kind of RNA, "transfer RNA," or tRNA, which looks like a clover leaf with three hairpin loops.

When you have a new thought, mRNA sends instructions to tRNA, which is like a little factory that physically builds the new set of hands, a protein. It starts building the protein by stacking amino acids one on top of the other, like beads on a string, in a specific order. It does this in milliseconds. When the chain of amino acids is complete, the tRNA stops stacking, and the chain folds itself into the proper shape and becomes a protein. That protein will become a new neurotransmitter receptor. This happens millions of times during millisecond intervals.

All these new neurotransmitter receptors give your brain the ability to make brand new neuronal connections, and this means you now have the ability to have a new thought. A new thought has a physical form. Connections between neurons are physical structures. They exist in the physical world. A new thought necessitates and leads to new connections; an old thought doesn't.

Neuroplasticity refers to your ability to build these new neurotransmitter receptors. If your brain can build lots of new receptors, you are considered highly plastic and you can have lots of new thoughts. If your brain cannot build lots of new receptors, you are considered less plastic. You cannot think as many new thoughts.

Here's how Jon Leiff described the life of a thought to us: With each mental event, dramatic structural changes occur inside large numbers of neurons, outside of neurons in the extracellular space, at the synapses between neurons, and in glial brain cells. Remarkably, these molecular changes occur instantaneously all over the brain in specific circuits using many different mechanisms.

For each different event, the same neuron can be used in completely different circuits. Signals in the circuits occur simultaneously with other types of electrical communication, including synchronous oscillations and changes in the extracellular electrical potentials. With each new learning event, new cells are minted from stem cells and incorporated into the neuronal circuits. This is just part of the life of a thought in the brain.

Why are neurotransmitter receptors so important to new thoughts, or thoughts at all, for that matter? Your neurons have these spindly arms called dendrites. Dendrites branch out from a neuron's cell and receive messages from other neurons. These messages come in the form of chemical neurotransmitters like dopamine and seratonin. When the dendrites make contact with the neurotransmitter, they send an electrical signal to the neuron's cell body. This is how your neurons speak to one another. Dendrites are the physical structures neurons use to reach out and listen to one another.

All up and down the length of these dendrites are these little heads. These are the neurotransmitter receptors. These are the specially shaped trapeze hands that receive the messages from the neurotransmitters. Plastic people tend to have large dendritic heads on their neurons. These larger heads hold more receptors. And the more receptors you have, the more information you can process. The more receptors you have, the more chances there are for your neurons to communicate, and the more bandwidth you have to think new thoughts.

When you are highly plastic, these dendritic heads with their neurotransmitter receptors are constantly being built. When you are less plastic, these dendritic heads are getting pruned.

. . . You'll find more at www.TheButterfly.net.

The Default Network

What is the default mode network?

First, let's talk about how the DN fits into the brain. The brain can't be understood simply as a set of specific regions doing specific tasks. No one brain region is an island. Instead, the brain is an "immensely complex interconnected system."[1] It is a sprawl of networks that connect to and overlap with other networks.

Neuroscientists Dardo Tomasi and Nora Volkow identified seven overlapping networks covering 80 percent of all the gray matter in the brain. These involved four major cortical networks (default mode, dorsal attention, visual, and somatosensory) linked to four major hubs (ventral precuneus/posterior cingulate, inferior parietal cortex, cuneus, and postcentral gyrus), and three subcortical networks (tied to hubs involving the cerebellum, thalamus, and amygdala).

The DN is one of the seven overlapping networks that cover 80 percent of all the grey matter in the brain. These seven networks split further into two groups: the major cortical networks and the three subcortical networks. The DN's associative power probably exists because it is made up of some of the brain's major hubs, its major crossroads and switching stations.

Our default network is one of several intrinsic brain systems functioning at all times without our conscious knowledge or effort. Just as we have systems that keep us breathing and keep our hearts beating, we also have systems that are exploring our environment, exploring our internal milieu, thinking about ourselves, and using all this information to make sense of the world. The energy devoted to intrinsic (unconscious) activity might be as high as 90 percent of our overall energy expenditure.

Now let's take a deeper look at some of these regions that make up the DN.

The posterior inferior parietal lobes, one on the left side and one on the right side of your brain, have millions of nerves that connect to your body's physical sensors: hands, fingertips, skin, balance. Thus your brain takes in all this physical information through the parietal lobes. The electrical impulses get interpreted by your brain to create a map of your physical experience. This map is then ready to be used by your DN.

If you are not focused on a task but doing something physical, that information goes to the anterior cingulate cortex, the posterior cingulate cortex, the precuneus, the medial prefrontal cortex, and other parts of the DN, and they all start sharing information.

Looking at this network in our brains helps explain the oddity of how such an internal, nonphysical thing like a breakthrough can so often be connected to physical activity. Your physical activity plays an important role in your innovative process. Taking a walk, running water over your hand, listening to music, exercising, any of these can make your default network spring to life, triggering a series of relations between concepts that lead to breakthroughs.

Think of Archimedes stepping into the bath, and Newton watching the apple fall. It was not happenstance that these physical actions led to insights.

Another part of the network is known as the temporal gyrus. You have one on either side of your brain, but when it comes to a moment of insight, it's the right gyrus that matters. The right side handles more of the abstract, context-oriented understanding. At the moment of insight, the breakthrough, the anterior superior temporal gyrus has a burst of gamma waves. Neuroscientists can actually see you have a breakthrough before you realize you've had it. The temporal gyrus is known to be engaged in the interpretation of metaphors, like those we often get in dreams or the kind that lead to breakthroughs.

The temporoparietal junction is a region associated with theory of mind, that is, our ability to gauge what others are thinking. The hippocampus is where we create memories, but also where we remember the past and imagine the future.

The cingulate gyrus is part of the so-called salience network, which switches internal attention from DN to EN. Most of the time, your DN is functioning below your level of awareness. When a threshold is reached, the salience network switches your attention from the DN to the EN, and suddenly the breakthrough enters your consciousness.

We would have thought the DN did the creating, the EN did the evaluating, and the salience network switched you back and forth across the awareness border. But it appears that both the EN and the DN are involved in the evaluation of the ideas.

The cingulate gyrus includes the anterior cingulate and insula, and is involved in a wide range of cognitive functions, initiation, motivation, and goal-directed behavior. The dorsal anterior cingulate has been associated with orienting attention to the most relevant environment, to stimuli involved with intra- and extrapersonal events.[2]

How does this system work to give us our breakthroughs? To be clear, no one is absolutely sure. As Dr. Raichle said, "We have a very narrow window on this. Our brain is insanely complex and has spent years as a prediction machine. We don't really know how it does it." But new research by Dr. Kalina Christoff at the University of British Columbia sheds light on this mysterious and powerful process that we all have access to and that gives us all the ability to be prediction machines, breakthrough machines.

Your hippocampus is the part of your brain that creates your memories. Its job is to encode new experiences so that you can remember them. When you are doing something, when you're on-task, your hippocampus is taking in information. It is creating packets of connected neurons that will become your memory. But that's just stage one. It is during this stage, when you are on-task, that your DN goes a little quiet.

Then comes the next stage. You stop doing what you were doing and you are now off-task. If you are resting, your hippocampus replays your experience. It sporadically fires, activates traces of memories, or a few traces that get recombined and form new events—events you've never experienced before. Sometimes it simulates future events.

All of this happens in your unconscious. The hippocampus seems to be related to the origin of thought. These thoughts originate in your unconscious, emerging out of your hippocampus while you rest, day-dream, sleep. Your hippocampus is recombining and reactivating traces and fragments of memories spontaneously. Then, and this is still a mystery for us, a certain threshold is reached, or a pattern is completed that reaches a certain level of meaning, and these traces and fragments of memories enter your DN.

When deliberate and goal oriented, the hippocampus is in input mode, encoding memories. When mind-wandering, the hippocampus goes into output mode, and this is when we start generating new thoughts, literally creating new neural connections. The current theory is that when the hippocampus is in output mode, sending out those spontaneous, random trace memories, it is training the cortical brain to be more plastic. By recombining experiences, the cortical brain creates new connections, and replays chunks of experience in new (and sometimes bizarre) ways.

Even Dr. Raichle's moment of discovering the DN was a spontaneous thought. To hear him describe it, he had left a meeting and was walking down the hall. He had spent many years thinking about the brain and its intrinsic systems. He was working at the lab that created the first PET scan and it was his job to figure out what to do with the scanner. The first thing scientists and cognitive psychologists did was start scanning for what different activities looked like in the brain. They looked at one activity versus another, but Dr. Raichle noticed that it wasn't black and white; one area didn't turn completely on while another turned completely off. What he noticed was that the brain is fully active all the time; the experiments were just torquing it here or there. He also noticed that no matter what activity the brain was asked to do, there were a collection of areas that always went quieter during a task. They seemed to be centered around the medial parietal cortex near the back of the brain. Dr. Raichle created a file called the MMPA, Mystery Medial Parietal Area. He started collecting data.

As he said, he'd been thinking about this phenomenon for a long time. And then after a meeting one day he was walking down the hall and he was thinking about computers and their default settings and spontaneously came up with the default mode for the brain. "The idea that the brain had a default mode of functioning just kind of fit the bill," he said.

Dr. Raichle's DN facilitated a spontaneous breakthrough about nothing less than the existence of the DN.

. . . You'll find more on the groundbreaking science of breakthroughs at www.TheButterfly.net.

Recommended Resources

Books on and About Breakthrough Thinking

Italo Calvino, *Invisible Cities* (New York: Harcourt, 1974). Recommended as a workbook to increase plasticity.

G. H. Hardy, *A Mathematician's Apology* (Cambridge, U.K.: Cambridge University Press, 1940). An excellent first-person account of the creative process for the rational, hard science–minded.

Jeff Hawkins, *On Intelligence* (New York: Times Books, 2004). An excellent introduction to the functioning of the brain.

Arthur Koestler, *The Act of Creation* (New York: Penguin, 1964). For a deep dive into the nature of having breakthroughs.

Rollo May, *The Courage to Create* (New York: W. W. Norton and Co., 1975). For a more artistic and psychological approach to breakthroughs.

Edward Slingerland, *Trying Not to Try* (New York: Broadway Books, 2015). For an excellent approach to accessing the DN through ancient Chinese practices.

Books on Design Thinking

Tim Brown, *Change by Design: How Design Thinking Transforms Organizations and Inspires Innovation* (New York: HarperBusiness, 2009).

Tom Kelley, *The Art of Innovation: Lessons in Creativity from IDEO, America's Leading Design Firm* (New York: Crown Business, 2001).

Tina Seelig, *inGenius: A Crash Course on Creativity* (New York: HarperOne, 2015).

Tina Seelig, *Insight Out: Get Ideas Out of Your Head and into the World* (New York: HarperOne, 2015).

Books on Removing
the Breakthrough Blockers

Tara Brach, *Radical Acceptance: Embracing Your Life with the Heart of a Buddha* (New York: Bantam, 2004). A great resource for emotional training. We have often called this one "graduate school for the heart."

Olivia Fox Cabane, *The Charisma Myth: How Anyone Can Master the Art and Science of Personal Magnetism* (New York: Portfolio, 2013). Charisma is not innate, it can be learned, and this book shows you how.

Robert B. Cialdini, *Influence: The Psychology of Persuasion*, rev. ed. (New York: Harper Paperbacks, 2006). Considered the "bible" of influence, Cialdini's book is required reading in most MBA programs.

Keith Ferrazzi and Tahl Raz, *Never Eat Alone, Expanded and Updated: And Other Secrets to Success, One Relationship at a Time* (New York: Crown Business, 2014).

Viktor E. Frankl, *Man's Search for Meaning*, rev. ed. (New York: Pocket Books, 1997). A great help in gaining equanimity, this is a worthwhile read for anyone facing a crisis. Few books can give you perspective like this one (and in so few pages).

Christopher K. Germer, *The Mindful Path to Self-Compassion: Freeing Yourself from Destructive Thoughts and Emotions* (New York: Guilford Press, 2009). A great resource if you'd like to focus on self-compassion.

Adam Grant, *Give and Take: Why Helping Others Drives Our Success* (New York: Viking, 2013). A fantastic primer on the power of altruism (pro-social behavior in technical terms).

Adam Grant, *Originals: How Non-Conformists Move the World* (New York: Viking, 2016).

Jonathan Haidt, *The Happiness Hypothesis* (New York: Basic Books, 2006). A fascinating look at the science of happiness.

Steven C. Hayes, *Get Out of Your Mind and Into Your Life* (Oakland, Calif.: New Harbinger Publications, 2005). One of the very best books we have found on how to handle your own mind.

Jon Kabat-Zinn, *Wherever You Go, There You Are*, tenth anniv. ed. (New York: Hyperion, 2005). The best introduction to mindfulness we have yet found. Just the introduction and first two chapters will already give you a breakthrough or two.

Hal Stone and Sidra Stone, *Embracing Your Inner Critic: Turning Self-Criticism into a Creative Asset* (New York: HarperOne, 1993). A great first start on getting to know the inner critic, and an easy read.

Mark Williams, John Teasdale, Zindel Segal, and Jon Kabat-Zinn, *The Mindful Way through Depression: Freeing Yourself from Chronic Unhappiness* (New York: Guilford Press, 2007). The best of the best on this difficult topic. A must-read for anyone who has experienced depression or whose loved ones have suffered from it.

Online Resources

We highly recommend this five-minute journal for daily gratitude work, and this productivity planner as a good all-around tool: www.intelligentchange.com.

Check out Annie Duke's courses covering decision strategy and critical thinking at annieduke.com.

Visit www.TheButterfly.net to access free downloadable content, audio recordings of many visualization exercises, and much more to help you get the most out of this book.

Speaking Engagements

Olivia and Judah are frequently requested keynote speakers, seminar leaders, and facilitators for executive leadership retreats. To book either of them for a speaking engagement, view highlights of live keynote speeches or learn about their topics of expertise, visit www.TheButterfly.net or contact them via e-mail at speaking@ thebutterfly.net.

Coaching and Consulting

For a more intensive or in-depth experience tailored to you or your organization's specific needs, you may also want to explore Olivia and Judah's extensive coaching and consulting practice, which has attracted clients such as Google, Deloitte, and the U.S. Army Special Forces. You will find more information at www.TheButterfly.net.

Acknowledgments

Over the past four years of researching and working on the book, we have had the great privilege of being guided by our science advisers: neuroscientists Dr. Kalina Christoff, Dr. John Kounios, Dr. Jonathan Schooler, and oxytocin expert Dr. Paul Zak; psychiatrists Dr. John Beebe, Dr. Jon Lieff, and Dr. Srini Pillay; biochemist Dr. Joseph Orgel; physical chemist Dr. Andrew Ouderkirk; systems scientist Dr. Dario Nardi; and theoretical physicist Dr. Geoffrey West.

To the many experts who have shared their experience and insights, and whose contributions will feature in our upcoming book on breakthrough organizations: Michael Arena, David Arkness, Gilles August, Patricia Carson, Pablo Cohn, Andrew Douglass, Regina Dugan, Alan Fine, Ken Gabriel, Dr. Temple Grandin, Dr. Eric Grigsby, David Hall, Courtney Hohne, Maggie Hsu, Andy Hunt Sara Johnson, Reg Kelly, Lisa Kimball, Michelle Kreger, Dr. Greg Maguire, Mark Monroe, Darya Pilram, Razz, Ron Ricci, David Shearer, Craig Silverstein, Vytus Sunspiral, Mary Uhl-Bien, Don Vaughn, and Jason Apollo Voss.

We would like to thank our contributors: Jennefer English, Kelly Lehman, Andrew Pederson, Kristin Posehn, Brian Sharp, Stephanie Sharp, Victoria Spadaro-Grant, Jeff Thomson, and Jeff Williams.

And the many reviewers whose comments provided great value: Linda Anderman, Safi Bahcall, Paul Bartley, Jennifer Basco, Kyle Bellin, Ali Binazir, Michael Burkett, Melanie Carter, Eric Cohen, Bob Covello,

David Desrochers, Franziska Deutsch, Danielle Dudum, Aaron Emigh, Debbie Falconer, Karen Fannin, Nathalie Felëus, Ella Frank, Paul Grew, Beth Hatchel, Doug Hathaway, Kaily Heitz, Teresa Jones, Jerry Keenan, Jeff Kleeman, Glenn Leifheit, Janet Lim, Mehul Mandania, Amy Merrill, Eden Moafy, Derek O'Leary, Henry Petty, Laurence Piubello-Coqueron, Dom Ricci, Saumitra Saha, Courtney Strobel Salazar, Tammy Sanders, Kevin Sauer, Ray Schmitz, Holleigh Schoors, Oscar Serra, John Shamberg, Felicia Spahr, Ken Shubin Stein, Daiki Sueyoshi, Jordan Thibodeau, Robin Turner, Bart Volger, Adrian Weekes, Ben Weston, and Mike Zwiefelhofer.

With great skill, dedication, patience, kindness, and generosity, Niki Papadopoulos and Leah Trouwborst led Penguin's impressive team effort.

Our most profound thanks to our Super Agent Jim Levine, for his wisdom, insight, and experience, his guidance and humor, and for knowing us so well.

Olivia Would Like to Give Thanks . . .

To four remarkable women: Carina Levintoff, Catya Martin, Elisabeth Puissant, and Natalie Risacher. Ladies, it all started with you.

To the mentors and teachers whose wisdom guided me along the path: Tina and Mitch Beranbaum, Tara Brach, David and Shoshana Cooper, Leil Lowndes, and Victoria Moran.

To my family and extended family: Guillaume, Marine, Ernie, and the entire Cabane clan; Dave and Doris Schoenfarber; the wonderful Bradoos; Barney Pell and Nadya Direkova; Devon and Pablo Cohn; Ana and Michael McCullough; Ava Reich and John Rigney; Serafim Batztoglou and Katya Stanton; Ruth Owades; Tom Breur.

To those who have kept me healthy and sane, supplying friendship, encouragement, caffeine, or a haven to work in: Alex Maki-Jokela; Joel Kraut; Ian Price; Semira Rahemtulla; Fernando Diaz and Vince Beaudet; Shauna Mei; Catherine Pernot; Kushal Chakrabarti; Steven Puri; Mark Herschberg; David, Brooke, Lenore, Dan, and Asa; Todd and Elaine; Tynan; and the entire games and chocolate gang.

To Marissa Mayer and Zack Bogue, who kindly took an unknown author under their wing, way back when, and whose patronage made such a difference. Thank you both.

I would also like to dedicate this book to my clients, as together we've shared discoveries, confessions, laughter, struggles, triumphs, pride, and joy. I'm looking forward to continuing our journey together.

To Fabian Cuntze, who first suggested that Judah and I collaborate. And, of course, to Judah, for your wisdom and your guidance, for being the voice of reason and saving my sanity more times than I can count.

To my husband, Brian, for frozen marshmallows and fresh coconuts, and to Devon Cohn, Natalie Philips, and Sunita de Tourreil. You each own a piece of my heart.

Judah Would Like to Give Thanks...

To my coauthor and dear friend, Olivia. Thank you for overcoming our mutual introversion and saying hi at that party that night, the one neither of us wanted to go to. It's been a fascinating ride.

To my friends in the army for teaching me more than a civilian has a right to know: Mark Monroe, Razz, Mike Rogan, JB, Patricia Carson, Darya Pilram, Dave Horan, Phillip Pattee, Angela DiGiosaffatte, Dan Hoeprich, Ryan Kranc, and Mike Loveall. To Dana Pittard for your reflection and insight.

To the OD masters of innovation and systems and the human variable within them: Regina Dugan, Ken Gabriel, Geoffrey West, Ron Ricci, Michael Arena, Mary Uhl-Bien, Lisa Kimball.

To Sara Johnson, for your kindness, intelligence, and willingness to tell me what's going on. To Cami Clark, for the future sight and conversations and laughter at the unbelievable come true.

To Dario Nardi, for your insights into the brain and personality. To John Beebe, for the lunches and for answering all my questions and for your encouragement to explore the entirety of one's personality. To Daniel Shapiro, for your friendship and humble brilliance, my brother from another mother. To Whitney Hirschier, for telling it like it is, never being fooled by the fools, and your true soul.

To the boys in the Lab for listening to me vent: Alex, Andrew, Vadik, Sergey, Keaton, Greg, Andrei and Andrey, and Cameron. And to Wren, for your smiles and joy. To Joe, for listening and for the genius cover design we didn't use. And to Esther, for the dim sum and knowing glance.

To Christos, the mystic, and Lieba, the seer, to Amanda, the honest one. To the Lambies, the Italian, and the Bengali for being awesome.

To the DJs: Kem, Stickybeats, Rus, Dave "MoFo" Simon, Betty-Ray, Mo Corleone, LeftCtrl, kev/null, Derek Ryan, Aaron Dyson Xavier, Adi Shanti, Ghost Squadron. To Nachi the magnificent.

To my teachers: Isa, the edge runner; Lori, the healer; and Rosenberg, the trickster. To Nicole W. for hanging at the rest stops on the journey.

And to so much family: Dr. Pants, Soul Sisters Katester and Darci, Soul Brothers Dov and Allan, and Allison, the best bike passenger ever Eyla T., my parents; and the coven, Meg the body, Sera the soul, and Tara the heart. And always to Tara, for ravishing my heart. So much love.

Notes

Introduction

1. Drawn from Albert Einstein's talks, letters, and the recollections of his son, Hans Albert. See Dennis Overbye, *Einstein in Love: A Scientific Romance* (New York: Penguin, 2001).
2. Salvador Dalí, *50 Secrets of Magic Craftmanship* (New York: Dover, 1948), 36–37.
3. Randy L. Buckner, Jessica R. Andrews-Hanna, and Daniel L. Schacter, "The Brain's Default Network," *Annals of the New York Academy of Sciences* 1124, no. 1 (2008): 1–38.
4. Aaron Kucyi, Michael J. Hove, Michael Esterman, R. Matthew Hutchison, and Eve M. Valera, "Dynamic Brain Network Correlates of Spontaneous Fluctuations in Attention," *Cerebral Cortex* (2016): bhw029.
5. John Stachel, "'What Song the Syrens Sang': How Did Einstein Discover Special Relativity?," in *Einstein from 'B' to 'Z'*, vol. 9 (Heidelberg: Springer Science & Business Media, 2001), 157.
6. Claire Suddath, "A Brief History of: Velcro," *Time*, June 15, 2010.
7. Wilson Greatbatch, *The Making of the Pacemaker: Celebrating a Lifesaving Invention* (Amherst, New York: Prometheus Books, 2000).

Chapter 1: The Four Wings

1. György Moldova, *Ballpoint: A Tale of Genius and Grit, Perilous Times, and the Invention That Changed the Way We Write* (n.p.: New Europe Books, 2012).
2. Martha Beck, "7 Ways to Spark a Major Breakthrough in Your Life," *O Magazine*, August 2014.

3. Amanda L. Boston and Lisa Burgess, "Helo Mechanics Draw Praise for NASCAR-Inspired Windshield Coatings," *Stars and Stripes,* March 6, 2005.

4. William Rosen, *The Most Powerful Idea in the World: A Story of Steam, Industry and Invention* (Chicago: University of Chicago Press, 2012), 137.

5. Robin McKie, "James Watt and the Sabbath Stroll That Created the Industrial Revolution," *Guardian,* May 29, 2015.

6. Stephen S. Hall, "The Age of Electricity," in *Inventors and Discoverers: Changing Our World,* ed. Elizabeth L. Newhouse (Washington, D.C.: National Geographic Society, 1988).

7. Electronic correspondence with Victoria Spadaro Grant, July–September 2016.

8. Joe Griffin and Ivan Tyrrell, *Why We Dream: The Definitive Answer* (Hailsham, U.K.: HG Publishing, 2014).

9. Thomas Waln-Morgan Draper, *The Bemis History and Genealogy: Being an Account, in Greater Part, of the Descendants of Joseph Bemis of Watertown, Mass.* (Washington, D.C.: Library of Congress, n.d.), 159–62, 1357 Joshua Bemis, FHL Microfilm 1011936 Item 2.

10. GreenerDesign Staff, "Oyster Glue Could Hold Secret to Safer Surgery," *GreenBiz,* September 22, 2010.

11. Tom D. Crouch, "On Wheels and Wings," *Inventors and Discoverers: Changing Our World.*

12. Tom Wolfe, *The Right Stuff* (New York: Farrar, Straus and Giroux, 1979).

13. Private conversations and e-mails with Tammy Sanders, January–March 2014.

14. Hall, "The Age of Electricity," *Inventors and Discoverers: Changing Our World.*

15. John Stachel, "'What Song the Syrens Sang': How Did Einstein Discover Special Relativity?," in *Einstein from 'B' to 'Z',* vol. 9 (Heidelberg: Springer Science & Business Media, 2001), 157.

16. Private communication with Dr. Barney Pell.

Chapter 2: The Chrysalis

1. Stacey Anderson, "When Keith Richards Wrote '(I Can't Get No) Satisfaction' in His Sleep," *Rolling Stone,* May 9, 2011, www.rollingstone.com/music/news/when-keith-richards-wrote-i-cant-get-no-satisfaction-in-his-sleep-20110509.

2. Discussions and interviews with Dr. Kalina Christoff, head of the Cognitive Neuroscience of Thought Laboratory at the University of British Columbia; Roger E. Beaty, Mathias Benedek, Scott Barry Kaufman, and Paul J. Silvia, "Default and Executive Network Coupling Supports Creative Idea Production," *Scientific Reports* 5 (2015); Kieran C. R. Fox, R. Nathan Spreng, Melissa Ellamil, Jessica R. Andrews-Hanna, and Kalina Christoff, "The Wandering Brain: Meta-Analysis of Functional Neuroimaging Studies of Mind-Wandering and Related Spontaneous Thought Processes," *Neuroimage* 111 (2015): 611–21; Melissa Ellamil, Charles Dobson, Mark Beeman, and Kalina Christoff, "Evaluative and Generative Modes of Thought During the Creative Process," *Neuroimage* 59, no. 2 (2012): 1783–94.

3. Steven L. Bressler and Vinod Menon, "Large-Scale Brain Networks in Cognition: Emerging Methods and Principles," *Trends in Cognitive Sciences* 14 (2010), 277–90.

4. Randy L. Buckner, Jessica R. Andrews-Hanna, and Daniel L. Schacter, "The Brain's Default Network," *Annals of the New York Academy of Sciences* 1124, no. 1 (2008): 1–38; also discussions with Dr. Marcus Raichle, Dr. Jonathan Schooler, Dr. John Kounius, and Dr. Kalina Christoff.

5. Conversations with Dr. Marcus Raichle, 2012–16. "I've never seen anyone suffer damage to that part of the brain from a stroke and survive." Every mammal down to the mouse has been found to have a default network. It has two blood supplies, a form of redundancy found in vital parts like the heart and the liver.

6. H. Berger, "*Über das Elektrenkephalogramm des Menschen*," Archiv Für Psychiatrie Und Nervenkrankheiten 87 (1929): 527–70. Berger demonstrated that the human brain remains electrically active even at rest while attention wanders.

7. Conversation with Dr. Marcus Raichle, March 2014.

8. The salience network is a network of regions that, among other things, focus our attention on the most salient information at any time. This network has been found to actually direct our attention either to people, facts, or events outside of, external to us, or to things happening inside of us. It mediates between our EN and our DN. It consists of the anterior insula (AI) and dorsal anterior cingulate cortex (dACC), the amygdala, the ventral striatum, and the substantia nigra/ventral tegmental area. Things that catch the salience network's eye include anything out of the ordinary, anything that breaks a pattern, anything surprising, pleasurable, rewarding, relevant to the self, or engaging the emotions. See Vinod Menon and Lucina Q. Uddin, "Saliency, Switching, Attention and Control: A Network Model of Insula Function," *Brain Structure and Function* 214, no. 5–6 (2010): 655–67.

9. O. T. Benfey, "August Kekulé and the Birth of the Structural Theory of Organic Chemistry in 1858," *Journal of Chemical Education*, 35 (1958): 21–23. doi:10.1021/ed035p21.

10. Conversations with Adam Cheyer, August 2014.

11. Kieran C. R. Fox, Savannah Nijeboer, Elizaveta Solomonova, G. William Domhoff, and Kalina Christoff, "Dreaming as Mind Wandering: Evidence from Functional Neuroimaging and First-Person Content Reports," *Frontiers in Human Neuroscience* 7 (2013): 412.

12. Conversations with Jeff Hawkins, September 2014.

Chapter 3: On the Hunt

1. Matt Kaplan, "Why Great Ideas Come When You Aren't Trying: Allowing the Mind to Wander Aids Creativity," *Nature*, May 22, 2012. www.nature.com/news/why-great-ideas-come-when-you-aren-t-trying-1.10678.

2. Randy L. Buckner, Jessica R. Andrews-Hanna, and Daniel L. Schacter, "The Brain's Default Network," *Annals of the New York Academy of Sciences* 1124, no. 1 (2008): 1–38.

3. Kimberly D. Elsbach and Andrew B. Hargadon, "Enhancing Creativity Through 'Mindless' Work: A Framework of Workday Design," *Organization Science* 17, no. 4 (2006): 470–83.

4. R. Wilkins, D. Hodges, P. Laurienti, M. Steen, M., and J. Burdette, "Network Science and the Effects of Music Preference on Functional Brain Connectivity: From Beethoven to Eminem," *Nature Scientific Reports* (2014), doi:10.1038 /srep06130.

5. Conversation with Dr. Kalina Christoff, based on her research. See also Science Appendix.

6. While at Stanford University's Graduate School of Education, Marily Oppezzo and colleague Daniel L. Schwartz, PhD, conducted studies involving 176 people, mostly college students. They found that those who walked instead of sitting or being pushed in a wheelchair consistently gave more creative responses on tests commonly used to measure creative thinking, such as thinking of alternate uses for common objects and coming up with original analogies to capture complex ideas. When asked to solve problems with a single answer, however, the walkers fell slightly behind those who responded while sitting, according to the study. Marily Oppezzo and Daniel L. Schwartz, "Give Your Ideas Some Legs: The Positive Effect of Walking on Creative Thinking," *Journal of Experimental Psychology: Learning, Memory, and Cognition* 40, no. 4 (2014): 1142.

7. Dan Rubinstein, *Born to Walk: The Transformative Power of a Pedestrian Act* (Toronto: ECW Press, 2015).

8. Kirk I. Erickson, Michelle W. Voss, Ruchika Shaurya Prakash, Chandramallika Basak, Amanda Szabo, Laura Chaddock, Jennifer S. Kim, et al., "Exercise Training Increases Size of Hippocampus and Improves Memory," *Proceedings of the National Academy of Sciences* 108, no. 7 (2011): 3017–22.

9. Fernando Gómez-Pinilla, Zhe Ying, Roland R. Roy, Raffaella Molteni, and V. Reggie Edgerton, "Voluntary Exercise Induces a BDNF-Mediated Mechanism That Promotes Neuroplasticity," *Journal of Neurophysiology* 88, no. 5 (2002): 2187–95.

10. Oppezzo and Schwartz, "Give Your Ideas Some Legs: The Positive Effect of Walking on Creative Thinking."

11. Alex Soojung-Kim Pang, *The Distraction Addiction: Getting the Information You Need and the Communication You Want, Without Enraging Your Family, Annoying Your Colleagues, and Destroying Your Soul* (New York: Little Brown, 2013), 198–215.

12. For all subsequent references to Mason Currey's work: Mason Currey, ed., *Daily Rituals: How Artists Work* (New York: Knopf, 2013).

13. Werner Heisenberg, *Physics and Philosophy: The Revolution in Modern Science* (New York: HarperPerennial, 1958).

14. Ibid.

15. Leo Babauta, "The No. 1 Habit of Highly Creative People," zen habits, May 27, 2010, zenhabits.net/creative-habit.

16. Ibid.

17. Orrin E. Dunlap Jr., "Tesla Sees Evidence That Radio and Light Are Sound," *New York Times*, April 8, 1934, 9.

18. M.P.M. Kammers, Frederique de Vignemont, Lennart Verhagen, and H. Chris Dijkerman, "The Rubber Hand Illusion in Action," *Neuropsychologia* 47, no. 1 (2009): 204–11.
19. Angela K.-Y. Leung, Suntae Kim, Evan Polman, Lay See Ong, Lin Qiu, Jack A. Goncalo, and Jeffrey Sanchez-Burks, "Embodied Metaphors and Creative 'Acts,'" *Psychological Science* 23, no. 5 (2012): 502–9.
20. Quote from Dean Hovey, designer of the original Apple mouse, from the PBS documentary *Steve Jobs: One Last Thing* (2012: London: Pioneer Productions).
21. Private correspondence with Kevin Sauer, July–August 2016.
22. Peter Biskind, *Easy Riders, Raging Bulls* (New York: Simon & Schuster, 1998).

Chapter 4: The Butterfly Process

1. Gary Wolf, "Steve Jobs: The Next Insanely Great Thing," *Wired,* February 1, 1996.
2. W. C. Klann, "Reminiscences," Henry Ford Museum & Greenfield Village Archives, n.d.. Accession 65.
3. No one is positive whether the use of rifling with feathers on arrows was the inspiration for rifling the inside of a gun barrel, but most people agree that given the overlap of projectiles used in war and hunting and both methods' need for accuracy, it is the most plausible explanation.
4. John R. Scherer, "Before Cardiac MRI: Rene Laennec (1781–1826) and the Invention of the Stethoscope," *Cardiology Journal* 14, no. 5 (2007): 518–19, PMID 18651515; R.T.H. Laennec, *De l'Auscultation Médiate ou Traité du Diagnostic des Maladies des Poumons et du Coeur* (Paris: Brosson & Chaudé, 1819). The complete title of this book, often referred to as the "Treatise," is *On Mediate Auscultation or Treatise on the Diagnosis of the Diseases of the Lungs and Heart.*
5. J. K. Lee, K. A. Grace, and A. J. Taylor, "Effect of a Pharmacy Care Program on Medication Adherence and Persistence, Blood Pressure, and Low-Density Lipoprotein Cholesterol: A Randomized Controlled Trial," *Journal of the American Medical Association* 296, no. 21 (2006): 2563–71, doi:10.1001/jama.296.21.joc60162.
6. Ibid.; N. Col, J. E. Fanale, and P. Kronholm, "The Role of Medication Noncompliance and Adverse Drug Reactions in Hospitalizations of the Elderly," *Archives of Internal Medicine* 150 (1990):841–45; M. C. Sokol, K. A. McGuigan, R. R. Verbrugge, and R. S. Epstein, "Impact of Medication Adherence on Hospitalization Risk and Healthcare Cost," *Medical Care* 43 (2005): 521–30.
7. Interviews with T. J. Parker, May 2015.
8. Charlie Connell, "Did Thomas Edison Invent the Tattoo Machine?," *Inked,* December 18, 2014.
9. Anna Winston, "French Designers Hack a 3D Printer to Make a Tattooing Machine," *Dezeen,* October 28, 2014.
10. Daniel E. Slotnik, "Tom Sims, Pioneer in Sport of Snowboarding, Dies at 61," *New York Times,* September 18, 2012.
11. This argument was made by Robert D. Ekelund, Robert F, Hébert, Robert D. Tollison, Gary M. Anderson, and Audrey B. Davidson, *Sacred Trust: The Medieval Church as an Economic Firm* (Oxford: Oxford University Press, 1996).

12. William C. Taylor, "What Hospitals Can Learn from the Ritz," *Fortune*, March 2, 2011.

Chapter 5: Cultivating Your Garden

1. Erik Weihenmayer, *Touch the Top of the World: A Blind Man's Journey to Climb Farther Than the Eye Can See* (New York: Plume, 2002), and many, many articles, including a *Time* magazine cover.
2. Mandy Kendrick, "Tasting the Light: Device Lets the Blind 'See' with Their Tongues," *Scientific American*, August 13, 2009, accessed March 15, 2014, www .scientificamerican.com/article/device-lets-blind-see-with-tongues.
3. Obituary, "Founder: Paul Bach-y-Rita," Tactile Communication and Neurorehabilitation Laboratory, Department of Biomedical Engineering, University Wisconsin-Madison, 2015, tcnl.bme.wisc.edu/laboratory/founder.
4. Tony T. Yang, C. C. Gallen, V. S. Ramachandran, S. Cobb, B. J. Schwartz, and F. E. Bloom, "Noninvasive Detection of Cerebral Plasticity in Adult Human Somatosensory Cortex," *Neuroreport: An International Journal for the Rapid Communication of Research in Neuroscience* 5, no. 6 (1994), 701–4; Judy H. Song, Erica Skoe, Patrick C. M. Wong, and Nina Kraus, "Plasticity in the Adult Human Auditory Brainstem Following Short-term Linguistic Training," *Journal of Cognitive Neuroscience* 20, no. 10 (2008), 1892–1902.
5. Helen Thomson, "Woman of 24 Found to Have No Cerebellum in Her Brain," *New Scientist*, September 10, 2014, www.newscientist.com/article/mg22329861 -900-woman-of-24-found-to-have-no-cerebellum-in-her-brain.
6. Christina M. Karns, Mark W. Dow, and Helen J. Neville, "Altered Cross-Modal Processing in the Primary Auditory Cortex of Congenitally Deaf Adults: A Visual-Somatosensory fMRI Study with a Double Flash Illusion," *Journal of Neuroscience* 32, no. 28 (July 11, 2012), 9626–38; Frédéric Gougoux, Robert J. Zatorre, Maryse Lassonde, Patrice Voss, and Franco Lepore, "A Functional Neuroimaging Study of Sound Localization: Visual Cortex Activity Predicts Performance in Early-Blind Individuals," *PLoS Biology* 3, no. 2 (2005): e27.
7. Frédéric Gougoux, Robert J. Zatorre, Maryse Lassonde, Patrice Voss, and Franco Lepore, "A Functional Neuroimaging Study of Sound Localization: Visual Cortex Activity Predicts Performance in Early-Blind Individuals," *PLoS Biology* 3, no. 2 (2005): e27.
8. Weihenmayer, *Touch the Top of the World*.
9. Bogdan Draganski, Christian Gaser, Volker Busch, Gerhard Schuierer, Ulrich Bogdahn, and Arne May, "Neuroplasticity: Changes in Grey Matter Induced by Training," *Nature* 427, no. 6972 (2004): 311–12; Arne May, Gören Hajak, S. Gänssbauer, Thomas Steffens, Berthold Langguth, Tobias Kleinjung, and Peter Eichhammer, "Structural Brain Alterations Following 5 Days of Intervention: Dynamic Aspects of Neuroplasticity," *Cerebral Cortex* 17, no. 1 (2007): 205–10.
10. Conversations with Dr. Jon Lieff, January–March, 2015.
11. Conversations with Astro Teller, May 2015.

12. Jeffrey A. Kleim and Theresa A. Jones, "Principles of Experience-Dependent Neural Plasticity: Implications for Rehabilitation After Brain Damage," *Journal of Speech, Language, and Hearing Research* 51, no. 1 (2008): S225–39.

13. Cyrus K. Foroughi, Samuel S. Monfort, Martin Paczynski, Patrick E. McKnight, and P. M. Greenwood, "Placebo Effects in Cognitive Training," *Proceedings of the National Academy of Sciences* 113, no. 27 (2016): 7470–74; Lucinda S. Spaulding, Mark P. Mostert, and Andrea P. Beam, "Is Brain Gym® an Effective Educational Intervention?," *Exceptionality* 18, no. 1 (2010): 18–30; Jennifer Stephenson, "Best Practice? Advice Provided to Teachers About the Use of Brain Gym® in Australian Schools," *Australian Journal of Education* 53, no. 2 (2009): 109–24.

14. Sharon Eldar and Y. Bar-Haim, "Neural Plasticity in Response to Attention Training in Anxiety," *Psychological Medicine* 40, no. 04 (2010): 667–77.

15. Leo Babauta, "Focus: A Simplicity Manifesto in the Age of Distraction" (Grand Haven, Mich.: Brilliance Audio, 2011).

16. For all subsequent references to Dr. Kelly McGonigal's work: Kelly McGonigal, PhD, *The Willpower Instinct* (New York: Avery, 2012), 42.

17. Susan Burton, "Terry Gross and the Art of Opening Up," *New York Times*, October 21, 2015.

18. Aymeric Guillot, Kevin Moschberger, and Christian Collet, "Coupling Movement with Imagery as a New Perspective for Motor Imagery Practice," *Behavioral and Brain Functions* 9, no. 1 (2013): 1.

19. Adapted from Italo Calvino's classic book *Invisible Cities*, in which Marco Polo is entertaining Kublai Khan with tales of the different and magical cities he has visited throughout the great Khan's lands. Italo Calvino, *Invisible Cities* (New York: Harcourt Brace, 1978).

20. "Bicycle History from the Late 19th Century," America on the Move Exhibit, National Museum of American History, Smithsonian Institution, amhistory.si.edu/onthemove/themes/story_69_3.html.

21. Jon Gertner, *The Idea Factory: Bell Labs and the Great Age of American Innovation* (New York: Penguin, 2012).

22. Dennis Overbye, *Einstein in Love: A Scientific Romance* (New York: Penguin, 2001).

23. Private communication with Nadya Direkova.

24. EarthSky editors, "Sunni Robertson on How a Kingfisher Inspired a Bullet Train," *EarthSky*, June 29, 2012.

25. Abigail Doan, "BioMimetic Architecture: Green Building in Zimbabwe Modeled After Termite Mounds," *Inhabitat*, November 29, 2012.

26. Janine M. Benyus, *Biomimicry: Innovation Inspired by Nature* (New York: William Morrow, 2002).

Chapter 6: What's in Your Net?

1. Conversations with Sandy Pentland, October 2014.

2. Stacey Anderson, "When Keith Richards Wrote '(I Can't Get No) Satisfaction'

in His Sleep," *Rolling Stone*, May 9, 2011, www.rollingstone.com/music/news /when-keith-richards-wrote-i-cant-get-no-satisfaction-in-his-sleep-20110509.
3. Conversations with Tom Chi, March 2014.

Chapter 7: The Spiders of Fear

1. Interestingly, high catastrophizers report higher levels of pain and may even differ in their physical neuroanatomy. See Claudia M. Campbell, Kenny Witmer, Mpepera Simango, Alene Carteret, Marco L. Loggia, James N. Campbell, Jennifer A. Haythornthwaite, and Robert R. Edwards, "Catastrophizing Delays the Analgesic Effect of Distraction," *PAIN®* 149, no. 2 (2010): 202–7; A new study reports: "Our data provide evidence that individuals who carry the NPSR1 T allele over-interpret their conditioned fear reactions compared with non-T carriers," Karolina A Raczka, Nina Gartmann, Marie-Luise Mechias, Andreas Reif, Christian Büchel, Jürgen Deckert, and Raffael Kalisch, "A Neuropeptide S Receptor Variant Associated with Overinterpretation of Fear Reactions: A Potential Neurogenetic Basis for Catastrophizing," *Molecular Psychiatry* 15, no. 11 (2010): 1067–74.
2. Rick Hanson, PhD, "Do Positive Experiences Stick to Your Ribs?," *Take in the Good*, June 1, 2015, www.rickhanson.net/take-in-the-good.
3. Private correspondence with Adam Berman, 2010–12.
4. More precisely: specific areas of our brain are used for both experiencing and imagining, and this economical use of the brain has the side effect of provoking some of the emotions of the real experience.
5. This effect is so powerful that athletes have found you can actually gain muscle mass through imagination. Erin M. Shackell, Lionel G. Standing, "Mind Over Matter: Mental Training Increases Physical Strength," *North American Journal of Psychology* 9, no. 1 (2007): 189–200.
6. For more on this topic, we enthusiastically recommend Robert Sapolsky's work, including his iTunes lecture, "Why Zebras Don't Get Ulcers."
7. Gretchen Cuda, "Just Breathe: Body Has a Built-in Stress Reliever," NPR, *Morning Edition*, December 6, 2010.
8. Private correspondence with Dr. Philippe Goldin, 2013.
9. David Rock, "SCARF: A Brain-Based Model for Collaborating With and Influencing Others," *NeuroLeadership Journal* 1 (2008).
10. Leonardo C. De Souza, Henrique C. Guimarães, Antônio L. Teixeira, Paulo Caramelli, Richard Levy, Bruno Dubois, and Emmanuelle Volle, "Frontal Lobe Neurology and the Creative Mind," *Frontiers in Psychology* 5 (2014); Bruce L. Miller, Kyle Boone, Jeffrey L. Cummings, Stephen L. Read, and Fred Mishkin, "Functional Correlates of Musical and Visual Ability in Frontotemporal Dementia," *British Journal of Psychiatry* 176, no. 5 (2000): 458–63; Bruce L. Miller, Marcel Ponton, D. Frank Benson, J. L. Cummings, and I. Mena, "Enhanced Artistic Creativity with Temporal Lobe Degeneration," *Lancet* 348, no. 9043 (1996): 1744–45; Bruce L. Miller, J. Cummings, F. Mishkin, K. Boone,

F. Prince, M. Ponton, and C. Cotman, "Emergence of Artistic Talent in Fronto-temporal Dementia," *Neurology* 51, no. 4 (1998): 978–82.

11. John Martyn Harlow, "Recovery from the Passage of an Iron Bar through the Head," *Publications of the Massachusetts Medical Society* 2, no. 3 (1868): 327–47 (Boston: David Clapp & Son, 1869, repr.).

12. "A Most Remarkable Case," *American Phrenological Journal and Repository of Science, Literature, and General Intelligence,* Fowler & Wells 13, no. 4 (April 1851): 89, col. 3.

13. P. R. Clance and S. A. Imes, "The Imposter Phenomenon in High Achieving Women: Dynamics and Therapeutic Intervention," *Psychotherapy: Theory, Research and Practice* 15, no. 3 (1978): 241–47.

14. In more technical terms, Robert Cialdini defines the self-image as a characterological view of the self formed through feedback that we get. Being successful on the physical field, we can gain a self-image of ourselves as athletes. Experiencing an internal feeling of anxiety when going to a party might reinforce the notion that "I am a shy person." Feedback we receive from others, who give us approval or disapproval, will also be integrated into the self-image. Private conversation with Robert Cialdini, 2015–16.

15. Microsoft's imposter syndrome blog is available at www.hanselman.com/blog /ImAPhonyAreYou.aspx.

16. Teresa Amabile and Steven J. Kramer, "The Power of Small Wins," *Harvard Business Review*, May 2011.

17. Brain scans show that remembering something turns on the same "circuits" in the brain as the original experience. The study, using MRI scanners, was the most detailed yet into how similar "reliving" an experience was to experiencing it in the first place. The scientists found that the real and remembered versions had "striking" similarities, with 91 percent of the same brain circuits activating. "When we mentally replay an episode we've experienced, it can feel like we are transported back in time and re-living that moment again," said Dr. Brad Buchsbaum, lead investigator. "Our study has confirmed that complex, multi-featured memory involves a 'repeat' of the whole pattern of brain activity that is evoked during initial perception of the experience. This helps to explain why vivid memory can feel so real." Researchers found that vivid memory and real experience share "striking" similarities at the neural level, although they are not "pixel-perfect" brain pattern replications. The two cognitive operations don't work exactly the same way in the brain—hence, even the most vivid memories don't "fool" us into thinking we are actually there. Bradley R. Buchsbaum, Sabrina Lemire-Rodger, Candice Fang, and Hervé Abdi, "The Neural Basis of Vivid Memory Is Patterned on Perception," *Journal of Cognitive Neuroscience* 24, no. 9 (2012): 1867–83, doi: 10.1162/jocn_a_00253.

18. Private conversations with Tara Brach.

19. Ellen Langer, *Counterclockwise* (New York: Random House, 2012).

20. Private communication and correspondence with Robert Cialdini, 2015–16.

21. Charles Duhigg, *The Power of Habit* (New York: Random House, 2014).

22. For all subsequent references to B. J. Fogg's work: Private communications and electronic correspondence with B. J. Fogg, 2015–16.

23. Private correspondence with Dr. Philippe Goldin, 2009–10.

24. Martha Beck, *Finding Your Own North Star* (New York: Harmony Books, 2002).

25. Stanley Milgram, *Obedience to Authority: An Experimental View* (New York: Harper & Row, 1975); N. J. Russell, "Milgram's Obedience to Authority Experiments: Origins and Early Evolution," *British Journal of Social Psychology* 50, part 1 (2011): 140–62.

26. Considered by many the greatest hitter of all time, Babe Ruth only managed to get a hit of any kind 34 percent of the time. In his career, Michael Jordan took 24,537 shots. He missed 12,345 times. You may as well have flipped a coin. He was just as likely to fail. Adapted from Benjamin Morris, fivethirtyeight.com.

27. From Tom Hanks interview in "Kevin Pollack's Chat Show" podcast, December 13, 2013.

28. John Varrasi, "The Man Behind the Vacuum Cleaner," ASME, December 2011; Nadia Goodman, "James Dyson on Using Failure to Drive Success," *Entrepreneur,* November 5, 2012; John Seabrook, "How to Make It," *New Yorker,* September 20, 2012.

29. For more on the principle of scarcity, see Robert Cialdini's excellent *Influence: The Psychology of Persuasion* (New York: HarperBusiness, rev. ed., 2006).

30. Private communications and electronic correspondence with Robert Cialdini regarding the combined effect of the principles of social proof and authority.

31. Barry Schwartz, *The Paradox of Choice: Why More Is Less* (New York: Harper-Collins, 2005).

32. Ibid.

33. D. R. Carney, A.J.C. Cuddy, and A. J. Yap, "Power Posing: Brief Nonverbal Displays Affect Neuroendocrine Levels and Risk Tolerance," *Psychological Science OnlineFirst,* September 21, 2010.

34. Benson is the Director Emeritus of the Benson-Henry Institute (BHI), and Mind Body Medicine Professor of Medicine, Harvard Medical School.

35. The results revealed significant changes in the expression of several important groups of genes between the novice samples and those from both the short- and long-term sets. Even more pronounced changes were shown in the long-term practitioners. Manoj K. Bhasin, Jeffery A. Dusek, Bei-Hung Chang, Marie G. Joseph, John W. Denninger, Gregory L. Fricchione, Herbert Benson, and Towia A. Libermann, "Relaxation Response Induces Temporal Transcriptome Changes in Energy Metabolism, Insulin Secretion and Inflammatory Pathways," *PLoS One* 8, no. 5 (2013): e62817.

36. R. A. Emmons and A. Mishra, "Why Gratitude Enhances Well-Being: What We Know, What We Need to Know," in *Designing Positive Psychology: Taking Stock and Moving Forward,* ed. K. Sheldon, T. Kashdan and M. F. Steger (New York: Oxford University Press, 2011), 248–58; R. A. Emmons, "Gratitude," in

Encyclopedia of Positive Psychology, ed. S. J. Lopez and A. Beauchamp (New York: Oxford University Press, 2009), 442–47.

37. Robert A. Emmons, PhD, *Thanks! How Practicing Gratitude Can Make You Happier* (New York: Houghton Mifflin, 2007); Alex M. Wood, John Maltby, Raphael Gillett, P. Alex Linley, and Stephen Joseph, "The Role of Gratitude in the Development of Social Support, Stress, and Depression: Two Longitudinal Studies," *Journal of Research in Personality* 42, no. 4 (August 2008): 854–71.

38. For more on this subject, see Olivia's book *The Charisma Myth* (New York: Portfolio, 2012).

39. Roy F. Baumeister and Brad J. Bushman, *Social Psychology and Human Nature* (Boston: Cengage Learning, 2014), 196; P. Brickman, R. Janoff-Bulman, and D. Coates, "Lottery Winners and Accident Victims: Is Happiness Relative?" *Journal of Personality and Social Psychology* 36, no. 8 (1978), 917–27.

40. George Hill, the Story Corps Project, storycorps.org/listen/george-hill.

41. Andrew Hunt, *Pragmatic Thinking and Learning: Refactor Your Wetware* (Raleigh, N.C.: Pragmatic Bookshelf, rev. ed. 2010).

42. Cialdini, *Influence*; B. J. Sagarin, R. B. Cialdini, W. E. Rice, and S. B. Serna, "Dispelling the Illusion of Invulnerability: The Motivations and Mechanisms of Resistance to Persuasion," *Journal of Personality and Social Psychology* 83, no. 3 (2002): 526–41.

43. Hunt, *Pragmatic Thinking and Learning.*

44. Bill Bryson, *A Short History of Nearly Everything* (New York: Broadway Books, 2004), 11.

45. Darya L. Zabellina and Michael D. Robinson, "Don't Be So Hard on Yourself: Self-Compassion Facilitates Creative Originality Among Self-Judgmental Individuals," *Creativity Research Journal* 22, no. 3 (2010): 288–93.

46. Communications with Dr. JoAnn Dahlkoetter, 2014–15.

47. K. D. Neff, "Self-Compassion," in *Handbook of Individual Differences in Social Behavior,* ed. M. R. Leary and R. H. Hoyle (New York: Guilford Press, 2009), 561–73.

48. K. D. Neff, "Self-Compassion, Self-Esteem, and Well-Being," *Social and Personality Compass* 5 (2011): 1–12; K. D. Ne and P. McGeehee, "Self-Compassion and Psychological Resilience among Adolescents and Young Adults," *Self and Identity* 9 (2010): 225–40; K. D. Neff, K. Kirkpatrick, and S. S. Rude, "Self-Compassion and Its Link to Adaptive Psychological Functioning," *Journal of Research in Personality* 41 (2007): 139–54.

49. K. D. Neff, "Self-Compassion."

50. Ibid. Self-compassion deactivates the threat system (which generates feelings of fear, insecurity, and defensiveness) and activates the soothing system instead.

51. T. Barnhofer, T. Chittka, H. Nightingale, C. Visser, and C. Crane, "State Effects of Two Forms of Meditation on Prefrontal EEG Asymmetry in Previously Depressed Individuals," *Mindfulness* 1, no. 1 (2010): 21–27; T. Barnhofer, D. Duggan, C. Crane, S. Hepburn, M. J. Fennell, and J. M. Williams, "Effects of

Meditation on Frontal Alpha-Asymmetry in Previously Suicidal Individuals," *NeuroReport* 18, no. 7 (2007): 709–12; B. R. Cahn and J. Polich, "Meditation States and Traits: EEG, ERP, and Neuroimaging Studies," *Psychological Bulletin* 132, no. 2 (2006): 180–211; G. Feldman, J. Greeson, and J. Senville, "Differential Effects of Mindful Breathing, Progressive Muscle Relaxation, and Loving-Kindness Meditation on Decentering and Negative Reactions to Repetitive Thoughts," *Behaviour Research and Therapy* 48, no. 10 (2010): 1002–11; A. Manna, A. Raffone, M. G. Perrucci, D. Nardo, A. Ferretti, A. Tartaro, et al., "Neural Correlates of Focused Attention and Cognitive Monitoring in Meditation," *Brain Research Bulletin* 82, nos. 1–2 (2010): 46–56.

52. Christopher K. Germer, *The Mindful Path to Self-Compassion* (New York: Guilford Press, 2009).

53. Paul Gilbert, Mark W. Baldwin, Chris Irons, Jodene R. Baccus, and Michelle Palmer, "Self-Criticism and Self-Warmth: An Imagery Study Exploring Their Relation to Depression," *Journal of Cognitive Psychotherapy* 20, no. 2 (2006): 183–200.

Chapter 8: The Failure Wasps

1. James J. Gross, "Emotion Regulation: Affective, Cognitive, and Social Consequences," *Psychophysiology* 39, no. 3 (May 2002): 281–9.

2. Ibid., 289.

3. Carol Dweck, *Mindset: The New Psychology of Success* (New York: Ballantine, 2006).

4. Elon Musk tweet: "Rocket made it to drone spaceport ship, but landed hard. Close, but no cigar this time. Bodes well for the future tho," January 10, 2015.

5. Conversation with Astro Teller, March 2014.

6. Conversation with Tina Seelig, September 2015.

7. Randy Komisar, *The Monk and the Riddle* (Cambridge, Mass.: Harvard Business Review Press, 2000).

8. D. J. Simons and C. F. Chabris, "Gorillas in Our Midst: Sustained Inattentional Blindness for Dynamic Events," *Perception* 28, no. 9 (1999): 1059–74.

9. Dr. Steven C. Hayes, *Get Out of Your Mind & Into Your Life* (Oakland, Calif.: New Harbinger Publications, 2005).

10. For all subsequent references to Dr. Shawn Achor's work: Electronic correspondence with Dr. Shawn Achor, June–November 2014.

11. The denial of grief reaction may have served an important purpose during our evolution, in allowing us to escape danger. In most cases, death would come from violence: war, predation, accident. And if you're that close to the danger, you really shouldn't stop to grieve. You need to get out of there first! So we can imagine that those of our ancestors who had this grief-denial period tended to survive more than others, because they got out of danger and then grieved. The others? Well, they're not our ancestors. For more on the evolutionary advantages of grief and depression, see Jonathan Rottenberg, *The Depths* (New York: Basic Books, 2014).

12. Above four, we must engage different, slower brain processes. It takes us more time to remember the items, and we do not remember them as accurately. Assessments of one to four items are rapid, accurate, and confident, through a process called subitizing. As the number of items increases beyond this amount, judgments are made with decreasing accuracy and confidence. In addition, response times rise in a dramatic fashion. See Douglas Clements, "Subitizing: What Is It? Why Teach It?," *Journal of the National Council of Teachers of Mathematics* 5, no. 7 (March 1999); Ernst von Glaserfeld, "Subitizing: The Role of Figural Patterns in the Development of Numerical Concepts," *Archives de Psychologie* 50 (1982): 191–218.

13. "Thomas Edison Quote—Tinfoil Phonograph 'Something There Was No Doubt Of,'" Today in Science History, todayinsci.com/E/Edison_Thomas/EdisonThomas-TalkingPhonograph-SciAm.htm.

14. Private correspondence with Dr. Andy Ouderkirk, 2010.

15. Nathan Furr, "How Failure Taught Edison to Repeatedly Innovate," *Forbes*, June 9, 2011.

16. For all subsequent Annie Duke quotes: Communication and correspondence with Annie Duke, 2015–16.

17. Conversations with Matt Brady, August 2013.

Chapter 9: Icy Uncertainty

1. Phillip G. Pattee, *At War in Distant Waters: British Colonial Defense in the Great War* (Annapolis, Md.: Naval Institute Press, 2013).

2. *Bartlett's Familiar Quotations,* ed. John Bartlett and Geoffrey O'Brien (New York: Little, Brown and Company, 2012), 707.

3. Mason Currey, ed., *Daily Rituals: How Artists Work* (New York: Knopf, 2013).

4. For all subsequent references to Tony Schwartz: Private communications and electronic correspondence with Tony Schwartz, 2014–15.

5. You'll find this free online habit-formation program at www.tinyhabits.com.

6. Kelly McGonigal, PhD, *The Willpower Instinct* (New York: Avery, 2012).

7. M. T. Gailliot, R. F. Baumeister, C. N. DeWall, J. K. Maner, E. A. Plant, D. M. Tice, et al., "Self-Control Relies on Glucose as a Limited Energy Source: Willpower Is More Than a Metaphor," *Journal of Personality and Social Psychology* 92, no. 2 (2007): 325–36.

8. R. F. Baumeister, "Ego Depletion and Self-Regulation Failure: A Resource Model of Self-Control," *Alcoholism: Clinical and Experimental Research* 27, no. 2 (2003): 281–84.

9. Eric J. Johnson and Daniel Goldstein, "Do Defaults Save Lives?," *Science* 302, no. 5649 (2003): 1338–39.

10. L. Roemer, S. M. Orsillo, and K. Salters-Pedneault, "Efficacy of an Acceptance-Based Behavior Therapy for Generalized Anxiety Disorder: Evaluation in a Randomized Controlled Trial," *Journal of Consulting and Clinical Psychology* 76, no. 6 (December 2008): 1083–9, doi: 10.1037/a0012720. Generalized anxiety disorder (GAD) is a chronic anxiety disorder, associated with comorbidity and

impairment in quality of life. At posttreatment assessment 78 percent of treated participants no longer met criteria for GAD and 77 percent achieved high end-state functioning; these proportions stayed constant or increased over time.

11. Electronic correspondence with Dr. Marie Pasinski, 2014–15.

12. Deepak Chopra, *The Seven Spiritual Laws of Success: A Practical Guide to the Ful-fillment of Your Dreams* (San Rafael, Calif.: Amber-Allen Publishing, 2010), 20.

13. S. Harris, S. A. Sheth, and M. S. Cohen, "Functional Neuroimaging of Belief, Disbelief, and Uncertainty," *Annals of Neurolology* 63 (2008).

14. Private conversation with William Bosl, 2011. Image generation has a powerful impact on emotions and physiological states and a high impact on brain function. See A. Hackmann, "Working with Images in Clinical Psychology," in *Comprehensive Clinical Psychology*, ed. A. Bellack and M. Hersen (London: Pergamon, 1998), 301–17.

15. T. J. Kaptchuk, E. Friedlander, J. M. Kelley, M. N. Sanchez, E. Kokkotou, et al., "Placebos without Deception: A Randomized Controlled Trial in Irritable Bowel Syndrome," *PLoS ONE* 5, no. 12 (2010): e15591, doi:10.1371/journal .pone.0015591

Chapter 10: The SuperTools

1. Nils Ringertz, "Alfred Nobel—His Life and Work". Nobelprize.org. Nobel Media AB 2014. Web. September 13, 2016, http://www.nobelprize.org/alfred_ nobel/biographical/articles/life-work.

2. Steve Blank, "The Secret History of Silicon Valley," Computer History Museum. November 20, 2008.

3. For all subsequent references to Dr. Meg Lowman: Private communications, interviews, and electronic correspondence with Dr. Meg Lowman, 2014–15.

4. Alan Mozes, "A Sense of Purpose May Benefit Your Brain," WebMD, March 19, 2015, accessed September 14, 2016, www.webmd.com/healthy-aging/news /20150319/a-sense-of-purpose-may-benefit-your-brain.

5. Communication and correspondence with Dr. Adam Grant, 2014.

6. For all subsequent references to Kevin Starr: Private communications, meetings, off-sites, electronic correspondence, more meetings, leadership retreats, heated debates, and coffee with Kevin Starr, 2012–present.

7. Communications and electronic correspondence with Josh Balk, 2015–16.

8. After meditating for eight weeks, scientists found increased grey matter in the brain regions that make up the default network. See Britta K. Hölzel, James Carmody, Mark Vangel, Christina Congleton, Sita M. Yerramsetti, Tim Gard, and Sara W. Lazar, "Mindfulness Practice Leads to Increases in Regional Brain Gray Matter Density," *Psychiatry Research* (2011), accessed September 13, 2016.

9. Eileen Luders, Florian Kurth, Emeran A. Mayer, Arthur W. Toga, Katherine L. Narr, and Christian Gaser, "The Unique Brain Anatomy of Meditation Practitioners: Alterations in Cortical Gyrification," *Frontiers in Human Neuroscience* 6 (2012): 34.

10. P. Goldin, M. Ziv, H. Jazaieri, K. Hahn, and J. J. Gross, "MBSR vs Aerobic Exercise in Social Anxiety: fMRI of Emotion Regulation of Negative Self-Beliefs," *Social Cognitive and Affective Neuroscience* 8, no. 1 (2013): 65–72.

11. F. Ferrarelli, "Experienced Mindfulness Meditators Exhibit Higher Parietal-Occipital EEG Gamma Activity during NREM Sleep," *Plos ONE* 8, no. 8 (2013): 1-9, doi:10.1371/journal.pone.0073417.

Science Appendix

1. Dardo Tomasi and Nora D. Volkow, "Association Between Functional Connectivity Hubs and Brain Networks," *Cerebral Cortex* 21, no. 9 (2011): 2003–13.

2. Steven L. Bressler and Vinod Menon, "Large-scale brain networks in cognition: emerging methods and principles." *Trends in Cognitive Sciences* 14, no. 6 (2010): 277–90.

Index